THE HEALING BRAIN
A Scientific Reader

THE HEALING BRAIN
A Scientific Reader

Edited by

ROBERT ORNSTEIN
CHARLES SWENCIONIS

THE GUILFORD PRESS
New York   •   London

1990

© 1990 The Guilford Press
A Division of Guilford Publications, Inc.
72 Spring Street, New York, NY 10012

Printed in the United States of America

This book is printed on acid-free paper.

Last digit is print number: 9 8 7 6 5 4 3 2 1

Library of Congress Cataloging-in-Publication Data

The healing brain : a scientific reader / edited by Robert Ornstein
    and Charles Swencionis.
        p.   cm.
    Includes bibliographies and index.
    ISBN 0-89862-394-4
    1. Psychoneuroendocrinology.   2. Healing.   3. Mind and body.
4. Brain.   I. Ornstein, Robert E. (Robert Evan), 1942–.
II. Swencionis, Charles.
    [DNLM: 1. Brain—physiology.   2. Psychoneuroimmunology.
3. Psychosomatic Medicine.   WM 90 H4334]
QP356.45.H43   1990
612—dc20
DNLM/DLC
for Library of Congress   89-16968
                                                                                    CIP

For the memory of Dave Ornstein, who kept himself
   alive with his work.

                                                    R.O.

For Stanley and Julia Swencionis, whose work and
   love allowed me to see this far.

                                                    C.S.

Contributors

REUBIN ANDRES, M.D. Gerontology Research Center, National Institute on Aging, Francis Key Hospital, Baltimore, Maryland.

AARON ANTONOVSKY, Ph.D. Department of the Sociology of Health, University Center for Health Sciences, Ben Gurion University of the Negev, Beer-Sheva, Israel.

JOHN CASSEL, B.Sc., M.D., B.Ch., M.P.H. (deceased). Department of Epidemiology, University of North Carolina, Chapel Hill, North Carolina.

MARIAN C. DIAMOND, Ph.D. Department of Physiology–Anatomy, University of California, Berkeley, California.

RENÉ DUBOS, Ph.D. (deceased). Department of Microbiology, Rockefeller University, New York, New York.

CHARLES M. GOOD, Ph.D. Department of Geography, Virginia Polytechnic Institute and State University, Blacksburg, Virginia.

SUZANNE C. OUELLETTE KOBASA, Ph.D. Graduate Center, City University of New York, New York, New York.

HARRIS R. LIEBERMAN, Ph.D. Department of Brain and Cognitive Sciences, Massachusetts Institute of Technology, Cambridge, Massachusetts.

RUTH LLOYD, M.S. Boston, Massachusetts.

JAMES J. LYNCH, Ph.D. Life Care Health Associates, Towson and Columbia, Maryland.

MEREDITH MINKLER, Dr. P.H. Health Education Program, School of Public Health, Department of Social and Administrative Health Sciences, University of California, Berkeley, California.

JEANNE MOSCA, Ph.D. Department of Psychiatry, Bronx Municipal Hospital Center, Health and Hospitals Corporation, Bronx, New York.

ROBERT ORNSTEIN, Ph.D. Institute for the Study of Human Knowledge, Los Altos, California; Department of Human Biology, Stanford University, Stanford, California.

CANDACE B. PERT, Ph.D. Section of Brain Chemistry, National Institute of Mental Health, Bethesda, Maryland.

DAVID S. SOBEL, M.D., M.P.H. Division of Regional Patient Education and Health Promotion, Kaiser–Permanente Health Plan, San Jose, California.

GEORGE F. SOLOMON, M.D. Department of Psychiatry, University of California, Los Angeles, California; Department of Psychiatry, University of California, San Francisco, California; Psychiatry Service, Veterans Administration Medical Center, Sepulveda, California.

BONNIE J. SPRING, Ph.D. Department of Psychology, University of Health Sciences, Chicago Medical School, North Chicago, Illinois.

CHARLES SWENCIONIS, Ph.D. Ferkauf Graduate School of Psychology; Departments of Epidemiology/Social Medicine and Psychiatry, Albert Einstein College of Medicine, Yeshiva University, Bronx, New York.

RICHARD J. WURTMAN, M.D. Department of Applied Biological Sciences, Massachusetts Institute of Technology, Cambridge, Massachusetts.

Contents

·I·

INTRODUCTION

· 1 ·

What Is the Healing Brain?

ROBERT ORNSTEIN
CHARLES SWENCIONIS

In these days of high technology and artificial intelligence, it is easy to imagine that the brain is only a computer, but that we just do not know the details of its hardware and software. The cognitive sciences and artificial intelligence researchers use computer models of the brain and the mind. Software companies foster the computer model of the brain with names such as Cognition Technology, Ideaform®, Macromind®, Mindscape®, and Dream Maker®.

Freud used a hydraulic model of the mind because hydraulics represented the dominant technology at the time he formulated his basic theories. There is some attraction in drawing a parallel between the human brain and whatever the leading technology is at the time. This is related to the love affair Western culture has carried on with technology since the Enlightenment. The promise that technology would solve the problems of humankind carries with it a corollary, that in a way we are nothing but machines. Descartes' separation of the body from the mind allowed medical scientists to study anatomy and physiology unimpeded by the Church, but it also lent a glamour to the machinery that persists today. American and European art of the 19th and 20th centuries is full of the metaphor of technology as a promise of a bright future.

The human brain is not a computer. The human brain is an irrational conglomeration of one system layered on another. All the animals we evolved from are there, in some fashion, in our brains. "Ontogeny recapitulates phylogeny" is true not merely of the development of an individual, but also as a summary of the mature state of our central nervous systems. We retain traces of earlier primates, earlier mammals, reptiles, fish, and so on down the phylogenetic scale in the systems of our brains that we have and use now.

3

Each system of the brain has as its primary function minding the health of the body. The primary responsibility of organisms is to keep themselves alive. Evolution has taken this rather seriously as a bottom line, which is reflected in all the body's and the brain's systems.

Rational thinking is a late development of the brain in terms of evolution, and the earlier systems can easily derail it. Since the cerebral cortex is built on top of the earlier structures and communicates with the rest of the body through them, rational thinking stops when a cinder gets in your eye.

The more we know about how the brain functions to control the health of the body, the more we should be able both to optimize that health and to free the brain to be more creative and understand more of the world around us. This is what we mean by "the healing brain." The brain is involved in maintaining the health of the body at all levels. The more we find out about the relationships between the brain and the body, the more connections relevant to health we discover.

USE IT OR LOSE IT

One principle that has been badly misunderstood is that the brain grows in response to experience. Our scientific notion about brain growth has been that we lose many brain cells every day from infancy onwards, until we come to the point in old age when we can no longer function. Actually, this notion is based on a few seriously flawed studies (Brody, 1955, 1978) that were cited throughout the neuroscience literature. It has been said that we lose 100,000 nerve cells per day after age 30. This is based on Brody's having counted the nerve cells in a single column of the cerebral cortex from an 80-year-old whose history he knew nothing about (we do not know whether the person had been sitting in an isolated room for many years) and the cells in that area of the brain from a 20-year-old person. He found that there was a 30% difference and reported that there is a 30% loss in neurons with aging. Leboucq (1929) measured the surface area of an 80-year-old's brain and the surface area of a 20-year-old's brain and said again that there was roughly a 20%–30% loss. Burns (1958) calculated from these data that human beings lose 100,000 nerve cells per day after age 30. Brody more recently acknowledged the prominence of this information in the lay literature, but rejected it as scientifically inaccurate. Furthermore, Brody reported that some areas of the brain do not lose cells at all. (For further details on these studies, see Diamond, 1988).

It now seems that the brain does not necessarily lose cells and can develop new dendrites through very old age. The commonplace experience of skills improving with practice is more than a psychological phenomenon, it is reflected in changes in brain structure as well. Brain cells grow new connections as a result of stimulation, and if we continue to stimulate organisms, dendrites continue to develop. Rat brains in an enriched environment actually grow heavier with time, even in very old rats. The brain does not grow new cells, but the connections between cells may be as important.

PSYCHOSOCIAL FACTORS IN HEALING

We have always known that psychological and social factors influence healing, and a close reading of the epidemiological literature yields support for this idea from many areas of research. Epidemiology has focused on pathogenic agents and on environment, but has left the resistance or susceptibility of the host largely to other disciplines. Psychosocial factors show themselves repeatedly to be able to powerfully alter human resistance and susceptibility to the ubiquitous agents in our environment. Disruption of the social milieu leads more to a rise in a wide range of diseases than to a rise in any one or any coherent class of diseases.

The healing process involves a subtle interweaving of cultural, interpersonal, and personality factors as well as physiological ones. Studying the ways healing occurs in different cultures can help us understand how these factors combine to engage the individual in the process of healing. The ethnomedical approach emphasizes the "meaning contexts of sickness" in joining different medical systems. In an ethnomedical analysis, one recognizes that people take on sick roles when they do not have organic diseases. Biological and social realities, while they affect each other, are not identical, and cultures define and structure their interactions.

From within the perspective of Western medicine, study of the placebo effect yields understanding of how expectation can unleash a person's own healing processes. Until about 1900, when the efficacy of biomedicine first rose above chance levels, the history of Western medicine was the history of the placebo. The effects of placebos are about two thirds as powerful as those of the drugs to which they are compared. This is not so impressive in the case of aspirin, but consider that a patient given a placebo he or she believes to be as powerful as morphine will experience pain relief equivalent to two thirds that of morphine. Placebo effectiveness varies with the expectations of both physician and patient, and some patients may be placebo responders in certain situations but not in others.

The social process is a theme running through all the work on healing. The social fabric is reflected in an individual's health. People without close contact with others have higher morbidity and mortality from many causes than people with intimacy. Communication can be a mechanism of both sickness and death through the cardiovascular system, and paradoxically, a mechanism of improving health. The Cartesian dualistic approach our society has adopted to divorce the body from the mind has had the consequence that people do not recognize the damage social isolation and conflict cause. We cannot communicate without affecting our bodies. There is no disease that kills people at the rate loneliness does. At all ages, for both sexes and all races in the United States, the single, widowed, and divorced die at rates from two to ten times higher than do married people younger than 70. People genuinely need each other. Yet, as a society we are moving away from traditions that have evolved over centuries to provide human contact and friendship for the lonely. No country spends more money on biomedical research than the United States. War has been declared on heart disease and on cancer, but we may be working feverishly to control diseases that we ourselves are causing.

The damage that social upheaval, conflict, and loss cause may be remediable by psychophysiological treatment to some degree, but such dislocation might also be prevented by improving social networks. When disconnected people band together and develop ties, their health improves. Forming and maintaining social support networks is very important to our health.

ENVIRONMENTAL INFLUENCES

People have long noted that they feel different at the seashore and in the mountains from the way they normally do. In addition to natural beauty, such places have a higher concentration of negative air ions. These ions have measureable influences on serotonin and cyclic adenosine monophosphate (AMP) levels and apparently affect mood and alertness. Respiratory cilia increase in activity in the presence of negative air ions. This seems to be the mechanism of the decrease they are associated with in airborne cross-infection. Rats exposed to negative air ions show increased cortical thickness, suggesting that negatively ionized air might accelerate maturation and aging, but concentrations of lipofuscin, an aging pigment, are lowered by exposure to negative ions.

Alertness, concentration, and sleepiness can also be manipulated in a matter of minutes by the foods we eat. Of the many compounds that function as neurotransmitters, it is now clear that some, at least, are synthesized at different rates depending on the composition of the food eaten. The rate of neurotransmitter synthesis affects the quantities released and can be related to mood and behavior.

It is surprising that three cookies could make a person sleepy, but carbohydrates affect serotonin synthesis. A high-carbohydrate, low-protein meal raises brain tryptophan and accelerates the synthesis of its product, 5-hydroxtryptophan into serotonin. A high-carbohydrate meal does this by increasing the secretion of insulin, which does little to serum tryptophan, but lowers serum levels of other large neutral amino acids such as tyrosine, phenylalanine, leucine, isoleucine, and valine. This has the effect of increasing fatigue and sleepiness, accelerating sleep onset, decreasing sensitivity to mild pain, and increasing errors on performance tests.

It is not surprising that caffeine will make a person more alert, but it is surprising that yogurt or turkey can have the same effect, and almost as quickly. A protein-rich meal reverses the effect of a carbohydrate-rich meal by reversing the ratio of tryptophan to the other large neutral amino acids by contributing many of these other amino acids to the blood, but little tryptophan. Eating pure tyrosine will raise brain tyrosine levels and increase catecholamine synthesis, but a high-protein meal alone will probably not raise blood and brain levels of tyrosine enough to affect catecholamine synthesis.

PSYCHONEUROIMMUNOLOGY

Healing does not merely restore the mind or the body to its condition before the illness, but more usually it brings about a lasting change. Even the most primitive cell is equipped with mechanisms for self-healing. It is reasonable that all healing practices should be evaluated in the light of this very widespread capacity for healing that exists in all living things and in every human being. Healing can be considered just a clinical correction of the damage that had been done. There is another kind of healing that implies a very different mechanism, however, a kind of permanent change in the patient or in the organism, whatever its nature, that makes it better able to cope with whatever new situation has arisen. René Dubos called this creative adaptation. The change can be negative, but it can also be adaptive. Adapting can be a change in the whole organism, making it better able to meet new challenges.

A developing field at the forefront of the study of how the body and mind interact in healing is psychoneuroimmunology. It now appears that neurons communicate with one another not merely in the relatively direct manner across synapses with which we are familiar, but via neuropeptides that can act far downstream from the producing neuron. The selectivity of the receptors is such that they can sort out messages. The brain, glands, and immune system are joined to one another in a bidirectional network of communication, with the neuropeptides the carriers of information. For example, peptide-producing neurons come from the brain and actually innervate bone marrow. In the other direction, some monocytes actually enter the brain and are transformed and become glial cells. Before this, monocytes are important parts of the immune system. They contain receptors for every neuropeptide they have been examined for. They communicate with B-cells and T-cells, fight disease, and distinguish between self and nonself. In addition to managing immune and endocrine functions, the neuropeptide system may underlie emotions.

THE BRAIN'S REGULATION OF THE BODY

We may have been brainwashed by the Metropolitan Life Insurance Company's tables of height and weight. Reanalysis of the data these tables are based on indicates that the tables may be correct for people about 40 years old, but that as people age, ideal weight may be heavier than the tables suggest. The healthiest people may be those who gain a little weight with age.

COPING WITH STRESS

Of two people under similarly demanding situations, why does one stay healthy and one become sick? The way we cope with stress must make a difference. The three C's, challenge, control, and commitment, appear to be part of the explanation. People who view the world as a challenge, who view themselves as in control, and who have a commitment to themselves seem to stay healthier under stress than people with the reverse traits. Another perspective finds that people who view the world as coherent are more resistant to stress-related illness than people who view it as chaotic.

The concept of the Type A behavior pattern initially held great promise as a new risk factor for coronary heart disease, but recent negative findings have cast some doubt on its validity. If interpreted carefully, these findings show that the hypothesis that behavior can cause heart disease has merely been developed and focused, but has not died.

Together, these articles describe a world of research that changes the way we think about the brain and health. Just because we can put together the words "What is the relationship between the mind, the body, the brain, and health?" does not mean there is a satisfactory answer to the question. Not only do the neuropeptides produced by the brain communicate with parts of the endocrine and immune system, but some immune system monocytes, which develop in bone marrow and circulate in the blood, enter the brain and are transformed into glial cells. This suggests the mind may reside partially in our monocytes and all the far-flung places they go. This is a long way from the belief many people still hold, that the mind is in the brain or is some sort of secretion of the brain.

REFERENCES

Brody, H. (1955). Organization of the cerebral cortex. III. A study of aging in the human cerebral cortex. *Journal of Comparative Neurology, 102,* 511–556.

Brody, H. (1978). Cell counts in cerebral cortex and brainstem. In R. Katzman, R. D. Terry, & K. L. Bick (Eds.), *Aging: Vol. 7. Alzheimer's disease, senile dementia and related disorders.* New York: Raven Press.

Burns, B. D. (1958). In E. Arnold (Ed.), *Monographs of the Physiological Society: The mammalian cerebral cortex.* London. Arnold.

Diamond, M. C. (1988). *Enriching heredity.* New York: Free Press.

Leboucq, G. (1929). Le rapport entre lipoids et la surface de l'hémisphere cerébrale de l'homme et les singes. *Mém. Acad. R. Méd. Belg., 10,* 55.

·2·

The Brain as a Health Maintenance Organization

ROBERT ORNSTEIN

DAVID S. SOBEL

"Real," organic diseases are linked to changes in one's belief about oneself and one's relationship to others. This only appears impossible, or at least irrelevant or unimportant, from the early and simplistic medical view that regards the body as a mindless automaton. Heart, lungs, stomach, immune system, and all other organs and systems are hardly independent and autonomous. Certainly they have autonomous functions, but they are to some degree regulated by and in communication with the brain.

Many different factors, from the cells to the self, from spouses to societies, can affect health. There may be specific disturbances in the organs of the body, an inborn error in the genes, a break in personal relationships, a radical change in one's company's prospects, a shift in the government, or an improvement in economic conditions, all of which can occur separately and independently, yet each one can destabilize the organism and contribute to the progress of disease.

Diseases and disorders have multiple causes and can occur for many different reasons, so any disease, mental or physical, is rarely all "in the mind" of those afflicted, nor is it solely a matter of simply determined germ attacks on the body. The patient is neither always responsible for the disease, nor always helpless. But all these factors, all these events, from the state of one's marriage to the current state of hormone production, are managed instant by instant by one 3-pound lump containing a hundred billion, give or take a few billion, cells.

The answers to questions about the relationships between the brain, the mind, health, and society are hardly all in, but the evidence from many different areas of research now available begins to make some of the connections clear. The heart cannot itself decide that a death is too much for it, the liver does not alone register the shame of embarrassment, the immune system does not know whether its client is employed or not, divorced or not.

The brain does.

The brain minds the body: the insides of the body, the safety and stability of the individual, and the maintenance of the social body of human society. In fact, health maintenance is the primary function of the brain, not rational thought, language, poetry, and other functions usually thought of as the brain's work. The brain has evolved complex systems, which we call bodyguards, to protect and maintain health and is the central agent in managing the stability of the person and resistance to disease.

THE TRIUNE BRAIN

A rather haphazard and seemingly disorganized set of structures makes up the brain because the brain was built, partly by design and partly by accident, by the processes of evolution over hundreds of millions of years. It can be thought of as an old ramshackle house, a house that was originally built long ago for a small family, then added on to over several generations of growth and changes.

So it is with the original structure of the brain, the old rooms. The brain contains room after room of different structures united only because they are in the same skull, side by side. The human brain is not like a well-designed modern house, one in which each cubic foot is well planned and organized. We were not built that way. We carry our evolution inside us, within the different structures of the brain, structures built in different eras. There are many different little brains inside there.

There is an archeology as well as an architecture to the brain, because it was built up over millions of years. As in an archaeological dig, there are layers to the brain. The human brain was not constructed of new elements. It is a compendium of circuits piled atop one another, most developed to serve a short-term purpose in millenniums past. Evolution does not work for the long term, but for the immediate exigencies of survival for individuals.

The brain evolved, as is well known by now, in different levels, each one designed to maintain stability in its organism as animals moved from the sea to land, to the trees, to the savannas of eastern Africa, to Fifth Avenue. The early layers and the "higher" brain structures share the same head, the same neurons, and the same blood supply. The neurochemicals that are activated for emergencies, for example, may course through the entire structure. An instability in one brain system can easily come to affect others, as a fire started in one dwelling of a large building affects the neighbors, even though they did not cause the fire.

The oldest and deepest area of the brain evolved more than 500 million years ago, before the evolution of mammals. Many scientists refer to this part of the brain as the reptilian brain, since the human brainstem looks like that of a reptile. The brainstem is primarily concerned with the biological stability of the organism and manages the first and most basic means of life support—such as the control of breathing and heart rate. This sufficed for ocean life in our ancestors.

Some 200 to 300 million years ago, during the transition from sea-dwelling animals to those that lived on land, a new brain had to evolve. Living off the land causes many problems for the brain. Life is more stable and relatively easy in the sea. There is no harsh winter, or at least there is extremely little temperature variation, so there is no need for the organism to regulate internal temperature. Gravity is not a problem. One also does not have to worry much about where one's next drink is coming from, so complicated systems for thirst regulation and fluid retention are hardly worth evolving.

But to maintain the stability of the body on land with its vagaries—the irregular supplies of food and drink, the extremes of climate, and new dangers unknown in the deep—a new and different brain developed. This area of the brain was named the limbic system, a group of cell structures in the center of the brain, immediately atop the brain stem. A person in a coma cannot respond to or interact with the outside world; but he or she continues to live, because the limbic system still operates, maintaining vital body functions.

It is often called the mammalian brain because the same brain structure is found in all mammals. The limbic system is the area of the brain that helps to maintain homeostasis, a stable environment within the body. Homeostatic mechanisms located in the limbic system regulate such functions as the maintenance of body temperature, blood pressure, heart rate, and blood sugar level. But it does much more than just control recurrent internal processes: The limbic system is involved in the emotional reactions that have to do with survival, such as self-protection through fighting or escaping. It contains the hypothalamus, the "brain of the brain," its most intricate and amazing structure. It regulates eating, drinking, sleeping, waking, body temperature, chemical balances, heart rate, hormones, sex, and emotions.

The hypothalamus operates through feedback. Body temperature is registered, for instance, in specialized neurons in the hypothalamus that respond to the temperature of incoming blood as it circulates through the brain. If the blood is too cool, the hypothalamus stimulates heat production and conservation. When one area of an animal's hypothalamus is injured, the animal does not eat or drink, no matter how long it has been deprived of food or water. Conversely, stimulation or destruction of other areas of the hypothalamus causes incessant eating, which can be fatal.

Through a combination of electrical and chemical messages, the hypothalamus directs the master gland of the brain, the pituitary. This gland regulates the body through hormones, chemicals manufactured and secreted by special neurons in the brain and carried through the blood to specific target cells in the body. The pituitary synthesizes most of the hormones used by the brain to communicate with the major glands of the body.

The latest level of the brain to develop, the cerebral cortex, made its appearance about 50 million years ago. It performs the functions that have increased our adaptability and that make us most human. In the cortex decisions are made, the world is organized, individual experiences are stored in memory, speech is produced and understood, paintings are seen, and music is heard.

The cortex is only about an eighth of an inch thick, and it is folded. If it were spread out, it would be about the size of a newspaper page. Of all mammals, human beings have the most enfolded cortex, perhaps because such a large cortex had to fit into a small head to permit passage through a narrow birth canal. The cortex is built in quite an interesting manner, with specialized cells arranged in columns—columns that seem to have specific functions, such as the detection of corners, or edges in the visual system. These "hard-wired" data-processing centers in the cortex and below serve as modules for the basic interpretation of information. The rooms of the brain have their own columns.

Inside the cortex lie separate centers for specific functions, which we like to call talents. Looked at this way, the brain is not a single organ, but is divided into different and well-defined areas, each of which possesses a rich concentration of certain abilities.

The cortex is responsible for making decisions and judgments on all the information coming into it from the body and the outside world. It receives information from the outside world, analyzes and compares it with stored information from previous experiences and knowledge, and makes a decision; then sends its own messages and instructions out to the appropriate muscles, glands, and other organs. The cortex is the seat of the rational abilities we develop.

THE BRAIN AVOIDS TROUBLE

As this tour of 500 million years in a few paragraphs might begin to indicate, the brain is not primarily designed for thinking. Those attributes we consider most human—language, perception, intelligence—represent only a small fraction of the brain's functions. The academic and scientific analysis of the brain has focused wrongly on this one, admittedly interesting, function of the brain.

In brain science the bulk of the research effort is on those attributes that are most uniquely human: language, thought, creativity, intelligence, and logic. Our models of the brain compare it with an information-processing machine, now the computer, years ago the switchboard. Brain scientists have confused our own ideal of what we would like to be—rational decision makers—with our analysis of what the brain is doing. Thought came very late in the development of the brain, intelligence came later, at least as we understand it, and it is a question whether rationality has come at all.

The brain is basically a system that helps the organism avoid trouble; thinking about it this way makes it unnecessary to worry whether there are systems of the body (like the immune system) that might run without the brain's management. This kind of thinking took hold in the era when both neurophysiology and medicine were at their beginnings. Those who were interested in the effects of "the organism" on health were considered unscientific, and the one discipline that did consider it, psychiatry, was relegated to a department separate from the "hard sciences" such as immunology. No matter the academic mistakes; it is all one organism in there, under real control of brain mechanisms. Asking whether the brain "knows" about the immune system is like asking whether President Richard Nixon knew about Watergate.

But the link between the brain and the other internal organs is not to be made by us in this book: It is already there, because the brain is another organ of the body, like a gland, like the adrenals or the pancreas. It grows and develops with the rest of the body. It does not grow up in the midst of silicon chips or disk drives to be inserted into the skull later on.

The brain has a body to manage. It controls temperature, blood flow, and digestion; it monitors every sensation, breath and heartbeat, movement, blink and swallow. It directs movement: walk this way; take the hand off the stove; lift the arm to catch the ball; smile. The tongue, the lungs, the mouth, and the pharynx all must be directed to move to produce speech. All these actions are not designed primarily for poetry or opera, but for the safety, stability, and health of the body that owns the brain.

If we followed this line of thought about the brain, our ideas and research efforts would undergo an important change; and we could completely turn around concepts of health and disease.

Ultimately, everything the brain does results in action or in motions. The brain directs all voluntary and involuntary movements. It communicates with the body via the glands of the endocrine system and three interconnected systems of nerves: the central nervous system, the peripheral nervous system, and the autonomic nervous system. Its job is complex enough. To function in a complex environment, actions must be planned, guided, and organized; and we must know when and where to walk; when to speak and what to say; when to eat, drink, eliminate, and sleep. These actions must be coordinated with events in the outside world.

THE ORGAN OF ADAPTATION

The brain responds to changes in the external and internal worlds. Through the senses the brain receives information about occurrences in the outside world. The internal state of the body, blood sugar level and internal pain, are controlled, in part, by the endocrine system. The stimulus that gets the brain's attention is one that signals a change from the existing state. The change may be as subtle as a change in air pressure or as jarring as a novel or unexpected statement. The brain constantly interprets information it receives, matching it against a model it develops of the world.

It is not enough for actions to be coordinated with events in the outside world, they must reflect internal needs. Thus there is an innate priority system in the brain: Certain events seem to enter our consciousness much more easily than others. Suppose you are having a discussion about your marriage. It may seem quite important at the moment, but what happens when you get a cinder in your eye, or put your hand over a flame? Even the most compelling argument disappears. Pain can flood consciousness in the same way that an emergency fills the front page of a newspaper. The priority system gives certain events, those affecting survival, fast access inside. Survival and safety come first—while hunger will not intrude as dramatically as does pain, the need will be felt if left unattended.

The brain is the major organ of adaptation. It tells the body what to do based on its information on the changing state of the world. The ability to respond quickly to change and to be flexible in responding are the primary ingredients of adaptability. The more complex the organism, the more adaptable it will be. Consider what happens when a frog is confronted by a fallen tree. The frog has such a specialized sensory system and brain that it probably would not notice the tree unless it ran into it. A human can cut it, play seesaw on it, make tables out of it, even make paper for this book. The greater flexibility of action that characterizes human adaptation is in large part due to a larger brain.

A PYRAMID OF PRIORITIES

Because we evolved on the biological underpinnings of the codfish, the rat, and the monkey and were elaborated in the early hominids, it should not be surprising that we have many different kinds of needs and many ways of satisfying them and that we are doing thousands of things at any moment. In dealing with this continuous flux of input and output, the brain must have evolved some sort of priority system to signal what is important or urgent to deal with and what can be safely ignored. The brain's job is to keep track of this continuous priority system and to keep things moving.

It is useful to picture these different kinds of requirements as forming a pyramid. At the bottom are the most basic needs; as one progresses to the top, the needs and the goals become more complex. The relative strength, or prepotence, of the different needs distinguishes the levels of the hierarchy. The stronger needs are lower: given the lack of both friendship and water, the need for water is stronger, prepotent. It will preempt consciousness until it is satisfied. The brain shifts up and down a constantly changing set of priorities, keeping balance, keeping the cells of the body properly hydrated and with a mineral content close to that of the sea, organizing parties with the family, adjusting heart rate after a meal, alerting the body when a loud noise is heard, shunting blood around the body, maintaining weight, and thousands more, wheeling and healing along.

The many different and separate systems within the brain, all cohabiting in the same skull, are there for the purpose of surviving biologically, for which health is the primary prerequisite. An organism that is sick is unlikely to reproduce. An organism that has accidents does not survive to do so. Remember, many organisms lived for quite a while before we came on the scene, and those that remain have to have done something correctly in order to keep themselves healthy for the last 500 million years. Note that this period begins 499,999,960 years before the effective administration of streptomycin and 499,999,920 years before Salvarsan (arsphenamine) marked the beginning of chemotherapy.

So, a long time ago, before the present physical and created world, when the world was very different, our ancestors had already evolved many different highly effective and interdependent programs, residing in different brain structures, to keep their bodies stable in the face of internal and external demands and disruptions, surviving, remaining healthy. Some of these responses remain effective under modern conditions, like the exquisite control of the oxygenation of the blood or the temperature of the body in widely different circumstances and the precise regulation of weight.

SYSTEMS OF HEALING

These intrinsic healing and self-regulatory systems of the brain may be commonplace but should not be overlooked in favor of striking medical successes; they are not trivial to our health. Many of them have evolved within the brain to aid survival and are so common and obvious that they attract little notice, personally or scientifically.

Why do people cry? Recent evidence suggests that the tears produced by emotional crying may be a way the body disposes of toxic substances. It may seem strange to think of crying as beneficial, yet many people say that a good cry makes them feel better.

The belief that crying has positive effects is of ancient origin. More than 2,000 years ago, Aristotle theorized that crying at a drama cleanses the mind of suppressed emotions by a process called catharsis. Catharsis is the reduction of emotional distress by releasing the emotion in controlled circumstances. Many people attend movies and plays that they know beforehand are, shall we say, elicitors of psychogenic lacrimation, or tearjerkers. Such people may cry freely in movies and not regret the experience at all. The experience that stimulated crying is sought out, and if the resultant crying is the behavioral release of suppressed grief, it is but a short step to a view of crying as therapeutic.

There have been a few studies of the effects of crying. Borquist (1906) obtained reports of the effects of crying, including the observation of 54 of 57 respondents that crying had positive results. Weiner found from reports that asthma attacks—long thought to be largely psychosomatic—cease as a result of crying.

While the research on the benefits of crying is intriguing but hardly decisive, other strands of evidence are becoming available. Tears produced by emotional crying, such as those elicited by tearjerker movies, differ in chemical content from those caused by irritants such as onion juice. Emotional tears contain more protein than tears induced by irritants. Frey and colleagues contend that emotional crying is an eliminative process in which tears remove toxic substances from the body (Frey, DeSota-Johnson, Hoffman, & McCall, 1981). Crying may cleanse the mind in a much more literal sense than even the catharsis theorists imagine. Other researchers are now examining the contents of emotional tears for substances such as endorphins, ACTH, prolactin, and growth hormone, all of which are released by stress. While the research on psychoactive substances in tears is just beginning, there is reason to think that emotional tears may perform a very important function in the maintenance of physical health and emotional balance.

Why do we develop a fever with infection? There is some evidence to suggest that the elevated temperature is part of a brain mechanism to help fight infection. When the body is infected, chemicals called pyrogens are released into the blood stream. These chemicals act on the temperature-sensing neurons in the hypothalamus to reset the thermostat at a higher temperature. Experiments in which animals are prevented from raising their body temperatures in response to an infection have demonstrated higher death rates, suggesting that the fever fights the infection. How this occurs is not known for certain. One theory holds that at higher body temperatures iron is less available in the blood stream and the replication of germs that require iron is impeded. Current medical thinking has shifted from reducing the fever with drugs such as aspirin (unless the fever is extremely high or the person is debilitated) to appreciating the role of this brain-controlled mechanism.

Pain, too, is information of great priority to the organism and is a special experience to the person. It is so important that it is organized as a separate system within the central nervous system. Pain information travels through circuitry that seems carefully designed, from quite special receptors into a special network of priority systems in transmission to the brain. Pain is one way we keep out of trouble. Similarly, sneezes, shivers, hiccups, and many other innate reactions have their own specific health functions. These are all controlled by brain mechanisms, responding to the need to keep the organism stable.

These common reactions are not accidents and are not trivial compared with rationality or our elaborate medical care system; they are important parts of the brain's management of the body. They guard us against diseases and disorders, maintain body weight and temperature, fight infections, avoid poisons, keep things stable, and build health.

HEALTH MAINTENANCE PROGRAMS

The brain is principally a health maintenance organization, and the bodyguards are certain sophisticated brain-body systems that have evolved to help the brain mind the body. These health maintenance systems evolved in our predecessors long before the higher levels of the brain developed. They are reliable since they are below conscious control and seem invulnerable to voluntary regulation. For instance, have you ever gone to a restaurant and found the food spoiled, so much that you have been unable to return, even though you have had many good experiences there, and would like to go back? This is the health maintenance system taking over and overriding any thoughts you might have. Why does it work that way?

It is generally considered a good thing across all cultures (and across all species as far as is known) not to get poisoned. Few species with an appetite for poisonous food would survive long enough to contribute their genes to our ancestors. Humans also seem to have many built-in guards against poisonings, and the effects can color preferences for travel, for what is aesthetically appealing, and more commonly for taste (and smell), since taste is intimately related to detecting nutritious versus poisonous things.

One of us (R.E.O.) can speak from experience about a well-developed food preference, for instance: I don't eat Mexican food. My friends always make fun of me because of this. You're so inconsistent, they tell me; you love hot food like Indian curry; you love tomatoes, onions, garlic, avocados. It seems strange to me too. It's not just that I don't care for the food, I simply can't bear the thought of eating it, no matter what, no matter how hungry I am. It seems quite odd.

I know when and where I developed my problem. About 25 years ago I was working as a deck hand on a freighter that stopped at the port of Zihuatanejo, on the west coast of Mexico. We arrived one night and I went ashore to enjoy a meal given for the ship's crew. The ship left early the next morning. It was my time to stand watch on the bow. Before the sun came up a violent storm arose. The rain poured, the wind blew, and the bow of the ship leaped time and again out of the water, crashing again and again into the sea. Again and again the ship heaved. The only way I could stand up to stand watch out there was to tie myself onto the little perch on the bow. So I bounced and heaved (in more than one sense of the word) along with the ship itself.

When all had calmed down, I returned to my quarters, sick and completely exhausted. I slept for 12 hours. When I awoke I was afraid of returning to the bow of the ship and I was completely disgusted by the idea of Mexican food. My fear of the bow was, I think, completely understandable, but I got over that fast. I returned to my regular watch two or three days later. However, I have never been able to eat Mexican food again, even though I knew the cause of my sickness was the storm, not the dinner, so deeply into the mind went the association of the dinner with the sickness.

There is a body of literature on how the brain is wired up to learn about certain health-related experiences. Martin Seligman proposed that there is a continuum of preparedness for different experiences. John Garcia has shown, in conditioning studies, that rats are "prepared" to associate nausea with taste but not with other external events. Doesn't this make sense? How well would a rat survive that decided it was sick because of something it heard or saw?

That is why I have, for all these years, been unable to eat Mexican food. Of the particular combination of events I experienced, only the meal and the stomach upset—not the storm and the tossing ship—became strongly associated, because the ability to quickly learn the relationship between a certain food and stomach upset is strongly built into us. The association is specific, just for Mexican food, not for Mexican clothing, furniture, art, or the Mayan ruins.

I behaved like a subject in one of those rat experiments. Even now that I know why I cannot eat Mexican food, I still cannot do anything about it—our prepared associations are stronger than I am. Even conscious knowledge of why this happened has made little difference, so dominant are these pieces of mind. I have had to play tricks on myself, not all of which are successful. I have convinced myself that guacamole is really California barbecue food and that chili is from Texas. Not only does the brain deter us from eating upsetting foods once experienced, it governs the metabolism of all the food we eat as part of its health maintenance.

There are numerous other bodyguards. Some, like the ones we have so far discussed are more reflexive, controlled by the lower brain structures, and others are more under cortical control and therefore more influenced by social and psychological changes.

We need to recognize that the brain is not primarily for educating, not for speaking and thinking, but is more like a gland, part of the body and a system to mind the body. The brain spends most of its time maintaining homeostasis, the stability of the body, not in preparing for rational discussions or for writing music. But homeostasis, a return to a static state also represents a misunderstanding. Things are never static within ourselves or in the outside world; our needs change, society changes, growth occurs.

What the brain tries to do is to keep the body continuously adapting, and somehow stable, but not static in a changing world. What is strong enough in youth is not so in maturity, blood supply that is adequate for resting does not suffice for running, metabolic processes that keep the energy supply adequate in winter do not do so in spring. There are countless systems within the brain orchestrating this rough and always moving stability, as the world changes, as the organism changes, as needs change. We don't yet know how our brain does all of it, but we should note that it has taken a long time to perfect these health maintaining routines, and modern science might still have a bit to learn from them. Appreciating and understanding the central role the brain plays in maintaining the health of the body will create new opportunities for medicine to work in concert with the powerful self-regulatory systems of the organism.

We are at the beginning of a new era, one in which the brain's central contribution to resistance to disease is being discovered and enhanced. It has not been done before because medical scientists, like most other human beings, want to tackle problems that are amenable to solutions within a short time. So they typically try to study the simplest systems available. Bacteria, for instance, are quite simple. As Salvador Luria once said to one of us (R.O.), "We know everything about them. They move." Understanding these simple structures has paid off, as has the understanding of viruses and other disease entities.

But the price of progress has too often been a severe limit on acceptable inquiry into what is currently understandable and a set of beliefs that, somehow, the current set of problems is the correct set, even though they might have been selected on the basis of solvability. It is easy to see why most scientists, brain and medical researchers certainly included, have had to limit their inquiry. The understanding of large and complex systems is extremely difficult, given the methods of 19th and early 20th century science. Billions of people make up the earth's population and their interaction is difficult to measure; this has made researchers in the hard sciences more comfortable with analysis of simple and small systems. Just as complex and just as difficult to fathom is how the billions of cells in the brain operate, how the brain developed and what it responds to.

It is only now, in the late 1980s that the different streams of research are beginning to merge. It has taken years of the research work of thousands of scientists to be able to determine the nature of the brain's communication circuitry that enables it to connect such events as the sudden loss of a spouse to the ability of the body to survive infection.

And there is more. Raising hope increases health; the attention of friends is an essential part of the brain's nutrition. Recent discoveries about the endorphin, immune, and cardiovascular systems, combined with new studies of brain physiology, human evolution, and cognitive psychology point to a new understanding of this most mysterious organ.

It is the central connection between the different worlds and the different systems each person lives in. It connects the output of nerve, muscle, and gland cells in the body. It monitors the operation of all other organ systems, orchestrating and selecting the way information from the outside environment gets inside.

It maintains stability in countless ways. It ultimately controls heart-beat, blood pressure, blood composition and volume, breathing, the entrance of oxygen into the blood stream, the production and combination of thousands of chemicals of the internal pharmacy, the integrity of the internal organs, the safety of the organism, the avoidance of danger, the attachments to family, to friends and to society, and the creation of mental processes, routines, and structures that guide the person safely through immediate and long-term crises.

It is a healing brain.

REFERENCES

Borquist, A. (1906). Crying. *American Journal of Psychology, 17,* 149–205.
Frey, W. H., DeSota-Johnson, D., Hoffman, C., & McCall, J. T. (1981). Effect of stimulus on the chemical composition of tears. *American Journal of Ophthalmology, 92*(4), 559–567.

·3·

How the Brain Grows in Response to Experience

MARIAN C. DIAMOND

The human brain has changed slowly over millions of years, yet we can demonstrate on histological sections that the brain can change its structure in but 4 days. One might then ask the question "Why hasn't the brain grown astronomically over millions of years if it is possible to change it so readily?"

The title of this book is *The Healing Brain: A Scientific Reader*, but in order to understand the healing brain, we have to understand the potential of the healthy brain. If one lies on the grass at the top of a hill on a clear day and watches the clouds drift slowly by, one can introspect and wonder how the cells inside one's head can be helping to appreciate the marvels of nature. What kinds of cells can carry out such functions?

Essentially, there are only two kinds of brain cells, nerve cells and glial cells. These cells interact within the skull to carry out the myriad functions attributed to the brain. Most people know about nerve cells but how many know about glial cells?

The word "glial" comes from the Greek for glue, and early anatomists thought the glial cells glued nerve cells together, that they were the structural support cells for nerve tissue. But we know now that nerve cells need glial cells to function efficiently; they are both metabolic and structural support cells. There is a symbiotic relationship between them that may involve nutrition, ion balance, or acting as scaffolding for the migration of nerve cells during development. Some glial cells form the myelin on a nerve fiber that increases the speed of conduction. Both nerve cells and glial cells are necessary for building a brain.

In all mammalian embryos the brain develops from a neural tube that forms the hindbrain, the midbrain, and the forebrain. The forebrain grows into the very large cerebral hemispheres. The left and right hemispheres together account for about 85% of the human brain. The hindbrain deals with modifying the cardiovascular, respiratory, and other systems, but the forebrain allows for abstract thinking, composing beautiful music or poetry, or sending a man to the moon.

The outer layers of the cerebral hemispheres are called the cerebral cortex, the gray matter that differs in thickness depending on whether it is on the surface or within a sulcus. Quantitative measurements of human cortical thickness, which do not vary by more than 5%, cannot be made easily at present.

No two human brains are alike, and we need large samples to obtain meaningful statistics. We do not yet have techniques that can differentiate very precisely gray matter from white. Nuclear magnetic resonance imaging offers promise for the future, but at present computed axial or positron emission tomographic scanning are not adequate. Thus, we must work with the rat brain, whose cerebral cortex is smooth, not folded, so we can make very accurate measurements. We can measure the cortex in different sections very precisely from one animal to another. We are as careful as possible in sampling a mammalian brain to get uniform samples because no two parts of the brain are alike and, as we shall see, they do not respond to the same environment in a similar manner.

Folded deep in the temporal cortex is the hippocampus. This structure deals with emotional behavior, sexual behavior, and with memory processing. I will also refer to the diencephalon, a part of which has connections with the hippocampus.

CORTICAL DEVELOPMENT

To examine cortical development and aging as a continuum we can look at the cortical thickness in males from 6 to 650 days of age. During the first few days after birth the growth of the cortex is phenomenal, increasing about 45% by 26 days of age, and then the cortical mantle decreases in thickness by about 9% until 650 days, the last time measured in this particular study (Diamond, Johnson & Gold, 1977; Diamond, Johnson, & Ingham, 1975). At least three factors can be functioning here. It is possible that cortical cells are being lost and the cortex is decreasing in actual structure, or the cells are losing their branches, or it could be that the subcortical mass is increasing.

Later we added the data from a very old rat, one that was 904 days old. From 650 days to 900 there was a very slight decrease in the thickness in the frontal cortex. In the somatesthetic area, that dealing with general sensory modalities such as touch, pain, temperature, and pressure, thickness did not decrease significantly from 600 to 900 days. In the visual cortex, however, there was about a 30% decrease between 650 and 900 days.

Thus, once an animal reaches very old age, the aging patterns change. The posterior part of the brain, which is most responsive to the environment, apparently ages more rapidly after the animal has lived two thirds of its lifetime.

Generally, the diencephalon continues to grow by about 9% in both length and width between day 100 and day 650 in the rat. Thus, the possibility that the cortex stretches over an increasing subcortical mass is quite real.

THE EFFECTS OF ENRICHED ENVIRONMENTS

Our animals are exposed to different kinds of environments. In the multifamily enriched environment, three mothers live with three pups each in a large cage. They are housed in this way starting when the pups are 6 days old because before this time if they are housed together with other mothers and pups, the mothers will eat their pups. Even at 6 days, the mothers will take the pink, inch-long pups, pile them in a corner, and go out to explore the environment. The environment consists not only of communal living, but also of objects with which the rats interact. These objects are changed twice a week. We found this to be important—the brain did not change as much if the rats lived with the same objects continuously. We believe the animals became bored and needed to explore new things.

By contrast, for every pup that lived in a multifamily enriched environment, there was one in a single-family impoverished environment. One mother and her three pups lived in a small cage and had no toys and no additional playmates. All animals had free access to water and food and lived in the same room so they could hear and see the other pups. The key factor to creating brain changes was the presence of the toys. After varying periods of time, the brains were coded and the cortical thickness measured.

After only 22 days in their respective environments, the enriched rats showed up to a 12% thicker cortex than the nonenriched rats. We attribute this finding to environmental stimulation while the brain is growing rapidly.

But we know that after 26 days of age, there is a decrease in cortical thickness. Can enriched environments alter this phenomenon? For these experiments, rats in an enriched environment are housed without their mothers in groups of 12 to a cage, with access to toys. From three rat pups in a litter, one is assigned to the enriched environment, one to the standard colony (three rats to a small cage), and one to an impoverished environment. The impoverished environment consists of only one rat in a small cage with no toys or companions. The impoverished rats live in the same room as the other rats and have similar access to food and water.

This particular rat strain (S_1) becomes sexually mature at about 45 days of age. If the impoverished rats are housed in the enriched or standard environments at 60 days of age, the young cortex shows a difference in thickness between the enriched and impoverished environments by 4% after only 4 days. This difference is found in the occipital cortex, which proves to be the most responsive area of the cortex to environmental alterations.

Walter Riga had previously shown that from up to 1 year of age, the environment can cause significant changes in cortical weight (Diamond, 1976). Our work showed that rats exposed to enrichment beginning at 766 days of age and ending at 904 days of age had significant increases in cortical thickness (Diamond, Johnson, Prott, Ott, & Kajisa, 1985). We found differences in the frontal lobe, the somesthetic area, and the occipital lobe, even though stimulation did not begin until the animals were three quarters of the way through their lifetimes.

Left-Right Dominance and Sex

We have also examined cortical thickness in the left and right hemispheres. For these studies we used both Tryon's S_1 strain of maze-bright rats and Long–Evans rats. Robert Tryon observed in the 1920s that some rats ran mazes better than others; in seven generations, he bred a new maze-bright strain (Diamond, 1982).

In male maze-bright and Long–Evans rats the right side was thicker than the left in the visual–spatial occipital area. But in female Long–Evans rats (no more maze-bright animals were available) there was only a nonsignificant trend for the left side to be thicker than the right. At the time we found marked male-female differences in laterality in rats at 6–7 days, 14 days, 21 days, 90 days, 180–185 days, 390–400 days, and 800–904 days. Why there should be such marked gender differences in a quadruped that does not live in a culture that tells it to use the right side of the body is unclear. Why should the male have right dominance and the female a slight left dominance? The findings were not only in the cortex; we found the same difference in the hippocampus as well. Such laterality patterns may extend further into the brain.

Dendrite Growth

We compared the length of the dendrites in 630-day-old standard colony animals and 630-day-old enriched animals. In the first branch coming off the cell, there was no significant differences. In the second through the fifth branches coming off the cell there were similarly no significant differences. But in the terminal dendrite we found that the enriched animal had longer dendrites than the standard colony animal. Two factors could be responsible for this difference. There could actually be dendritic growth in the old animals; or we could be retaining a certain length in the enriched animals and the dendrites could be shrinking in the standard colony animals. There is no way now to determine which process is occurring in these animals (Connor, Melone, Yuen, & Diamond, 1981).

Another measure we examined was the dendritic spines. Not only does the nerve cell grow by extending processes of its cell membrane into dendrites, but on these dendrites there are small projections called dendritic spines. On each one of these little spines or projections, nerve fibers synapse from other nerve cells. A synaptic junction is found on the spines. We do not know yet why some nerve fibers called axons coming to a dendrite will synapse with a spine versus with the shaft of the dendrite proper. But we were interested to find out whether we could change the number of spines by placing animals in an enriched environment. We classified the spines into two types: one is called the lollipop spine because it has a long spine with a little bulbous ending; the second a nubbin spine because it has just a small projection off the dendritic shaft with the head as wide as the shaft of the spine. Reportedly the lollipop spine represents a healthy growing spine, the nubbin spine, a degenerating one.

We examined the spines in animals exposed to the different environments. We found no changes in the numbers of the lollipop spines and of nubbin spines in comparing 90-day-old standard animals with the enriched animals. However, in 630-day-old impoverished animals, there were more nubbin, degenerating spines than in those animals exposed to the standard colony condition (Connor, Diamond, & Johnson, 1980a).

You may not believe that a 630-day-old rat is old, but when we had caretakers caring for out rats, we began to lose them at 600 days. However, since we began taking care of the rats ourselves, we have been able to get them to live to 900 days. We believe it is because we really cared about these animals when we handled them. We call it the TLC effect.

What we are saying is that a very simple principle, use it or lose it, applies to stimulation for a nerve cell. We can show that the nerve cell can retain its healthy characteristics if it receives stimulation. Why do we bring this up? Because in essence, we are fighting old people's homes, where people are isolated from stimulation. The nervous system is not receiving much input. No wonder people become senile. Mental exercise helps the cerebral cortex as it does muscles, bones, and other organs of the body.

BIBLIOGRAPHY

Brody, H. (1955). Organization of the cerebral cortex. III. A study of aging in the human cerebral cortex. *Journal of Comparative Neurology, 102,* 511–556.

Brody, H. (1978). Cell counts in cerebral cortex and brainstem. In R. Katzman, R. D. Terry, & K. L. Bick (Eds.), *Aging: Vol. 7. Alzheimer's disease, senile dementia and related disorders.* New York: Raven Press.

Burns, B. D. (1958). In E. Arnold (Ed.), *Monographs of the Physiological Society: The mammalian cerebral cortex.* London: Arnold.

Connor, J. R., Diamond, M. C., & Johnson, R. E. (1980a). Aging and environmental influences on two types of dendritic spines in the rat occipital cortex. *Experimental Neurology, 70,* 371–379.

Connor, J. R., Diamond, M. C., & Johnson, R. E. (1980b). Occipital cortical morphology of the rat: Alteration with age and environment. *Experimental Neurology, 68,* 158–170.

Connor, J. R., Melone, J., Yuen, A., & Diamond, M. C. (1981). Terminal segments length of dendrites in aged rats: An environmentally induced response. *Experimental Neurology,* 827–830.

Diamond, M. C. (1967). Extensive cortical depth measurements and neuron size increases in the cortex of environmentally enriched rats. *Journal of Comparative Neurology, 131,* 357–364.

Diamond, M. C. (1976). Anatomical brain changes induced by environment. In J. McGaugh & L. Petrinovich (Eds.), *Festschrift: Knowing, thinking, and believing.* New York: Plenum Press.

Diamond, M. C. (1982). The aging rat forebrain: Male–female, left–right, environment and lipofuscin. In S. Scheff (Ed.), *Aging and recovery of function.* New York: Plenum Press.

Diamond, M. C., & Connor, J. R. (1981). A search for the potential of the aging brain. In S. J. Enna et al. (Eds.), *Aging: Vol. 17. Brain neurotransmitters and receptors in aging and age-related disorders.* New York: Raven Press.

Diamond, M. C. Krech, D., & Rosenzweig, M. R. (1964). The effects of an enriched environment on the histology of the rat cerebral cortex. *Journal of Comparative Neurology, 123,* 111–120.

Diamond, M. C., Johnson, R. E., & Gold, M. W. (1977). Changes in neuron and glia number in the young, adult and aging rat occipital cortex. *Behavioral Biology, 20,* 409–418.

Diamond, M. C., Johnson, R. E., & Ingham, C. A. (1975). Morphological changes in young, adult and aging rat cerebral cortex, hippocampus and diencephalon. *Behavioral Biology, 14,* 163–174.

Diamond, M. C., Johnson, R. E., Protti, A. M., Ott, C., & Kajisa, L. (1985). Plasticity in the 904-day-old male rat cerebral cortex. *Experimental Neurology, 87,* 309–317.

Leboucq, G. (1929). Le rapport entre lipoids et la surface de l'hemisphere cérébrale de l'homme et les singes. *Mém. Acad. R. Méd. Belg., 10,* 55.

·II·

PSYCHOSOCIAL FACTORS IN HEALING

· 4 ·

The Contribution of the Social Environment to Host Resistance

JOHN CASSEL

Wade Hampton Frost's introduction to the reprinting of John Snow's papers (Frost, 1936) starts, "Epidemiology at any given time is something more than the total of its established facts. It includes their orderly arrangement into chains of inference which extend beyond the bounds of direct observation." It is this "orderly arrangement into chains of inference" which intrigues me and which I think distinguishes creative epidemiologic studies from studies which may display considerable rigor in their methods but which are essentially pedestrian.

The question then is, what guides us in developing these chains of inference? Unquestionably, in large part the answer is the model of disease causation which we (implicitly or explicitly) espouse. In Frost's day this model, stated in its most general form, was that disease occurred as a result of new exposure to a pathogenic agent. It was recognized, of course, that the consequences of such exposure would be determined both by the pathogenicity of the agent and the degree of resistance or susceptibility of the host. This relationship has now been extended and formalized into the well-known triad of host, agent, and environment in epidemiologic thinking. Since Frost, the elucidation of host resistance factors has largely been the responsibility of the vastly expanded fields of biomedical research, such as genetics, molecular biology, immunology, biochemistry and endocrinology; while epidemiology has continued to search for the effects of a vastly

This chapter originally appeared in the *American Journal of Epidemiology*, 1976, 140(2), 107–123. It is reprinted here with permission from The Johns Hopkins University School of Hygiene and Public Health.

expanded array of pathogenic agents in the environment. The inference drawn on the basis of such findings has been that, given a certain level of resistance (for whatever reasons), we should be able to explain the occurrence of disease as a result of exposure to these pathogenic agents.

René Dubos (1965) has pointed out, however, that this formulation which may have provided a satisfactory basis for inferences in the 19th and early part of the 20th century when most diseases of interest (such as typhoid, cholera, smallpox, or the plague) were the result of agents of overwhelming pathogenicity and virulence, is no longer of particular use in a technologically developed society. In a modern society the majority of the citizens are protected from these overwhelming agents and most of the agents associated with current diseases are ubiquitous in our environment. Dubos (1965) stated it quite succinctly: "The sciences concerned with microbial diseases have developed almost exclusively from the study of acute or semi-acute infections caused by virulent microorganisms acquired through exposure to an exogenous source of infection. In contrast, the microbial diseases most common in our communities today arise from the activities of microorganisms that are ubiquitous in the environment, persist in the body without causing obvious harm under ordinary circumstances, and exert pathological effects only when the infected person is under conditions of physiological stress. In such a type of microbial disease, the event of infection is of less importance than the hidden manifestations of the smoldering infectious process and than the physiological disturbances that convert latent infection into overt symptoms and pathology."

Thus Dubos is stating that in societies where most disease agents are ubiquitous in the environment (and I believe his statement would cover most physiochemical agents, not only microbiologic ones), a full understanding of the distribution and determinants of disease requires that we know both the prevalence and toxicity of these agents and the determinants of those factors that change the relationship between the host and these agents, thus transforming an innocuous, possibly symbiotic, relationship to one in which clinical disease is the outcome.

The question facing epidemiologic inquiry then is, are there categories or classes of environmental factors that are capable of changing human resistance in important ways and of making subsets of people more or less susceptible to these ubiquitous agents in our environment? When we have thought of these questions at all, we have been accustomed to think in rather general terms of such things as nutritional status, fatigue, overwork, or the like. I would suggest, however, that there is another category of environmental factors capable of producing profound effects on host susceptibility to environmental disease agents, and that is the presence of other members of the same species, or more generally, certain aspects of the social environment.

The problem is that as soon as one introduces the concept of the potential role of the social environment in disease etiology, the almost inevitable response is that this means stress and stress disease. I think the simple-minded invocation of the word stress in such thinking has done as much to retard research in this area as did the concept of the miasmas at the time of the discovery of microorganisms. While there can be no question regarding the use of the concept of stress in the hands of the originators of this term (as applied in a scientific sense to medicine), and that Selye and Wolff (cited in Hinkle, 1973), for instance, have made a significant contribution to our ideas about the nature of disease and its causes, the current uncritical subscription to what are thought to have been the ideas of these investigators and the often erroneous interpretation of their theories by modern investigators have frequently led to contradictory findings and inappropriate inferences.

First, it is important to recognize the semantic difficulties surrounding the use of the word "stress." Selye and Wolff envisaged stress as a bodily state, not as a component of the environment. Thus Wolff states, "I have used the word stress in biology to indicate that state within a living creature which results from the interaction of the organism with noxious stimuli or circumstances, i.e., it is a dynamic state within the organism; it is not a stimulus assault, load symbol, burden, or any aspect of environment, internal, external, social or otherwise" (quoted in Hinkle, 1973). While Wolff demonstrated that this stress state (evidenced by neuroendocrinal changes) can be produced by a variety of noxious stimuli, physical as well as psychologic, he did not attempt to define the characteristics or the properties of these nonphysical (psychologic and/or social) noxious stimuli. Despite such formulations, subsequent investigators have tended to apply the term "stress" to these postulated noxious social or psychologic stimuli, often quoting Wolff for their justification. The use of the word "stressor" to indicate the environmental noxious stimulus and "stress state" or more frequently "stress disease" to indicate the postulated consequences of such exposure clarifies the semantic difficulty but highlights the more important conceptual issue. Stated in its most general terms, the formulation subscribed to (often implicitly) by most epidemiologists and social scientists working in this field is that the relationship between a stressor and disease outcome will be similar to the relationship between a microorganism and the disease outcome. In other words, the psychosocial process under investigation is envisaged as a stressor capable of having a direct pathogenic effect analogous to that of a physicochemical or microbiologic environmental disease agent. The corollaries of such a formulation are that there will be etiologic specificity (each stressor leading to a specific stress disease) and that there will be a dose-response relationship (the greater the stressor, the more likelihood of disease). There is serious doubt as to the utility or appropriateness of either of these notions.

Wolff himself stated quite explicitly that the action of physicochemical disease agents is different from psychosocial factors in that the former have a direct pathogenic effect by damaging and distorting structure and function, while the latter act indirectly (or, as he termed it, conditionally) by virtue of their capacity to act as signals or symbols (cited in Hinkle, 1973). Thus, disease can occur by virtue of a disturbance in the balance between the organism and various disease agents, as maintained by Dubos (1965), and if this balance is mediated largely by the neuroendocrine system, as has been maintained by Cannon (1935) and Schoenheimer (1942) and widely accepted since, then the mechanism through which the signals and symbols produced by the conditional noxious stimuli work presumably will be one of altering neuroendocrine secretions and levels in the body and thus changing the balance. As will be referred to later, there is evidence from both animal and human experiments indicating that variations in the social milieu are indeed associated with profound endocrine changes in the exposed subjects.

Viewed in this light, it is most unlikely that any given psychosocial process or stressor will be etiologically specific for any given disease, at least as currently classified. In other words, it no longer becomes useful to consider a subset of existing clinical entities as "stress" diseases as all diseases can in part be due to these processes. Hinkle (1973), arguing from the biologic evidence, supported this point strongly when he stated: "At the present time the 'stress' explanation is no longer necessary. It is evident that any disease process, and in fact any process within the living organism, might be influenced by the reaction of the individual to his social environment or to other people."

A more reasonable formulation would hold that psychosocial processes acting as "conditional" stressors will, by altering the endocrine balance in the body, increase the susceptibility of the organism to direct noxious stimuli, that is, disease agents. The psychosocial processes thus can be envisaged as enhancing susceptibility to disease. The clinical manifestations of this enhanced susceptibility will not be a function of the particular psychosocial stressor, but of the physicochemical or microbiologic disease agents harbored by the organism or to which the organism is exposed. Presumably, the disease manifestations will also be determined by constitutional factors, which in turn are a function of genetic endowment and previous experience.

Some reasonably convincing data exist to support this point of view. For example, one of the striking features of animal studies concerned with demonstrating the health consequences of a changed social environment has been the wide range of diseases that have followed such changes. Alteration of the social environment by varying the size of the group in which animals interact, while keeping all aspects of the physical environment and diet constant, has been reported to lead to a rise in maternal and infant mortality rates; an increase in the incidence of arteriosclerosis; a marked reduction in the resistance to a wide variety of direct noxious stimuli, including drugs, microorganisms, and x-rays; an increased susceptibility to various types of neoplasia; alloxan-produced diabetes; and convulsions (Ader & Hahn, 1963; Ader, Kreutner, & Jacobs, 1963; Andervont, 1944; Calhoun, 1962; Christian & Williamson, 1958; Davis & Read, 1958; King, Lee, & Visscher, 1955; Ratcliffe & Cronin, 1958; Swinyard, Clark, Miyahara, et al., 1961). Thus, in animals at least, no specific type of "stress disease" appears in response to changes in the social milieu-changes which have been interpreted as "stressors." Rather, the animals appear to respond with a variety of diseases, the particular manifestation being determined by factors other than the disturbed social process. The evidence from human studies is somewhat less direct but nevertheless still consistent with this idea. A remarkably similar set of social circumstances characterizes people who develop tuberculosis (Holmes, 1956) and schizophrenia, (Dunham, 1961; Mishler & Scotch, 1963), become alcoholics (Holmes, personal communication, 1963), are victims of multiple accidents (Tillmann & Hobbs, 1949), or commit suicide (Durkeim, 1951). Common to all these people is a marginal status in society. They are individuals who for a variety of reasons (e.g., ethnic minorities rejected by the dominant majority in their neighborhood; high sustained rates of residential and occupational mobility; broken homes or isolated living circumstances) have been deprived of meaningful social contact. It is perhaps surprising that this wide variety of disease outcomes associated with similar circumstances has generally escaped comment. To a large extent this has probably resulted because each investigator usually is concerned with only one clinical entity so the features common to multiple disease manifestations have tended to be overlooked.

One exception to this has been the study by Christenson and Hinkle (Christenson & Hinkle, 1961). In an industrial study in the United States, they have shown that managers in a company who, by virtue of their family background and educational experience were least well prepared for the demands and expectations of industrial life, were at greater risk of disease than age-matched managers who were better prepared. They found that this increased risk included all diseases, major as well as minor, physical as well as mental, long-term as well as short-term. A further example illustrating this point is the health consequences that follow the disruption of important social relationships, particularly death of a spouse. It has been shown that widowers have a death rate three to five times higher than married men of the same age for every cause of death (Kraus & Lilienfeld, 1959). It is difficult to conceive of a specific etiologic process responsible for the increased death rate from such diverse conditions as coronary heart disease, cancer, infectious diseases, and peptic ulcer, and it would appear more reasonable to consider that the loss of the spouse increases the susceptibility of such men to other disease agents.

Of course this position that psychosocial factors act as conditional or predisposing factors rather than as direct pathogenic agents is no different from the position taken by the psychosomasists, who have maintained quite specifically that psychologic factors should be regarded as predisposing rather than direct etiologic agents in disease. Where it does differ is in its suggestion that these order of factors will not be etiologically specific for any given disease (at least given the current clinical classification of diseases) and that research aimed at searching for a specific subset of "stress diseases" or attempting to link one type of stressor to a single clinical manifestation is likely to be unproductive.

My position on this complete absence of etiologic specificity (or putting it in another way, that the function of these psychosocial processes is to enhance susceptibility to all disease in general) may have to be modified somewhat by relatively recent developments. Henry and colleagues (1974) have shown that, in animal colonies, animals in the process of establishing their dominance show a sympathetic adrenal medullary catecholamine response and persistent elevated blood pressures. The ones forced into subordination, however, show more of the pituitary adrenal cortical response pattern, a pattern he feels is more consistent with depression and all the disease manifestations that have been associated with depression and hopelessness. If this is true it might be necessary to modify my stance and admit there may be several clusters of diseases associated with different psychosocial situations.

Clarification of the outcomes to be expected from exposure to these psychosocial processes is, however, only one of the dilemmas facing research in this area. It provides no guide as to what these processes might be, much less how they are to be measured.

One of the unfortunate controversies that has clouded research in this area has been the one about whether such stressors are invariant, affecting all people in a similar manner, or whether they are idiosyncratic, affecting each person differently depending upon his personality, interpretation of the situation, and so forth. The position for the latter point of view (which might be summarized as "what is one man's meat is another's poison") has recently been stated quite succinctly by Hinkle (1973): "In view of the fact that people react to their 'life situations' or social conditions in terms of the meaning of these situations to them, it is difficult to accept the hypothesis that certain kinds of situations or relationships are inherently stressful and certain others are not." Others, including perhaps the majority of investigators, have treated these factors not only as if they were invariant but as if they were unidimensional, the presence of the factor being stressful, its absence beneficial.

Quite clearly, if the idiosyncratic point of view is correct, much of the work to identify universal or general stressors will be futile and lead to contradictory and confusing results. But equally clearly, the contrary point of view ignores the proposition that these processes do not have a direct pathogenic action but operate in their capacity as signals or symbols triggering responses in terms of the information they are perceived to contain. And as this perception will almost certainly be a function of the differing personalities and the salience of the experience to different individuals, it is hard to accept the notion that certain social circumstances will always, or even in the majority of cases, be "stressful." This dilemma can best be resolved, I believe, by two changes in our thinking, changes which appear consistent with most of the data and which conceivably explain some of the existing contradictions. The first of these is that the extent to which the postulated psychosocial processes are generally noxious versus idiosyncratic in their action is largely a function of our level of abstraction. If we can identify the characteristics or properties of those signals or symbols which generally evoke major neuroendocrinal changes in the recipients, we will have identified a general class of stressors even if the particular circumstances or relationships creating those types of signals or symbols differ for different people. Furthermore, if we can identify the attributes of this class of stressors, it may well be that the same relationships or social circumstances within a given culture (or, perhaps, subculture) regularly produce such a class of signals. Secondly, the existing data have led me to believe that we should no longer treat psychosocial processes as unidimensional stressors or non-stressors, but rather as twodimensional, one category being stressors and another being protective or beneficial.

The evidence supporting these points of view comes from both animal and human research. As has been indicated earlier, altering the social milieu of animals by increasing the number housed together leads to marked changes in health status, even when all relevant aspects of the physical environment and diet are kept constant. The biologic mechanisms through which such changes are produced have also been identified. Changes in group membership and the quality of group relationships in animals have been shown to be accompanied by significant neuroendocrinal changes affecting the pituitary, the adrenocortical system, the thyroid and gonads (Mason, 1959; Mason & Brady, 1964). These same endocrines are those responsible in large part for maintaining what Schoenheimer (1942) has termed "the dynamic steady state" of the organism, and thus, presumably, its ability to withstand changes that would result from the action of disease agents.

The questions of concern are, what are the properties of the changes in this social milieu, and are there analogues in the human social system? The usual notion that the crowding itself (that is, the physical density of the population) is responsible for the deterioration in health status has not been sustained in human studies. Despite the popularity of the belief that crowding is harmful to health, a review of the literature shows that for every study indicating a relationship between crowding and some manifestation of poor health, there is another equally good (or bad) investigation showing either no relationship or even an inverse one (Cassel, 1971, 1973). Furthermore, Hong Kong, one of the most crowded cities in the world, and Holland, one of the most crowded countries, enjoy some of the highest levels of both physical and mental health in the world (Dubos, n.d.).

A careful review of the data reported from animal studies may hold a clue to these puzzles. In animals, an almost inevitable consequence of crowding is the development of a set of disordered relationships among the animals. These, while manifested by a wide variety of bizarre and unusual behaviors, often have in common a failure to elicit anticipated responses to what were previously appropriate cues. Thus, habitual acts of aggression (including "ritualized aggression" in defending the nest), or evidence of acceptance of subordination on the part of one animal, fail to elicit appropriate reciprocal responses on the part of another. In social animals under wild conditions, for example, the occupier of a nest will define a zone around that nest as "home territory." Invasion of this territory by another animal of the same species will lead to a set of highly ritualized aggressive moves and countermoves, rarely leading to bloodshed, but culminating in one or the other animal "signaling" capitulation. Under crowded conditions the defending animal may initiate this ritual "dance," but the invading animal fails to respond in the anticipated fashion. Instead he may lie down, go to sleep, attempt to copulate, walk away, or do something which, for the situation, is equally bizarre.

This failure of various forms of behavior to elicit predictable responses leads to one of three types of responses on the part of the animals involved, the most common of which is repetition of the behavioral acts. Such acts are always accompanied by profound neuroendocrinal changes, and presumably their chronic repetition leads eventually to the permanent alterations in the level of the hormones and to the degree of autonomic nervous system arousal reported under conditions of animal crowding. The fact that these behavioral acts are in a sense inappropriate, in that they do not modify the situation, can be expected to enhance such hormonal changes. Under these conditions it is not difficult to envision the reasons for the increased susceptibility to environmental insults displayed by such animals.

An alternative response on the part of some animals is to withdraw from the field and to remain motionless and isolated for long hours on end. It is not uncommon to observe some mice under crowded conditions crouched in most unusual places, on top of the razor-thin edge of a partition or in the bright light in the center of the enclosure, completely immobile and not interacting with any other animals. Such animals do not exhibit the increased pathology demonstrated by the interacting members (Calhoun, 1962).

The third alternative is for animals to form their own deviant groups that apparently ignore the mores and codes of behavior of the larger group. Thus, "gangs" of young male rats have been observed invading nests, attacking females (the equivalent of gang rapes has been reported), and indulging in homosexual activities. I am not aware of any data on the health status of these gang members, but according to this hypothesis they also should not exhibit any increase in pathology.

These observations would suggest that at least one of the properties of stressful social situations might be that the actor is not receiving adequate evidence (feedback) that his actions are leading to anticipated consequences. While we do not as yet have the appropriate instruments to measure in any direct fashion the extent to which such a phenomenon is occurring in humans, it is not unreasonable to infer that this phenomenon is highly likely to occur under certain circumstances. First, it is probable that when individuals are unfamiliar with the cues and expectations of the society in which they live (as in the case of immigrants to a new situation, or of individuals involved in a rapid change of social environment, such as the elderly in an ethnic enclave caught up in urban renewal), many of their actions and the responses to these actions would fall into this category. Thus, if this suggestion is correct, they should be more susceptible to disease than those for whom the situation is familiar. Another circumstance in which this lack of feedback might occur would be under conditions of social disorganization. This, while still being far from a precise term which can be measured accurately, has proved to be a useful concept in a number of studies.

As indicated earlier, however, a fuller explanation of the potential role of psychosocial factors in the genesis of disease requires the recognition of a second set of processes. These might be envisioned as the protective factors buffering or cushioning the individual from the physiologic or psychologic consequences of exposure to the stressor situation. It is suggested that the property common to these processes is the strength of the social supports provided by the primary groups of most importance to the individual. Again, both animal and human studies have provided evidence supporting this point of view. Conger et al. (1958), for example, have shown that the efficacy with which an unanticipated series of electric shocks (given to animals previously conditioned to avoid them) can produce peptic ulcers is determined to a large extent by whether the animals are shocked in isolation (high ulcer rates) or in the presence of litter mates (low ulcer rates). Henry and Cassel (1969) have been able to produce persistent hypertension in mice by placing the animals in intercommunicating boxes all linked to a common feeding place, thus developing a state of territorial conflict. Hypertension only occurred, however, when the mice were "strangers." Populating the system with litter mates did not produce these effects. Liddell (1950) found that a young goat isolated in an experimental chamber and subjected to a monotonous conditioning stimulus will develop traumatic signs of experimental neurosis while its twin in an adjoining chamber and subjected to the same stimulus, but with the mother present, will not.

If such research were to support these ideas, it would suggest the need for a radical change in the strategies used for preventive action. Recognizing that throughout all history, disease, with rare exceptions, has not been prevented by finding and treating sick individuals, but by modifying those environmental factors facilitating its occurrence, this formulation would suggest that we should focus efforts more directly on attempts at further identification and subsequent modification of these categories of psychosocial factors rather than on screening and early detection.

Of the two sets of factors, it would seem more immediately feasible to attempt to improve and strengthen the social supports rather than reduce the exposure to the stressors. With advancing knowledge, it is perhaps not too far-reaching to imagine a preventive health service in which professionals are involved largely in the diagnostic aspects—identifying families and groups at high risk by virtue of their lack of fit with their social milieu and determining the particular nature and form of the social supports that can and should be strengthened if such people are to be protected from disease outcomes. The intervention actions then could well be undertaken by nonprofessionals, provided that adequate guidance and specific direction are given. Such an approach would not only be economically feasible, but if the notions expressed in this paper are correct, would do more to prevent a wide variety of diseases than all the efforts currently being made through multiphasic screening and multirisk-factor cardiovascular intervention attempts.

REFERENCES

Ader, R., & Hahn, E. W. (1963). Effects of social environment on mortality to whole-body x-irradiation in the rat. *Psychological Reports, 13,* 211-215.

Ader, R., Kreutner, A., & Jacobs, H. L. (1963). Social environment, emotionality and alloxan diabetes in the rat. *Psychosomatic Medicine, 25,* 60-68.

Andervont, H. B. (1944). Influence of environment on mammary cancer in mice. *Journal of the National Cancer Institute, 4,* 479-581.

Calhoun, J. B. (1962). Population density and social pathology. *Scientific American, 206,* 139-148.

Cannon, W. B. (1935). Stresses and strains of homeostasis. *American Journal of Medical Sciences, 189,* 1-14.

Cassel, J. (1971). Health consequences of population density and crowding. In National Academy of Science (Ed.), *Rapid population growth. Consequences and policy applications* (pp. 462-478). Baltimore: Johns Hopkins Press.

Cassel, J. (1973). The relation of the urban environment to health: Implications for prevention. *Mount Sinai Journal of Medicine, 40,* 539-550.

Christenson, W. N., & Hinkle, L. E. (1961). Differences in illness and prognostic signs in two groups of young men. *Journal of the American Academy of Medicine, 177*, 247–253.

Christian, J. J., & Williamson, H. O. (1958). Effect of crowding on experimental granuloma formation in mice. *Proceedings of the Society for Experimental Biology and Medicine, 99*, 385–387.

Conger, J. J., Sawrey, W., & Turrell, E. S. (1958). The role of social experience in the production of gastric ulcers in hooded rats placed in a conflict situation. *Journal of Abnormal Psychology, 57*, 214–220.

Davis, D. E., & Read, C. P. (1958). Effect of behavior on development of resistance in trichinosis. *Proceedings of the Society for Experimental Biology and Medicine, 99*, 269–272.

Dubos, R. (1965). *Man adapting.* New Haven: Yale University Press.

Dubos, R. (n.d.). *The human environment in technological societies.* Unpublished article.

Dunham, H. W. (1961). Social structure and mental disorders: Competing hypotheses of explanation. *Milbank Memorial Fund Quarterly, 39*, 259–311.

Durkheim, E. (1951). *Suicide: A study in sociology.* Glencoe, IL: The Free Press.

Frost, W. H. (1936). Introduction. In *Snow on cholera.* New York: Commonwealth Fund.

Henry, J. P., & Cassel, J. (1969). Psychosocial factors in essential hypertension: Recent epidemiologic and animal experimental evidence. *American Journal of Epidemiology, 90*, 171–200.

Henry, J. P., Ely, D. L., & Stephens, P. M. (1974). The role of psychosocial stimulation in the pathogenisis of hypertension. *Verhandlungen der Deutschen Gesellschaft für Innere Medizin, 80*, 107–111.

Hinkle, L. E. (1973). The concept of "stress" in the biological and social sciences. *Science, Medicine and Man, 1*, 31–48.

Holmes, T. (1956). Multidiscipline studies of tuberculosis. In P. J. Sparer (Ed.), *Personality, stress and tuberculosis.* New York: International Universities Press.

King, J. T., Lee, Y. C. P., & Visscher, M. B. (1955). Single versus multiple cage occupancy and convulsion frequency in C₃H mice. *Proceedings of the Society for Experimental Biology and Medicine, 88*, 661–663.

Kraus, A., & Lilienfeld, A. (1959). Some epidemiologic aspects of the high mortality rate in the young widowed group. *Journal of Chronic Diseases, 10*, 207–217.

Liddell, H. (1950). Some specific factors that modify tolerance for environmental stress. In H. G. Wolff, S. G. Wolff, Jr., & C. C. Hare (Eds.), *Life stress and bodily disease.* Baltimore: Williams and Wilkins.

Mason, J. W. (1959). Psychological influences in the pituitary-adrenal-cortical system. *Recent Progress in Hormone Research, 15*, 345–389.

Mason, J. W., & Brady, J. V. (1964). The sensitivity of the psychendocrine systems to social and physical environment. In P. H. Leiderman & D. Shapiro (Eds.), *Psychobiological approaches to social behavior* (pp. 4–23). Stanford: Stanford University Press.

Mishler, E. G., & Scotch, N. A. (1963). Sociocultural factors in the epidemiology of schizophrenia: A review. *Psychiatry, 26*, 315–351.

Ratcliffe, H. L., & Cronin, M. I. T. (1958). Changing frequency of arteriosclerosis in mammals and birds at the Philadelphia Zoological Garden. *Circulation, 18*, 41–52.

Schoenheimer, R. (1942). *Dynamic state of body constituents*. Cambridge: Harvard University Press.

Swinyard, E. A., Clark, L. D., Miyahara, J. T., et al. (1961). Studies on the mechanism of amphetamine toxicity in aggregated mice. *Journal of Pharmacology and Experimental Therapeutics, 132*, 97–102.

Tillman, W. A., & Hobbs, G. E. (1949). The accident-prone automobile driver: A study of the psychiatric and social background. *American Journal of Psychiatry, 106*, 321.

·5·

Medical Pluralism

CHARLES M. GOOD

Pluralistic medical configurations are in no sense limited to the technologically less-developed countries. Despite the technological brilliance of scientific bio-medicine, the behavior of people seeking health care in Western societies suggests that the scope for mutual understanding and fruitful cooperation among a variety of contemporary alternative therapy systems is possibly greater than ever before. Both East and West Germany, for example, have evolved unique solutions for reconciling the criteria of "science" and "efficacy" in biomedicine with the continued demand from their populations for alternative drug therapy provided by homeopathy, anthroposocial healing, and herbal healing (Unschuld, 1980). In the United States today, orthodox biomedicine does not singularly fulfill either the demand or the need for health care. The preeminent medical model, of course, remains strongly wedded to molecular biology, to increasingly sophisticated and costly equipment, and to physician-dominated definitions and control of standards and access to health care resources. Yet there is considerable evidence that the boundaries of "legitimate" medical practice (as defined by medical associations, health insurance compa-nies, and other centers of influence in the medical industry) are expanding once again to include systems such as chiropracty and psychological counsel-ing. Other evolutionary trends, including modifications and additions to medi-cal school curricula such as community health and social science, are also under way. Today, many laypersons and some medical professionals are reexamining the biomedical model—particularly the therapeutic limitations of the narrow, mechanistic view of the human organism that has so infused medical practice in most of the United States.

This chapter originally appeared in *Ethnomedical Systems in Africa* by Charles M. Good, 1987, pp. 7-22. It is reprinted here with permission from Guilford Press.

Maybe

Whereas biomedicine continues to be widely perceived as the only legitimate basis of therapy in the United States, the revival of awareness and increasing acceptance of a wide variety of "folk" and popular health care strategies is decidely "medical chic" (Atkinson, 1979). There is a genuine interest in alternative medicine that runs deeper than passing fads or fancies, and it is increasingly political in outlook. Many concepts and practices have long historical roots, and it is evident that large numbers of people believe them to be potentially efficacious and beneficial to health. Whether the desired outcome is achieved through pharmaco-organic, physical, or psychological therapy, or some combination of these, may be of little concern to the person or family seeking relief from sudden, inexplicable, or persistent illness. Among the numerous examples of these alternative or competing therapies are botanical healing and various forms of psychotherapy among rural and urban black (de Albuquerque, 1979; Varner & McCandless, 1979), Native American, Hispanic, and other ethnic communities (Kunitz, 1981); transcendental meditation, yoga, and other forms of mysticism and techniques of mastering mind and body processes derived from Asian religions; the physical fitness movement, Alcoholics Anonymous, vitamin therapy, and special dietary regimens with restorative and preventive goals; and even such "deviant" belief systems as astrology and palmistry. We have recently witnessed the emergence of special centers in the United States and Mexico where persons chronically ill with diseases such as cancer and arthritis are treated with controversial and sometimes illegal medications (i.e., not sanctioned by the Food and Drug Administration or the American Medical Association) such as dimethyl sulfoxide (DMSO), Laetril, and snake venom compounds. Homeopathy, "Rolfing," acupuncture, Christian Science, naturopathy, community paramedical training, and midwifery are also receiving attention from many quarters. Not the least important is the spiritual healing movement which recently gained currency in American Episcopal and Catholic churches (Vecsey, 1978).

At present there is very limited systematic knowledge of the alternative therapies that are in fashion in the United States (Hulke, 1979). Little is known about regional variations in acceptance and patronage; locational features and spatial patterns created by the circulation of patients, therapists, and materia medica; or the extent of their complementarity and competition with other therapy systems.

MEDICAL PLURALISM AND COOPERATION IN THIRD WORLD SOCIETIES

Coexistence of various traditional medical systems, such as Yoruba, Unani-Tibbi, Ayurvedic, or classical Chinese, with each other and with biomedicine is a well-documented phenomenon in many parts of Africa, Asia, and Latin America. Together these different modes of interpreting and responding to sickness form what Charles Leslie describes (Janzen, 1978, p. xiv) as "more or less pluralistic, more or less integrated, and more or less syncretistic regional systems."

International awareness of the role and contributions of traditional therapy systems in African societies is primarily a postcolonial development. This emerging consciousness coincides with a growing realization that the kind of biomedical delivery system introduced by colonial administrations and subsequently inherited by independent African governments does not and cannot meet many of their societies' most pressing health care requirements. Rooted in the old colonial system, the Western-inspired blueprint for medical care is inefficiently designed, dependent on expensively trained personnel working in budget-absorbing hospitals, and too often grossly overwhelmed by the unrealistic expectations and demands placed upon it. In many ways it is inappropriate and of limited relevance to the conditions of life of people in developing countries (Dorozynski, 1975). It renders insufficient care even in central urban areas, and practically no care in large rural areas. Nevertheless, even where biomedical health services are physically present, prevailing social and cultural values and actual attendance patterns indicate that biomedicine is not preferred for many illnesses or for common events such as childbirth.

Although they are undeniably complementary, the pluralistic medical systems of the technologically less-developed countries are inequitably distributed and poorly interconnected. As is well known, biomedical health services are typically so thinly scattered that they are physically unavailable and inaccessible to rural populations that lack efficient motorized transport. In the Ivory Coast, Lasker (1981) found that the choice of therapy is more dependent on relative accessibility than on any traits associated with the individual patient. Similarly, a recent study from northern Nigeria (Stock, 1980) reveals that as distance from a health facility increases, people delay seeking institutional treatment, fail to complete a prescribed course of treatment, and are more prone to resort to alternative forms of therapy. Measures of this distance–decay relationship show that visits for the treatment of common symptomatic illnesses decline at an approximate rate of 25% per kilometer away from a dispensary. Thus "the effective range of the dispensary is only about four kilometres; at this distance the utilization rate is only about one-third of the zero kilometre value" (Stock, 1980, p. 426).

As the preceding example suggests, a large proportion of Africa's people suffer a critical lack of even the "aspirin and bandages" variety of Western health services. This situation is expected to continue well into the 21st century, regardless of incremental expansion of health personnel with biomedical training and the construction of additional physical facilities. The overall shortfall in biomedical health care is exacerbated by a shrinking supply of traditional medical practitioners in some rural areas; to some extent by a dehumanizing commercialization of both traditional and Western-type therapeutic services; by radical political, social, and economic upheavals of the sort Ugandans, Ethiopians, and Ghanaians have recently endured; and, as in Kenya, by unprecedented rates of population increase and diminishing budgetary resources for the health sector (Republic of Kenya, 1986).

Until quite recently, there has been a widespread tendency in Western societies to subscribe to one of two fallacies about health beliefs and behavior indigenous to other societies. Steven Polgar (1962) labeled one of these the "empty vessel fallacy," whereby a territory and people are assumed to lack systematic health beliefs and a therapy system until Western medicine arrives on the scene and fills the void. Alternatively, the "fallacy of the separate capsule" recognizes the existence of indigenous medical resources and theories of disease, but maintains that they are inferior and not a viable alternative to Western professional health practices (Scrimshaw, 1979). Barbara Pillsbury, a medical anthropologist, offers an eloquent response to those who hold these stereotypes and suggests important theoretical and practical reasons for redefining and expanding the study of "medical systems" in the field. She observes that:

> Nowhere do people live in a health care vacuum. In all cultures people become ill; in no cultures do others stand idly by. Each culture has produced over the centuries its own adaptive methodologies for coping with illness. These embody an indigenous etiology, that is, a system explaining the occurrence of illness and disease based on the worldview and religious beliefs of the particular people in question. It is the underlying explanatory system, in interaction with features of the ecological niche of the population, that dictates local strategies for coping with ill-health. These are strategies that international medicine has all too long ignored. (1978, p. 1)

"'Dead as the dodo.' That is what many health professionals and authorities would wish traditional medicine to be and what an even greater number of them believes it to be" (Vuori, 1982, p. 129). Yet it is evident today that traditional medical systems remain one of the major resources used by Third World populations to cope with their problems of poor health. Certainly in Africa, and in much of Asia and Latin America, there is a huge number and striking variety of traditionally based healers including herbalists, diviners, midwives, fertility specialists, and spiritualists. According to the World Health Organization (WHO) and other authorities, they form the main source of assistance with health problems for at least 80% of rural inhabitants (Bannerman, Burton, & Wan-Chieh, 1983). However, it should be kept in mind that neither traditional medical practitioners (TMPs) nor their various specialties are evenly distributed across the landscape. Traditional midwives deliver 60% to 90% of all children born in these regions. In addition, traditional healing continues to retain and expand its influence in towns and cities, side-by-side with biomedical services. Assessing the current pattern of medical pluralism in India, for example, Dunn (1976, p. 155) states emphatically that "whatever the development of cosmopolitan health care" in that country, "there can be little doubt that popular traditional medicine will indefinitely survive." Recent studies by the geographer Surinder Bhardwaj clearly illustrate the complementary roles and competitive aspects of multiple therapy systems in South Asia (Bhardwaj, 1975, 1980; Bhardwaj & Paul, 1986).

Ahmed and Kolker (1979) identify seven general functions, both psychological and sociological, that traditional indigenous medical systems perform independently of the local presence or adequacy of biomedicine. These are (1) relief of stress and anxiety created by the uncertainties of illness; (2) low cost (a questionable assertion addressed later) and convenience; (3) reinforcement of the patient through primary group involvement in diagnosis and treatment; (4) control of deviance; (5) minimization of the trauma of cultural change; (6) alleviation of personal stress in urban areas caused by social dislocation, uprooting, and anomie; and (7) promotion of ethnic identity. Nchinda (1976) has argued that traditional African medical systems survive because they satisfy the following four basic users' requirements (each of which has an important locational dimension): accessibility, availability, acceptability, and dependability.

At the urging of the WHO, biomedical opinion has recently begun to shift toward a more open stance regarding the validity and potential efficacy of elements of the traditionally based medical systems (Akerele, 1984). Although heated controversy continues and opposition by biomedical practitioners is widespread, there is increasing interest in the potential benefits to be obtained from stimulating cooperative therapeutic activities between biomedically oriented and traditional-style healers (Neumann & Lauro, 1982). In Africa, given "the inescapable reality that Western medicine will not be available to the masses for years to come" (Miller, 1980, p. 98), it is imperative to ask: Can formal cooperation among practitioners of biomedicine and traditional medicine promote health care that is culturally more appropriate, more accessible, and more effective than is currently available without such collaboration?

In the mid-1970s the WHO began to develop policy guidelines to assist Third World health ministries to conduct research, initiate pilot programs, and subsequently to implement cooperative training programs and treatment strategies. One World Health Organization contribution is the publication of a handbook for health administrators and practitioners, edited by R. H. Bannerman, J. Burton, and C. Wen-Chieh, entitled *Traditional Medicine and Health Care Coverage* (1983).

A synopsis of the strengths and weaknesses of African TMPs and traditional medicine is presented in Table 5.1. It will be noted that some of the "weaknesses" of traditional medicine are also applicable in varying degree to biomedicine.

While the concept of cooperation is attractive in the abstract to many, and numerous limited experiments have occurred—most often with traditional midwives (Pillsbury, 1982; World Health Organization, 1982)—few countries have actually taken the positive steps necessary to innovate and rationalize their health delivery systems within the framework of their own medical pluralism. Careful examination of the general health care situation in Kenya and elsewhere in Africa suggests that a formal policy decision to pursue specific areas of collaboration with traditional medicine could yield positive health benefits to both rural and urban populations (Good, 1987).

Despite their individual and collective strengths, probably no single therapy system, or combination of systems, is today adequately meeting even the most basic health care needs in the Third World. Separately or together, all fall short (Good et al., 1979). In their quest for health, people attempt to compensate for these deficiencies by utilizing both traditional and biomedical services. Such joint use is made concurrently or sequentially for the same or different aspects of the same illness. In this sense the pluralistic medical systems are informally but rather haphazardly integrated. In the great majority of cases, however, the traditionally based therapies and practitioners continue to be ignored by their country's ministry of health and thus by its Western-trained medical and health planning establishment.

COMPETING PARADIGMS: BIOMEDICAL AND PSYCHOSOCIAL

Any attempt to encourage formal cooperation between traditional and Western medicine and to promote their appropriate integration will encounter basic conflicts. Wherever scientific, profession-centered biomedicine has penetrated there is a confrontation between fundamentally different paradigms of health and illness. While I recognize the pitfalls of oversimplification, it may be said that the *biomedical* paradigm continues to dominate thought and behavior in Western, or bio-medicine. Disease and illness are reduced to essentially Newtonian, mechanical, or organismic states—to physical manifestations that can be successfully diagnosed and treated separately from a person's psychological condition and social milieu (Kleinman, 1978b). Consequently, throughout the Third World people usually assign biomedicine the limited function of treating organic disease or acute illness symptoms.

TABLE 5.1. Strengths and Weaknesses of African Traditional Medicine and TMPs

Strengths
1. TMPs perform positive psychological and sociological functions (e.g., stress reduction, social control) regardless of the local adequacy of biomedical services.
2. TMPs have acceptability through cultural continuity.
3. TMPs are generally adaptive and open to innovation.
4. TMPs collectively possess a large body of indigenous technical knowledge, ranging from individual and group psychology to the properties, actions, and applications of plant medicines.
5. TMPs treat a broad spectrum of physiological and mental ill-health, including conditions which are not diagnosed, misdiagnosed, and incompletely diagnosed by biomedical practitioners—or are not manageable according to biomedical standards.
6. Many TMPs recognize and will refer serious diseases and conditions such as malaria, tuberculosis, and trauma to biomedical facilities.
7. TMPs are available in all rural and urban communities.

Weaknesses
1. Knowledge of bodily diseases dependent on perceptible signs of dysfunction that are difficult to verify
2. Limited repertoire of diagnostic techniques.
3. Much variation in length and quality of training of TMPs.
4. Procedures with patients are highly idiosyncratic and quality of care rendered varies greatly due, in part, to lack of standardized training.
5. Standards of hygiene and sanitation are low.
6. Conceptualization of illness etiologies in terms of witchcraft and sorcery is widespread among certain types of TMP. Despite possible value in social control, these "fear systems" are potent sources of mental stress and physiological insult.
7. Few mechanisms exist for systematically evaluating the outcome of therapy.
8. Recruitment of *bona fide* TMPs in rural areas is increasingly problematic.
9. TMPs lack cohesiveness, and exchange of technical information and practical experience is rare.
10. TMPs are ineffective at correcting negative stereotypes and false information about their roles (e.g., the "witchdoctor" caricature of "skins, beads, and backwardness"; traditional medicine as a game of "con artists" pursuing self-enrichment schemes; and the "unyielding secrecy" associated with the methods and medicines of TMPs).
11. Inarticulate/weak response to the paradigm conflict with biomedicine.

Rappoport (1980) observes that the biomedical treatment model, among other features, gives precedence to "technique" over "person": to the replication of scientific procedures and to "objectivity." Its value structure tends to ignore if not disvalue the therapist as an individual whose unique charismatic qualities and style, and capacity to communicate and generate hope, are crucial to healing. In effect, the biomedical model also minimizes the length of time considered "necessary" for routine diagnosis and patient consultation. In practice, despite truly noteworthy exceptions, little premium attaches to really knowing a patient in terms of his or her social network and identity in a community, or the physical and psychological conditions of the patient's life space. Broad-ranging counseling of the sort that is typical, for instance, of *bona fide* traditional African therapy procedures, would be an extraordinary occurrence. Whereas in traditional medical practice time itself is virtually an organic part of therapy, in biomedicine time is measured and compressed by organizational and economic pressures. Biomedical clinical procedure is thus well adapted to processing a heavy patient load, a pressure that is particularly burdensome on medical assistants, nurses, and doctors. In the overcrowded and underequipped outpatient clinics of African hospitals and health centers there is usually little dialogue between clinician and patient, and the mean doctor-patient contact time is commonly less than 2 minutes (Family Health Institute, 1978; Lasker, 1981). The biomedical model is thus inadequate to the clinical realities in such circumstances. This is particularly apparent if, as Dr. T. A. Lambo, Deputy Director General of the WHO asserts, 70% to 80% of patients "are not suffering from any discernible organic disorder" (Singer, 1977, p. 246). Most importantly, few doctors and medical assistants have the theoretical and practical training in cultural analysis and psychology that is crucial to providing an appropriate diagnosis for most sick people they encounter. My own field observations suggest that the biomedical system of health care misses a broad spectrum of disease and illness. A significant proportion of the conditions presented in African hospitals, clinics, and dispensaries are not recognized or are misdiagnosed and consequently not treated appropriately (Gatere, 1980).

In contrast, the conceptual frameworks of traditional medical systems that evolved outside the Euro-American realm emphasize psychological, social, spiritual, humoral, pharmaco-organic, and other biophysical phenomena and processes in varying degrees and combinations. "Person" and place of therapy are both considered crucial elements in the successful treatment of illness. In most African societies situated south of the Sahara, for instance, what I term the dominant *psychosocial* paradigm illustrates the clearest and most pronounced area of conceptual and cognitive divergence from the biomedical paradigm. Its core features illustrate why there are significant constraints to achieving formal cooperation between traditional and biomedical systems.

In the *psychosocial* paradigm, a person's body, mind, and soul are conceived as an indivisible whole, and at any time the condition of one is mirrored in the others (Swift & Asuni, 1975). The etiology and symptoms of disease are not interpreted as isolated or simply probabilistic occurrences as so often happens in the biomedical approach; instead, the source lies beyond the ill person's physical being and reflects discord in his or her "social body" (Swantz, 1979) and a "rupture of life's harmony" (World Health Organization Regional Committee for Africa, 1976). Illnesses tend to fall into two general categories: *natural* or *God-given illnesses*, which are unrelated to human will or actions; and *illnesses of man*, caused by bad will or hostile conduct of one person or group against another, the commission of various indiscretions, or the activation of supernatural forces (Janzen, 1978). Illnesses of humans are manifested in the phenomena of witchcraft and sorcery, magic, ghosts, and disturbances of the ancestral spirits (Mbiti, 1970), and as consequences of broken taboos (cursing a child and intergenerational sexual relations are examples) and unmet religious obligations. In popular culture the root causes of much illness and misfortune are directly attributed to conflicts and tensions in interpersonal relationships. These feature both *horizontal* (kinfolk, neighbors, co-workers) and *vertical* dimensions (relations with the "living-dead" ancestral kin) (Mbiti, 1970).

Illness as it is conceived in the psychosocial paradigm thus has important moral implications. As a theory of causation, it integrates the spiritual with the physical universe. Quite logically, the appropriate therapy for "illnesses of humans" is rarely limited to brief bilateral consultation between a specialist and the sufferer. Instead, treatment frequently extends over several days or longer, may require meetings in more than one physical location (e.g., an urban migrant's rural homestead may be in need of special ritual purification or protective measures), and involve a supporting cast of kinfolk and other associates of the patient who act as a therapy managing group (Janzen, 1978). In this kind of system, illness and misfortune are essentially religious experiences, demanding a religious approach and a qualified specialist whose therapeutic techniques reflect the patient's cultural beliefs. The traditional healing process in Africa often evolves into a kind of psychosocial drama, with the goal of restoring the sufferer to a therapeutic community (Onoge, 1975). In coastal Tanzania, for example, the Swahili greeting *u mzima*, "are you whole, well?", captures the meaning of health interpreted as wholeness in the context of a community, a group of people related by bonds of kinship, neighborhood, or common work and interdependent with one another (Swantz, 1979).

In northern Nigeria, the common Hausa proverb *lafiyar jiki arzikine* ("health is wealth") parallels the ideal definition of health espoused by the World Health Organization. *Lafiyar* symbolizes much more than the absence of disease. It connotes "a general state of physical and social well-being which incorporates such characteristics as good relations with family and social contacts, a settled religious and moral state, freedom from danger and fear, success at work and in personal affairs, and the absence of sickness" (Stock, 1980, p. 73).

PARALLEL OR JOINT USE OF DIFFERENT THERAPY SYSTEMS

As Leslie (1980, p. 193) points out, it is "the experience of illness, not the biological reality of disease, [that] causes people to consult others about their health." Despite the fact that many individuals hold strong ambivalent feelings toward it, biomedicine does hold a respected position in the Third World because of its greater effectiveness—relative to traditional medicine—in identifying and treating many clinical symptoms of disease, particularly acute ailments. Nevertheless, even if fully staffed and equipped biomedical facilities were placed within easy access of everyone, people would still make use of traditional healers and others available to them who are skilled at treating illness if not a particular disease (Good et al., 1979; Leslie, 1980).

The cognitive linkage of people's beliefs about the etiology of disease and illness with particular and often sequential therapeutic options is a factor that should command attention from health professionals. Parallel use of biomedical and traditional medical specialists, as well as other sources of therapy, is often pronounced where large segments of the society conceptually separate the treatment of overt symptoms of illnesses from what are perceived as their underlying root causes. In Nairobi, for instance, a mother whose child experiences a sudden loss of weight and alertness may take him to the pediatric filter clinic at Kenyatta National Hospital to be seen by a doctor; and a man injured in an industrial accident will recuperate as an inpatient at the hospital. Assuming that both individuals are soon "cured" in a biomedical sense, neither the adults directly affected nor their families may consider the respective cases resolved until there is a satisfactory explanation as to *why* they were singled out for distress and injury. At this stage a diviner or other medicoreligious specialist is frequently consulted. In other cases, medical doctors are unable to identify or relate to the patient's complaint and send him or her away; or treatment is unsuccessful despite several return visits. Any of these three kinds of everyday experiences with the biomedical services serves to increase the flow of ill persons toward traditional healers and other kinds of therapists who are reputed to have skills in treating illness in its broader social context (Good, 1980, 1987).

The necessity for cultural mechanisms to deal with the healing of illness is a universal characteristic of health care systems. There is no evidence that such devices are a vestigial stage to be "passed through" in the succession to a modern biomedical system. Indeed, as Kleinman (1978a, p. 88) proposes, "we can look upon the legitimated role of social workers, psychiatrists, pastoral counselors, and patient advocates, as well as folk healers, in fully modern societies such as the United States as using a language of experience and treatment for illness which would otherwise go untalked about and untreated when sickness extends beyond the context of the family into the professional biomedical domain."

In view of the fundamentally different paradigms and behavioral correlates that distinguish traditional psychosocial and biomedical therapy systems, effective formal collaboration that actually enhances the health of individuals and communities cannot be expected to evolve on its own. Rather, cooperation will depend initially on the ethnomedical approach being cultivated, adopted, and infused into professional biomedical praxis— including a reformed academic medical curriculum. Because of shortages of both biomedical personnel and the health resources they require, bold and progressive initiatives are necessary to bring about a better allocation and utilization of those resources already available in the biomedical sector.

On the other hand, traditionally based practitioners are ubiquitous; those among them who are genuinely concerned about their patients' welfare have an unrealized potential to contribute more effectively to individual and community well-being. Nevertheless, serious reservations about the likelihood of a new role for traditional medicine persist. The orthodox biomedical system is, everywhere, intertwined and symbiotic with the established political and socioeconomic systems of a country. It is thus oriented toward serving the affluent, powerful, and mostly urban classes that are able to appropriate public resources. This political context of the health system will ultimately determine whether the "upgrading" and utilization of traditional healers in cooperative health care delivery will be of real value or if it will simply become another means of perpetuating so-called "second-rate" medical care to the already underserved masses. Might the price of legitimacy and other support for the traditional sector mean diminished service to the general population? The questions must be asked—who will benefit, and who will gain (McDonald, 1981)?

The health care systems of Kenya and other Third World countries are not static. Everywhere, improved access to appropriate health care depends less on huge injections of capital and more on innovative ideas for decentralizing and optimizing the use of health resources already at hand. Adoption of intensive experimentation with the concept and practice of ethnomedical analysis offers a realistic, feasible, and low-overhead approach to the formulation of rational policies for health service development in the 1980s and beyond. It holds out the prospect of linking multiple, spatially overlapping and interacting but poorly articulated therapy systems; and of facilitating better health care for the general population.

THE ETHNOMEDICAL MODEL: ITS RELEVANCE TO
MEDICAL PRACTICES AND HEALTH

Despite scattered experiments with traditional birth attendants and traditional healers, such as in the Techiman District of Ghana (Warren, Bova, Tregoning, & Kliewer, 1982), formally structured collaboration among various types of practitioners in pluralistic medical environments of Africa is not yet a realistic expectation of national health services. Also, the cooperative ethic is unlikely to spread if Western medical science and technology continue to be perceived as omnipotent systems with benign ideological biases. Prospects for effective experimental programs of cooperation between TMPs and biomedicine are also unlikely if key decision makers are reluctant to promote or to motivate real community participation in local health matters. Bureaucratic "turf" considerations and/or personal career and family considerations on the part of persons responsible for implementing health programs at district or subdistrict levels constitute a third stumbling block to cooperation. Finally, the changing political priorities of external funding agencies (e.g., U.S. A.I.D.) can also interfere with schemes to utilize TMPs (Pillsbury, 1982).

Leslie (1980) observes that even though biomedicine is almost always less scientific than it appears, health professionals throughout the world tend to translate proposals for cooperation with practitioners of alternative therapies as advocating the legitimization of quackery (Imperato, 1977). They contend such collaboration would require acceptance of procedures whose efficacy is at best difficult to evaluate according to conventional scientific criteria. These external, superficial interpretations of unfamiliar therapies (which may lead to conclusions of "quackery") and assumptions about their efficacy tend to screen out significant behavioral and semantic issues that are crucial to better professional communication and health care. At the same time, the difficulties of differentiating between genuine healers and those who have few skills apart from extracting their client's money must not be underestimated (International Development Research Center, 1980).

In all societies, medical systems function as social systems that attach meaning to and structure the experience of sickness (Fabrega, 1977; Leslie, 1980). Medical anthropologists and most other social and behavioral scientists now recognize the analytical and practical value of distinguishing between disease and illness as two elements of *sickness*. *Disease* connotes the impairment of biological and/or psychological processes, whereas *illness* can be described as "the psychosocial experience and meaning of perceived disease" (Kleinman, 1980, p. 72).

Because most biomedical practitioners restrict the focus of their work to disease, the distinction between disease and illness is for them rarely more than a secondary consideration. Consequently, neither the patient's interpretations of particular sickness episodes nor the rationale and qualities of therapies that are available from other healing systems are routinely taken into account in clinical activities. This observation is especially applicable to the practice of biomedicine in Africa and other Third World regions where many fundamental and subtle cultural differences commonly separate patients and practitioners.

The work of Kleinman (1980), Leslie (1980), and others suggests that the purposes of biomedicine, insofar as these are directed toward individual and community health can be advanced by integrating the principles of the "ethnomedical" model into biomedical practice. Building upon recent developments in semantic anthropology, ethnomethodology, and comparative medical studies, the *ethnomedical approach* places particular emphasis on the "meaning contexts of sickness," and joins different systems of medical knowledge. Health, disease, and illness are interpreted in the light of the many ways these terms are perceived by patients, families, practitioners, and communities. In practice, the "ethnomedical analyst," whether medical practitioner or social scientist, recognizes that people adopt sick roles when they do not have diseases, and experience diseases without being ill or taking on sick roles (Leslie, 1980). As already noted, the biological and psychosocial realities, while interdependent, are not the same thing; and their relationship is culturally defined and structured.

In the ethnomedical approach, episodes of sickness are interpreted in terms of explanatory models (EMs) that are used by patients and practitioners in all health care systems. Explanatory models are formed from a variable cluster of cultural symbols, experiences, and expectations associated with a particular category of sickness; and all EMs reveal sickness labeling and a cultural idiom for expressing the experiences of illness. They provide interpretations of sickness "to guide choices among available therapies and therapists and to cast personal and social meaning on the experience of sickness" (Kleinman, 1980, p. 105). *The nature of the exchange between patients' EMs and practitioners' EMs is therefore crucial* because it influences the entire procedure and outcome of health care.

Coping with sickness is a process organized for an ill person and his or her family within culturally composed networks of routine everyday meanings, symptom perception, and interpersonal relationships—what Kleinman (1980) calls the "semantic sickness networks." In patient and family EMs, these networks link a variety of experiences and beliefs about symptoms, causality, and significance. Quite often specific types of interpersonal problems and social tensions that are believed to trigger or accompany particular illnesses also form an important element of a network. These semantic sickness networks thus provide the basis for decisions regarding the selection and phasing of treatment options. Consequently, from the ethnomedical point of view, "it is the EM and the semantic sickness network it constitutes and expresses for a given sickness episode that socially produce the *natural history of illness* and assure that it, unlike the *natural history of disease*, will differ for different health care systems" (Kleinman, 1980, p. 107; emphasis in the original).

A number of culture-specific syndromes, identified in Western, non-Western, and transcultural ethnographic and medical anthropology studies, provide useful illustrations of "semantic sickness networks" (e.g., Hand, 1976). These include *susto* among selected Latin American groups; pathologies linked to an excess of "hot" or "cold" somatic qualities (such syndromes are nonsensical in the framework of a biomedical clinician's EM, who might in turn recommend a course of treatment the patient considers incompatible and even dangerous) (Kleinman, 1980); "rootwork" among southern Black Americans; "heart disease" in Iran; and *ching* ("fright") in Taiwan or Hong Kong. Concepts of infection (e.g., "evil eye" in North Africa and the Middle East) and specific "folk" therapy prescriptions (e.g., "feed a cold, starve a fever" in a middle-class English or American suburb) produce distinct lay patterns of choice among alternative therapies that may be utilized according to hierarchies of resort.

Contemporary American popular culture also illustrates the relevance of the ethnomedical approach. It contains a rich but largely unsurveyed variety of culturally constructed patterns of symptom perception, labeling, communication, and behavioral responses. For example, terms such as "nervous breakdown," "male menopause," "professional burnout," "shell shock," "rape," "lump in the breast," "upset stomach," and even "cancer" have profound personal, cultural, and social meanings that are crucial to establishing a basis for the provision of psychologically and culturally appropriate clinical care. They also reflect changing beliefs about the cause and severity of illness; yet there are few systematic accounts of popular American or other EMs and "networks" in the literature of social science and medicine.

Most functional social science studies of medical systems reflect definitions of health and sickness legitimated by the biomedical model and are concerned with these states primarily as they relate to professional and bureaucratic health care interests. Examples include defining disease and biological malfunction, an emphasis on technological innovation, and compliance with curative and preventive programs.

In contrast, ethnomedical analysis employs an interdisciplinary and interpretive methodology. It rejects the truncated, compartmentalized, and preselective approach to sickness in favor of examining a broad range of culture-specific and transcultural experiences in both clinical transactions and in the extraclinical domain of healing. Analysis is focused on the actual illness experiences of people and examines how they are perceived, labeled, communicated, and managed in interactions with family, social network, and therapists. In terms of this framework the social *geography* of therapy systems assumes much greater complexity, dynamism, and spatial range through the redefinition of "relevant" actors and through assessment of their locational behavior. For these reasons the ethnomedical model elaborated by Kleinman and others is an essential tool for nurturing successful collaboration between health care traditions.

Extending well beyond the horizon of conventional biomedical practice, the ethnomedical approach offers several distinct practical advantages to health professionals, social scientists, health planners, and, not least, the lay public.

First, analysis of recurring semantic sickness networks aids in understanding the logic of lay health resources and their utilization patterns. Such information can help detect key differences and areas of conflict between the various local folk, popular, and biomedical systems of health care. Health planners in Africa, the United States, and elsewhere will be better informed about the total environment of health-related behavior. They will also be able to mediate more realistically and effectively between the different systems when planning new programs or redesigning the configurations of existing resources for health.

Second, knowledge of semantic illness networks is directly applicable to the goals of disease prevention and health maintenance. Byron Good's (1977) analysis of a local Iranian explanatory model, for example, revealed information of great value to health authorities who were proposing to expand the use or oral contraceptives. Noncompliance with this program by village women was due chiefly to fear of "heart distress," which they perceived as a side effect of the pill. In Kenya, attempts by medical authorities to treat childhood malnutrition among the Digo people of coastal Kenya have often been unsuccessful because the ultimate cause is locally understood and treated in social terms. Rickets, marasmus, kwashiorkor, and loss of strength (*nguvu*) in children are given a signal label, *chirywa*, which the Digo attribute to parents' sexual misbehavior ("Witchcraft Warning," 1978; Gerlach, 1959).

Third, semantic network analysis of health-related concepts and transactions in any society can aid in creating a base of practical knowledge about typical sources of stress and the transition periods in the life of the individual that are popularly associated with changes in health status. It can also help identify diseases and illnesses that are perceived to be the most common and threatening (Pfifferling, 1975). Evaluation of usual family and social network patterns of coping with illness and maintaining health should help uncover which coping strategies are adaptive or maladaptive (Kleinman, 1978a). Ethnomedical knowledge of this kind is probably at least as important to local health authorities interested in developing appropriate preventive and maintenance programs as is orthodox epidemiological data on the prevalence and causes of various diseases. Indeed, Kleinman (1978b, p. 79), citing Kunstadter, urges that "both sources of information are needed to specify epidemiological webs of pathogens, vectors, host susceptibility, and behavioral and environmental contingencies promoting certain sicknesses and resisting specific public health interventions."

There are at least three other factors that should finally convince social scientists (and biomedical professionals) of the usefulness of the ethnomedical approach. First, its applications are not restricted to traditional and "non-Western" medical systems. It is also appropriate to the analysis of both lay and professional health behavior in societies where biomedicine is dominant, co-dominant, or only a variant (as in Kenya). Second, it serves to demystify and make more interpretable the otherwise exotic and perplexing aura (especially for Westerners) that typically surrounds the practices of both traditional and popular healers and their clientele (Rappoport, 1980). Finally, it should directly lead to more psychosocially *and* biomedically sophisticated models of health problems and therapeutic alternatives, and to more effective utilization of health services (Kleinman, 1978a).

DEFINITION AND CLASSIFICATION OF FOLK MEDICINE

Western biomedicine arrived in Kenya about 80 years ago. Today its appeal is widespread, but because of its restricted availability it is a practical alternative for only a small town-dwelling and periurban minority since nine out of ten Kenyans live in rural areas. As in many other technologically less-developed countries, biomedicine's bureaucratic structure, professionalization, and extensive resource requirements clearly inhibit its emergence as the dominant medical system accessible to the masses. Indeed, even where it is readily accessible, biomedicine often is not perceived by Kenyans as a comprehensive or final solution to health problems. Its diagnostic and therapeutic successes are limited because in practice its concepts, outlook, and institutional features lack the necessary "goodness of fit" with those of the local culture. Partly for this reason, a rich variety of traditionally based modes of therapy remain in use in Kenya and in virtually every other part of Africa (Lasker, 1981; Mullings, 1984). They are collectively and locally the dominant medical systems throughout Kenya today, cutting across both ethnic and class differences. Formalized, functional relationships between the local systems and biomedicine do not exist. Nevertheless, concurrent or serial utilization of traditional medicine and clinical medicine as treatment strategies is often more the rule than the exception.

Kenya's traditional and biomedical systems of healing are all undergoing change and adaptation from within and without in response to interaction with each other, and to the more general process of capitalistic modernization. One of the difficulties in analyzing and comparing these different therapy systems in Kenya, as in the rest of the world, stems from the imprecise terminology that is used to describe them in the literature and in general speech. For example, traditional medical systems are typically labeled "folk medicine," an ethnocentric term which has several different meanings, including: (1) any system other than Western biomedicine, (2) all unwritten systems, and (3) any "simpler" system at variance with Western biomedicine (Press, 1980). Press proposes a standardized definition of "folk medicine" that, by eliminating vague, stereotyped notions about its content and complexity, gives the concept sharpness and utility. Thus "folk medicine" is limited to "systems or practices of medicine based upon paradigms which differ from those of a dominant medical system of the same community or society" (Press, 1980, p. 48). According to this definition, which I adopt in this study, autochthonous medical systems such as Ayurveda, classical Chinese, precontact Navajo, or Kamba are not "folk," although any ethnic group's medical system can be so labeled if it is not the dominant practice of the community.

On the other hand, when folk medicine is freed from its non-Western or nonbiomedical implications it becomes possible to "label and approach *Western biomedicine as folk medicine* in many tribal and peasant areas of Africa, Asia, and Latin America where it operates in the presence of a locally dominant medical system" (Press, 1980, p. 49; emphasis added). Thus in Kenya, biomedicine may be viewed as a "variant" or folk medical system because it is subordinate to and, as an operational model, departs in fundamental ways from the traditionally based medical systems of the Kamba, Luo, Boran, Giriama, and others that remain dominant in terms of spatial coverage, accessibility, and frequency of utilization. A key distinction here in differentiating medical systems is their geographic sphere of influence. This dimension, which is seldom noted in the study of medical pluralism, concerns "the actual presence and availability of the constituent systems 'on the ground'" (Press, 1980, p. 47) in a specific locality.

REFERENCES

Ahmed, P. I., & Kolker, A. (1979). The role of indigenous medicine in WHO's definition of health. In P. I. Ahmed & G. V. Coelho (Eds.), *Toward a new definition of health.* New York: Plenum.

Akerele, O. (1984). WHO's traditional medicine programme: Progress and perspectives. *WHO Chronicle, 38,* 76–81.

de Albuquerque, K. (1979). Non-institutional medicine on the Sea Islands. In M. S. Varner & A. M. McCandless (Eds.), *Proceedings of a Symposium on Culture and Health: Implications for Health Policy in Rural South Carolina.* Charleston, SC: Center for Metropolitan Affairs and Public Policy, College of Charleston.

Atkinson, P. (1979). From honey to vinegar: Levi-Strauss in Vermont. In P. Morley & R. Wallis (Eds.), *Culture and curing.* Pittsburgh, PA: University of Pittsburgh Press.

Bannerman, R. H., Burton, J., & Wan-Chieh, C. (Eds.). (1983). *Traditional medicine and health care coverage*. Geneva: World Health Organization.

Bhardwaj, S., & Paul, B. K. (1986). Medical pluralism and infant mortality in a rural area of Bangladesh. *Social Science and Medicine, 10*, 1003–1010.

Bhardwaj, S. (1975). Attitude toward different systems of medicine: A survey of four villages in the Punjab-India. *Social Science and Medicine, 9*, 603.

Bhardwaj, S. (1980). Medical pluralism and homeopathy: A geographic perspective. *Social Science and Medicine, 14B*, 209–216.

Dorozynski, A. (1975). *Doctors and healers* (IDRC-043e). Ottowa: International Development Research Center.

Dunn, F. L. (1976). Traditional Asian medicine and cosmopolitan medicine as adaptive systems. In C. Leslie (Ed.), *Asian medical systems*. Berkeley: University of California Press.

Fabrega, H. (1977). The scope of ethnomedical science. *Culture, Medicine and Psychiatry, 1*, 9–23.

Family Health Institute. (1978). *A working paper on health services development in Kenya: Issues, analyses, and recommendations* (for USAID, Technical Assistance Program to the Government of Kenya). Washington, DC: Author.

Gatere, S. G. (1980). Traditional healing methods in psychiatry, Kenya. In A. Kiev, W. Muya, & N. Sartorius (Eds.), *The future of mental health services*. Amsterdam: Excerpta Medica.

Gerlach, L. (1959). Some basic Digo conceptions of health and disease. In *One-day Symposium on Attitudes to Health and Disease among Some East African Tribes*. Kampala, Uganda: East African Institute of Social Research.

Good, B. (1977). The heart of what's the matter: The semantics of illness in Iran. *Culture, Medicine and Psychiatry, 1*, 25–58.

Good, C. M. (1980). Ethnomedical systems in Africa and the LDC's: Key issues for the geographer. In M. Meade (Ed.), *Conceptual and methodological issues in medical geography: Studies in Geography No. 6*. Chapel Hill, NC: Department of Geography, University of North Carolina.

Good, C. M. (1987). Community health in tropical Africa: Is medical pluralism a hindrance or a resource? In R. Akhtar (Ed.), *Health and disease in tropical Africa: Geographical and medical viewpoints* (pp. 13–50). Chur, Switzerland: Harwood Academic Publishers.

Good, C. M., Hunter, J. M.,, Katz, S. H., & Katz, S. S. (1979). The interface of dual systems of health care in the developing world: Toward health policy initiatives in Africa. *Social Science and Medicine, 13D*, 141–154.

Hand, W. D. (Ed.). (1976). *American folk medicine: A symposium*. Berkeley: University of California Press.

Hulke, M. (1979). *The encyclopedia of alternative medicine and self-help*. New York: Schocken Books.

Imperato, P. J. (1977). *African folk medicine. Practices and beliefs of the Bambara and other peoples*. Baltimore, MD: York Press.

International Development Research Center. (1980). *Traditional medicine in Zaire. Present and potential contribution to the health services* (IDRC-137e). Ottawa: Author.

Janzen, J. M. (1978). *The quest for therapy in lower Zaire.* Berkeley: University of California Press.

Kleinman, A. (1978a). Concepts and a model for comparison of medical systems as cultural systems. *Social Science and Medicine, 12,* 85–93.

Kleinman, A. (1978b). International health care from an ethnomedical perspective: Critique and recommendations for change. *Medical Anthropology, (Spring),* 91–112.

Kleinman, A. (1980). *Patients and healers in the context of culture.* Berkeley: University of California Press.

Kunitz, S. J. (1981). Underdevelopment, demographic change, and health care on the Navajo Indian Reservation. *Social Science and Medicine, 15A,* 175–192.

Lasker, J. (1981). Choosing among therapies: Illness behavior in the Ivory Coast. *Social Science and Medicine, 15A,* 157–168.

Leslie, C. (1980). Medical pluralism in world perspective. *Social Science and Medicine, 14B,* 191–195.

Mbiti, J. S. (1970). *African religions and philosophy.* Garden City, NY: Anchor Books.

McDonald, C. A. (1981). Political-economic structures—approaches to traditional and modern medical systems. *Social Science and Medicine, 15A,* 101–108.

Miller, N. (1980). *Traditional medicine in East Africa* (American Universities Field Staff Reports, No. 22, Africa). Hanover, NH: American Universities Field Staff.

Mullings, L. (1984). *Therapy, ideology, and social change. Mental healing in Ghana.* Berkeley: University of California Press.

Nchinda, T. C. (1976). Traditional and western medicine in Africa: Collaboration or confrontation? *Tropical Doctor, (July),* 133–135.

Neumann, A. K., & Lauro, P. (1982). Ethnomedicine and biomedicine linking. *Social Science and Medicine, 16,* 1817–1824.

Onoge, O. F. (1975). Capitalism and public health: A neglected theme in the medical anthropology of Africa. In S. R. Ingman & A. E. Thomas (Eds.), *Topias and utopias in health.* The Hague: Mouton.

Pfifferling, J. H. (1975). Some issues in the consideration of non-Western and Western folk practices as epidemiologic data. *Social Science and Medicine, 9,* 655–658.

Pillsbury, B. L. K. (1978). *Traditional health care in the Near East.* Washington, DC: United States Agency for International Development.

Pillsbury, B. L. K. (1982). Policy and evaluation perspectives on traditional health care practitioners in national health care systems. *Social Science and Medicine, 16,* 1825–1834.

Polgar, S. (1962). Health and human behavior: Areas of interest common in the social and medical sciences. *Current Anthropology, 3,* 159–205.

Press, I. (1980). Problems in the definition and classification of medical systems. *Social Science and Medicine, 14B,* 45–57.

Rappoport, H. (1980). The integration of scientific and traditional healing: The problem of demystification. In P. R. Ulin & M. H. Segal (Eds.), *Traditional health care delivery in contemporary Africa* (Africa Series No. 35). Syracuse, NY: Maxwell School of Citzenship and Public Affairs, Syracuse University,

Republic of Kenya. (1986). *Development plan for the period 1984 to 1988.* Nairobi: Government Printer.

Scrimshaw, S. C. M. (1979). *A technical manual for private and indigenous health care assessment: Guidelines for health sector analysis.* Berkeley, CA: University of California School of Public Health.

Singer, P. (1977). *Traditional healing: New science or new colonialism?* Buffalo, NY: Conch Magazine, Ltd.

Stock, R. F. (1980). *Health care behaviour in a rural Nigerian setting with particular reference to the utilization of Western type health care facilities.* Unpublished doctoral dissertation, Department of Geography, University of Liverpool.

Swantz, M. L. (1979). Community and healing among the Zaramo in Tanzania. *Social Science and Medicine, 13B,* 169–173.

Swift, C. R., & Asuni, T. (1975), *Mental health and disease in Africa.* Edinburgh: Churchill Livingstone.

Unschuld, P. U. (1980). The issue of structured coexistence of scientific and alternative medical systems: A comparison of East and West German legislation. *Social Science and Medicine, 14B,* 15–24.

Varner, M. S., & McCandless, A. M. (Eds.). (1979). *Proceedings of a Symposium on Culture and Health: Implications for Health Policy in Rural South Carolina.* Charleston, SC: Center for Metropolitan Affairs and Public Policy, College of Charleston.

Vecsey, G. (1978, June 18). Spiritual healing gaining ground with Catholics and Episcopalians. *The New York Times,* p. 20.

Vuori, H. (1982). The World Health Organization and traditional medicine. *Community Medicine, 4,* 129–137.

Warren, D. M., Bova, G. S., Tregoning, M. A., & Kliewer, M. (1982). Ghanian national policy toward indigenous healers: The case of the Primary Health Training for Indigenous Healers (PRHETIH) Program. *Social Science and Medicine, 16,* 1873–1881.

Witchcraft warning . . . (1978, January 27). *Daily Nation.*

World Health Organization Regional Committee for Africa. (1976). *Traditional medicine and its role in the development of health services in Africa* (AFR/RC26/TO/1, June 23). Brazzaville: Author.

World Health Organization. (1982). The extension of health service coverage with traditional birth attendants: A decade of progress. *WHO Chronicle, 36,* 92–96.

·6·

The Placebo Effect: Using the Body's Own Healing Mechanisms

DAVID S. SOBEL

An abundance of evidence is now available to show that psychological stress in both animals and humans can produce physiological changes that suppress the immune system and may make us more prone to illness. There is a reverse of that same mechanism, however, that has happier effects on our health. It has been less well studied, perhaps, but we do now have a strong suggestion that positive emotion, positive feelings and states of expectancy, can work not only to enhance our health but to eliminate disease, sometimes counter to all odds.

We can see this most clearly in what has been termed the placebo effect. The word "placebo" is often used to refer to sugar pills, pills that are apparently chemically inert, or to any procedure that has no intrinsic therapeutic value. That is a rather limited and even incorrect view of what a placebo is. Arthur K. Shapiro (1964), a pioneer in placebo research, has suggested a broader, more useful definition of the placebo as any therapeutic procedure, or particular component of any therapeutic procedure, for which there is no objective evidence of a specific activity for the condition that is being treated.

Far from being considered worthy of study, the placebo has been seen for a long time as simply a nuisance, at least in research where we have tried to control or minimize its effects rather than understand and use them. In a way, our attitude toward the placebo has been a little like our original attitude toward penicillin. A contaminate in a biological experiment, penicillin was treated as such until it was noted that the contaminate itself had some rather interesting properties. It was only when it was finally investigated that we came up with the antibiotic that is now one of our most powerful therapeutic tools. If we start to pay the placebo the same serious attention, we may derive some understanding of why it too is a powerful and therapeutic tool in its own right.

Shapiro has often been quoted as saying that the history of medical treatment can be characterized as the history of the placebo effect since almost all medications until recently were placebos. At the turn of the century the prominent physician and father of Supreme Court Justice Oliver Wendell Holmes, also named Oliver Wendell Holmes, said that if most of the drugs in the pharmacopeia were sunk in the ocean, it would be all the better for mankind and all the worse for the fishes. For, throughout the ages, we have seen a variety of unlikely medications in use—animal dung, powdered mummies, sawdust, lizards' blood, dried vipers, frog sperm, unicorn horns, and so forth. Yet in spite of—or perhaps even because of—these potions, people managed to get better. They also managed to attribute their cures to the person who had given them these medications and, despite all the purging and poisoning and cutting and leeching, they revered the healers or medical men who had done it.

There are many reasons why those who are stricken ill become well. The first is that the unlikely remedies did contain some physiologically active ingredients. Leeches used in the medieval practices of bloodletting contain, by modern chemical analysis, at least four specifically active biochemical substances that counter different diseases. However, most of the remedies in the long history of medicine were probably much less effective than leeches.

A more likely explanation is that most ailments are self-limited. If a doctor does nothing or merely tells the patient to take two aspirin or two frog sperm pellets, the chances are fair that the patient will feel better in the morning, or at some time later during the course of most illnesses. Many illnesses follow their own specific natural history, and people are most likely to seek help at the worst point. Then, when they improve, they naturally attribute their improvement to the treatment they have received.

Another explanation for unexpected recovery is that perhaps it is not the remedy itself but belief in the remedy and belief in the healer that mobilize some very powerful self-healing mechanisms within the body. If this is so, the placebo may be very aptly named. The word is derived from the Latin for "I shall please" and the implications of that are interesting. Does it refer to the doctor or healer giving something to patients to please or placate them, even though the medicine has no specific activity? Or does it refer to the patient's decision to get better in order to please the doctor, so that the doctor will not feel that his or her efforts have gone for naught? This interaction may be exactly what is important.

The placebo is a tangible symbol that something is being done to help the patient. It evokes a network of strong personal and cultural expectations that the patient will improve. In our society, with its belief in better living through chemistry and worship of technology, what better symbol than a pill? It satisfies our need for something tangible, visible, which can be credited for the improvement. Norman Cousins (1980) observed:

> The placebo is not so much a pill as a process, beginning with the patient's confidence in the doctor and extending through the full functioning of his own immunological system. The process works not because of any magic in the tablets but because the human body is its own best apothecary and because the most successful prescriptions are those that are filled by the body itself. (p. 56)

If the placebo is to take its rightful place in medicine, we first must dispel some myths. The first is that placebos are essentially physiologically inert and that they therefore work only for psychological symptoms. There is clear evidence that this view is a fallacy. Henry Beecher of Harvard Medical School reviewed a wide range of studies and found that, on average, a third of the people who were given placebos reported satisfactory relief of their symptoms (Beecher, 1955). The symptoms included postoperative wound pain, seasickness, headache, cough, anxiety, and other problems. Even though we know that the perception and experience of pain is subjective, it would be inaccurate to claim that postoperative wound pain, for instance, is not organic.

Placebos have had effect on hypertension, angina, depression, acne, asthma with bronchospasm, arthritis, gastric acidity, ulcers, bleeding, common colds, warts, hay fever, insomnia, chronic urticaria, obesity, migraine, constipation, smoking behavior, etc. Although some symptoms are more amenable to placebo influence than others, it appears that no particular system in the body is immune to the placebo effect. So it is impossible for a clinician to use a placebo to distinguish between psychogenic ("not-real" pain) and pain due to organic causes.

The second myth is that the placebo effect is a very weak effect. On the contrary, there are at least some suggestions that the placebo effect is strong enough to overcome even the known pharmacological activity of another given drug. Stewart Wolf (1950) described an interesting case history of a woman who had such severe nausea and vomiting during pregnancy that nothing the doctors gave her seemed to help. Measurement of her gastric contractions confirmed that these were disrupted in a way consistent with the severe nausea she had reported. The doctors then offered her a new and extremely powerful drug that, they said, would unquestionably cure her nausea. Within 20 minutes of taking this drug, the patient reported relief and tests showed that her gastric contractions had returned to normal. The drug she was given was not a new drug designed to relieve nausea, however. It was syrup of ipecac, which is generally used to *induce* vomiting. In this case the placebo effect associated with the suggestion that the drug would relieve vomiting was powerful enough to counteract the direct and opposite pharmacological action of the drug itself. The syrup of ipecac when presented with the strong suggestion of relief of nausea acted as a cue to the brain which triggered a series of self-regulatory responses.

Not all of the effects of placebos are positive and therapeutic. A range of unpleasant symptoms including palpitations, drowsiness, headaches, diarrhea, nausea, and rashes have been produced by placebos. One classic placebo experiment is often done with medical students in a pharmacology class. The professor lectures about stimulant drugs and antidepressant drugs, describing in detail the effects each has on the body, and then invites the students to participate in a blind trial. The students take either a pink pill, the "stimulant," or a blue pill, the "depressant," and then measure one another's blood pressure and heart rate and record one another's symptoms.

About half of the students usually experience specific and measurable physiological reactions such as decrease in blood pressure and heart rate, and dizziness, watery eyes, and abdominal pain. But in fact, of course, all students have been given placebos and what we are seeing is the reaction to the expectation created when the professor described the relevant symptoms.

The placebo effect is not confined to sugar pills. It may extend to any therapeutic procedure, and surgery provides a particularly impressive example of placebo power in action. For instance, in the mid-1950s, a new surgical procedure was introduced to provide relief from the symptoms of chest pain due to coronary heart disease. The procedure was called internal mammary artery ligation, the tying off of an artery in the chest. About 40% of those who underwent this operation reported complete relief of chest pain, while 65%–75% showed considerable improvement. There were also electrocardiographic improvements and increases in exercise tolerance.

Despite these enthusiastic reports many clinicians doubted the physiological basis of the procedure. Two independent groups of skeptics decided to carry out a controlled trial with a unique experimental design the ethics of which would be questionable today.

Patients were randomly allocated to undergo either a real or a mock operation. Half had the mammary arteries ligated; the rest had incisions made in the chest wall under anesthesia in the operating room, but were then simply stitched together again. The benefits of the mock operation were found to be as great as those of the real one. The procedure was finally abandoned, but not before some 10,000 to 15,000 operations had been performed (see Frank, 1975).

As we have seen, the situations in which the placebo effect take place are surprisingly wide-ranging. But what governs whether or not a placebo will work and who will be the ones to respond? Unfortunately there are more opinions than facts here as yet. For instance, there is a considerable amount of evidence that suggests that persons who respond to placebos—called placebo responders—are usually highly suggestible, hysterical, neurotic, dependent, weak-willed, and introverted. But there is an equally impressive number of studies that indicate quite the opposite findings from these. We can only conclude that we do not at the moment have a good or reliable description of the personality type that is likely to respond to a placebo. In fact, what we find is that a person who is a responder in one situation or setting may turn out to be a nonresponder in a completely different situation or setting.

Placebo response seems to have more to do with the set of expectations or the meaning of the symptoms that a person brings to a particular situation than to enduring personality characteristics, though these may interact. Beecher (1956) did a study of soldiers who were wounded on a beachhead in the Pacific during World War II. He found that only a quarter of the soldiers required medication for the pain from severe wounds, whereas all civilians, if they had suffered those wounds, would have needed it. Part of the explanation that Beecher advanced was that the meaning of the pain for a soldier severely wounded on a beachhead was significantly different from that experienced by a man severely hurt in a car accident, for instance. For the soldier the wound was a ticket home, a way to get out of the war. For the civilian an accident would mean loss of work, hospital bills, etc. The one could welcome the pain, the other would not.

It is interesting in light of this that less badly hurt soldiers experienced more pain and required more pain medication than extremely hurt soldiers—because these men knew their wounds would be patched up and they would be sent back to fight. So whether a placebo response will take place or not may well be connected with the meaning of a symptom, the seriousness of the symptom, and perhaps the fear or anxiety level of the person experiencing that symptom.

There is an interesting study that demonstrates the power of expectation, another of the probable explanations for why placebos so often work. It is an anecdotal study carried out in Germany by a physician called Rheder (1955). He tried a test with three hospitalized patients: one had chronic gall bladder disease; one had severe pancreatitis with accompanying weight loss, depression, and constipation; and the third had inoperable cancer of the uterus, with massive collections of fluid in her body and accompanying anemia and weakness.

Rheder visited a faith healer in the neighborhood who practiced absent healing and asked him to attempt to treat his three patients. He supplied the necessary information about them, and the healer tried during 12 sessions in the few weeks that followed to project a healing force to the patients. Rheder did not tell the patients what was going on, but he and his associates monitored them carefully for any significant change in their clinical condition over the next few weeks. There was none.

When the healer was no longer working on their cases, Rheder then told the patients that he had located a very powerful absent healer who was prepared to project his healing energy for them at such and such a time on such and such a date. He made it clear that the healer had been highly successful on many other occasions.

Within a few days of the appointed "healing" time the patient with chronic gall bladder disease became free of pain and was symptom free for about a year. The patient with pancreatitis had a restoration of normal bowel function, was able to leave her bed, and gained 30 pounds. The patient with inoperable cancer experienced a decrease in swelling and fluid in her abdomen, an increase in appetite, and a dramatic improvement of her anemia. Within 5 days she was sent home from the hospital and, although she died about 3 months later as expected, she was able to live quite an active life until the end and was in very good spirits. It would seem, from this study, that more important than the distant projection of the healer was the patients' belief in and expectation of improvement (although it could be argued that the benefits were due to the delayed effects of the healing energy).

A less anecdotal piece of evidence for the power of expectation in recovery of health is provided by a study by R. C. Mason and colleagues (Mason, Clark, Reeves, & Wagner, 1969). They looked at patients' speed of recovery from surgery for a detached retina. About 98 patients were interviewed through questionnaires designed to assess their degree of trust in the surgeon, optimism that the outcome of the operation would be good, and readiness to accept the outcome even if it was not good. The surgeon also independently rated what he thought would be the degree of each patient's trust, optimism, and acceptance and the speed of recovery. The conclusion drawn was that rapid healing occurs when patients have faith in the healer and feel that the healer's methods are relevant to the cause of the illness, and that the way to help slow-healing patients is to enhance their trust and their faith.

Belief not only in the doctor or healer but also in the nature of the treatment can affect placebo outcome. For example, the physical characteristics of the medications seem to play a part in potentiating the placebo effect. Although evidence is scanty and often contradictory, it appears that placebo injections are more potent than pills and that capsules are more effective than pills but less effective than injections. Small yellow pills seem to work well for depression while larger blue pills have a better effect as sedatives. Further, the more bitter-tasting the medicine or unpleasant the treatment, the more likely it is that the placebo effect will be induced.

A recent British study (Brantwaithe & Cooper, 1981) even found that brand names can play a part in the placebo response. Researchers at Keele

University gave women who regularly had headaches aspirin or placebo in a familiar well-known branded package or in an unfamiliar unbranded package. Approximately 40% of the group receiving unbranded placebos reported the pain was considerably or completely better; 50% reported relief with branded placebos, 56% with unbranded aspirin, and 60% with branded aspirin. So although the active ingredient, aspirin, was slightly more effective than the sugar-pill placebo, as one would expect, the effectiveness of both was enhanced by the expectation engendered by the familiar brand name.

The way in which treatment is given, that is, the confidence of the therapist and the enthusiasm with which he or she promotes a particular treatment, also shapes the placebo response. Researchers Steven Gryll and Martin Katahn (1978) made a study of placebo influence on the painfulness of dental injections. Two groups of patients were given a placebo pill before an injection but a different message about the effects of the pill. Some were informed that it was a new drug that the dentist himself had found to be very effective in reducing patients' tension, anxiety, and sensitivity to pain. It was harmless and effective almost instantly. The other patients were told by the dentist that, although the drug was new and reduced tension, anxiety, and sensitivity in some people, he personally had not found it to be very effective. However, it was certainly harmless and, if it did work, would do so almost at once. The pill was significantly more effective when offered by the confident, enthusiastic practitioner. It was confidence that affected the response of the patient rather than the warmth or coldness with which the message was delivered or the status of the person delivering it (for example, if the dental assistant instead of the dentist proffered the pill), neither of which had a particular effect on the response.

The influence of confidence was noted as far back as 1833 when the French physician Armand Trousseau advised: "You should treat as many patients as possible with new drugs while they still have the power to heal" (cited in Shapiro, 1974, p. 222).

Although confidence on the part of the physician or healer may be helpful, it is not always necessary. In the final analysis all that seems to matter is what the patient believes, whether that belief is objectively correct or not. Lawrence D. Egbert (1985), an anesthesiologist, recalls the case of a patient undergoing an amputation of her foot for diabetic gangrene.

She was 85 years old, poor and close to illiterate. She accepted spinal anesthesia. Three surgeons were operating while talking about things of considerable social interest in their personal lives. The surgeons were asked to lower their voices but would not. The patient wondered what was going on and seemed only slightly mollified when I told her a birthday party was being held in the office nearby. The young surgeons simply would not quit their joking and horseplay. Finally, the senior surgeon was pouring an antibiotic wash over the raw stump, and the junior surgeon was citing data to show that this activity was a waste of time, when the third surgeon began a loud and humorous pseudoreligious incantation over the ablutions. The patient jumped and again was confused, wondering what was going on. The surgeons stopped the horseplay. The patient, however, took a completely new attitude about the entire business. She thought it was wonderful. Imagine how nice it was to have fine young surgeons praying over her foot and she just a poor old lady from the country! She was completely impressed with what a fine hospital we had and how nice we all were, and she went on to make a satisfactory recovery. I have no doubt that her recovery was helped by the spiritual support she thought she was receiving. (p. 57)

The importance of the suggestions given with any treatment is further illustrated by a case described by psychologist Neil Fiore (1979). He described his own experience when he was treated with chemotherapy for cancer. He suggested that the distress from side effects such as hair loss, extreme nausea, and vomiting might be reduced if the treatment were introduced with a positive rather than a negative message:

Physicians, by their attitudes and words, can lead patients to imagine and expect a hopeless situation with much pain. Examples of this approach are, 'You will have a lot of pain but we have the drugs to help you,' or 'Chemotherapy is highly toxic and you will lose your hair and become nauseated.' By the same token, aware physicians can use the patient's suggestible state to calm and to increase the chances for a positive outcome.

They can say, 'You will be receiving some very powerful medicine capable of killing rapidly producing cells. Cancer is the most rapidly producing cell, but there are other rapidly producing cells such as hair. And since the medication cannot tell the difference between hair and cancer cells, you may lose some hair temporarily. Fortunately, your normal, healthy cells can recover from the medication and reproduce themselves, but the weak, poorly formed cancer cells cannot.'

The positive statement uses the word 'medication' instead of 'drugs' to emphasize the helpful nature of chemotherapy, and uses 'powerful' instead of 'toxic' to emphasize the point that this is a strong ally to the body. The loss of hair and other side effects are presented as possible, and not certain, to avoid self-fulfilling prophecies. Most importantly, the statement allows patients to conceptualize the side effects as a sign that their powerful ally is working at killing rapidly producing cells. Without this kind of intervention, patients often conclude that the side effects are proof that they are dying—if not from cancer, from its treatment. (pp. 286–287)

The message given with a treatment can also influence how rapidly it takes effect. In a study of 30 patients undergoing relaxation training to lower blood pressure, half of the patients were told their blood pressure would begin to decline immediately following the first training session while the others were instructed that their blood pressure response would be delayed until at least after the third session. Those who expected an immediate response showed a seven times greater reduction (17.0 versus 2.4 mm Hg) in systolic blood pressure when compared with those led to expect a delayed response. The relaxation training was otherwise identical in both groups (Agras, Horne, & Taylor, 1982).

The mechanism by which the belief in a placebo is translated into beneficial physiological changes is not known. However, some recent research by Jon Levine and colleagues at the University of California in San Francisco links placebo analgesia and endorphins (Levine & Gordon, 1984; Levine, Gordon, & Fields, 1978). Levine's series of experiments on patients after wisdom tooth extraction suggested that placebo pain relief involves a turning on of the body's intrinsic pain regulation system mediated, in part, by endorphins. The better the physiology of the placebo is understood, the more we will be able to devise therapeutic interventions and supports that mobilize and work in concert with these intrinsic healing systems.

Despite the findings I have reviewed here demonstrating the power of the placebo, I certainly am not advocating that placebos should be used in clinical practice. That is a course fraught with serious ethical problems, particularly deception. The argument has been put forward that to use placebos in practice is not deception because the intent of the physician is still to heal, not to deceive. However, if there were widespread use of placebos based on that understanding, they would soon lose their effectiveness anyway because patients, believing any pills likely to be placebos, would cease to believe in them or have faith in those who provided them.

There is one study, however, that demonstrates that deception may not have to be an element in the placebo response and that may point the way toward a method by which it could be mobilized both ethically and efficaciously. The study, published in the *Archives of General Psychiatry* in 1965 by Lee C. Park and Lino Covi of the Johns Hopkins University School of Medicine, tested the "honest" approach to using placebos. Fifteen anxious patients attending a psychiatric outpatient clinic were given sugar pills for 1 week. They were told that they were receiving sugar pills but that these pills had been helpful to many people. At the end of the week, 14 of the 15 had reported significant improvement of their symptoms and nine attributed the benefits directly to the pills even though eight of them believed they were placebos. Six thought the pills must contain an active ingredient because they were working so well and three even reported side effects of dry mouth and blurred vision.

It might be possible perhaps to set up a kind of double-blind trial with some patients where, if they agreed, they would receive either a drug or a placebo, neither they nor the doctors knowing at the time who was receiving which. The patients would monitor what happened to their pain during the experiment, and if it turned out that they had responded to placebo, they could discuss with the doctor the positive implications: that is, that if people see that they can control pain themselves, they might also obtain relief from other methods of pain control over which they could have some measure of self-regulation, such as relaxation training, hypnosis, or biofeedback.

This, then, is the real import of the placebo effect. It gives testimony to the fact that we have within us certain self-healing mechanisms, intrinsic healing systems, that can be mobilized and elicited if given appropriate situational and environmental cues. There could well be alternative ways in which we could begin to understand the dynamic mechanisms of these intrinsic systems and then learn to mobilize or trigger them in ways that have fewer side effects than conventional drugs.

The work of Dr. Carl Simonton and Stephanie Matthews-Simonton with cancer patients is a case in point (Simonton, Matthews-Simonton, & Creighton, 1978). They developed the idea of visualization as a way to help trigger the body's self-healing mechanism. While patients were receiving orthodox treatments such as surgery, chemotherapy, and radiation, they were also encouraged to participate in group and family therapy and, while in a state of relaxation, to visualize their cancers and their body defenses fighting them. The Simontons achieved this by lecturing on and discussing the role of the body's white blood cells in attacking and destroying cancer cells as part of the normal surveillance system of the body. They found that the descriptions or visualizations did not have to be physiologically exact to be effective. For instance, some people chose to imagine white light dissolving the cancer cells or schools of piranhas attacking them. An increased survival rate has been reported among patients, which is interesting and suggestive, although there have been no controlled trials.

A preliminary report by Howard Hall (1983) at Pennsylvania State University of the effect of hypnosis and visualization on the immune system does begin to show some of the possibilities ahead. Twenty healthy men and women volunteers, aged from 20 to 85, were given blood tests to check their white cell function. They were then hypnotized and told to visualize their white blood cells as strong, powerful sharks swimming through their blood streams, attacking and destroying the germs that caused colds and influenza. They were told by posthypnotic suggestion that these sharklike cells would continue to protect them, and they were required to do self-hypnosis twice a day for a week, at home, while carrying on working with the imagery. The researchers found that in younger subjects there was a slight increase in responsiveness of white blood cells to stimulation.

While the results were not dramatic, they did show that it may be possible to harness some of the powers seen in the placebo effect and stimulate them by other means. Other researchers are just beginning to look at the physiological effects of position emotions, laughter, relaxation, and visualization (Ornstein & Sobel, 1987; Ornstein & Sobel, 1989). The findings may take us well beyond the placebo effect and allow us deliberately to exploit our bodies' own healing mechanisms by hitherto unrealized means.

BIBLIOGRAPHY

Agras, W. S., Horne, M. & Taylor, C. B. (1982). Expectation and the blood-pressure-lowering effect of relaxation. *Psychosomatic Medicine,, 44*, 389–395.

Beecher, H. K. (1955). The powerful placebo. *Journal of the American Medical Association, 159*, 1602–1606.

Beecher, H. K. (1956). Relationship of significance of wound to pain experienced. *Journal of the American Medical Association, 161*, 1609–1613.

Beecher, H. K. (1961). Surgery as placebo. *Journal of the American Medical Association, 176*, 1102–1107.

Benson, H., et al. (1975). The placebo effect: A neglected asset in the care of patients. *Journal of the American Medical Association, 232*, 1225.

Branthwaite, A., & Cooper, P. (1981). Analgesic effect of branding in treatment of headaches. *British Medical Journal, 282*, 1576–1578.

Buckalew, L. W., & Ross, S. (1981). Relationship of perceptual characteristics to efficacy of placebos. *Psychological Reports, 49*, 955–961.

Cousins, N. (1980). *Anatomy of an illness as perceived by the patient.* New York: Norton.

Egbert, L. D. (1985). Postscript. *Advances, 2*, 56–59.

Fiore, N. (1979). Fighting cancer—One patient's perspective. *New England Journal of Medicine, 300*, 284–289.

Frank, J. D. (1973). *Persuasion and healing.* Baltimore: Johns Hopkins University Press.

Frank, J. D. (1975). The faith that heals. *The Johns Hopkins Medical Journal, 137*, 127–131.

Gryll, S. L., & Katahn, M. (1978). Situational factors contributing to the placebo effect. *Psychopharmacology, 57*, 253–261.

Hall, H. (1983). Hypnosis and the immune system: A review with implications for cancer the psychology of healing. *American Journal of Clinical Hypnosis, 1983*, 92–103.

Jospe, M. (1978). *The placebo effect in healing.* Lexington, MA: Lexington Books.

Levine, J. D., & Gordon, N. C. (1984). Influence of the method of drug administration on analgesic response. *Nature, 312*, 755–756.

Levine, J. D., Gordon, N. C., & Fields, H. L. (1978). The mechanism of placebo analgesia. *Lancet, 2*, 654–657.

Mason, R. C., Clark, G., Reeves, R. B., & Wagner, B. (1969). Acceptance and healing. *Journal of Religion and Health, 8*, 123–142.

Ornstein, R., & Sobel, D. (1987). *The healing brain.* New York: Simon & Schuster.

Ornstein, R., & Sobel, D. (1989). *Healthy pleasures.* New York: Addison-Wesley.

Park, L. C., & Covi, L. (1965). Nonblind Placebo Trial. *Archives of General Psychiatry, 12*, 336–345.

Rheder, H. (1955). Wunderheilungen: Ein experiment. *Hippokrates, 26*, 577–580.

Shapiro, A. K. (1964). Factors contributing to the placebo effect. *American Journal of Psychotherapy, 73*(Suppl.), 73–88.

Shapiro, A. K. (1974). Contribution to a history of the placebo effect. In T. X. Barber, L. V. DiCara, J. Kamiya, D. Shapiro, & J. Stoyva (Eds.), *Biofeedback and self-control 1973.* Chicago: Aldine.

Shapiro, A. K., & Morris, L. A. (1978). The placebo effect in medical and psychological therapies. In S. L. Garfield & A. E. Bergin (Eds.), *Handbook of psychotherapy and behavior change.* New York: John Wiley.

Simonton, O. C., Matthews-Simonton, S., & Creighton, J. (1978). *Getting well again.* Los Angeles: J. P. Tarcher.

Sobel, D. S. (Ed.). (1979). *Ways of health: Holistic approaches to ancient and contemporary medicine.* New York: Harcourt Brace Jovanovich.

White, L., Tursky, B., & Schwartz, G. E. (Eds.) (1985). *Placebo: Theory, research, and mechanisms.* New York: Guilford Press.

Wolf, S. (1950). Effects of suggestion and conditioning on the action of chemical agents in human subjects—The pharmacology of placebos. *Journal of Clinical Investigation, 29,* 10–109.

· 7 ·

The Broken Heart:
The Psychobiology of
Human Contact

JAMES J. LYNCH

This chapter first reviews the material on the broken heart, trying to show
that the way we live together and do not live together or are isolated from one
another is a major cause of increased morbidity and mortality in our society;
then it focuses on cardiovascular disease in terms of interpersonal isolation.
Finally, it examines how communication can be, paradoxically, both a
mechanism of sickness and death through the cardiovascular system and a
mechanism of improving health.

   Communication is vitally linked to our bodies and is probably the single
most important force that influences our health or lack of health. We can now
deal clinically with a broad range of cardiovascular diseases by focusing on
links between the cardiovascular system and communication. For example,
although some of our patients have been taking antihypertensive medication
for 10 to 15 years, we have been able to regulate their blood pressure and help
them withdraw from medication by teaching them how to communicate in a
healthful way and instructing them about relations between the cardiovascular system and their communications.

   The paradox is how to understand the collision of paradigms about the
body that now exist in society. On the one hand we have the first human
beings with artificial hearts, a medical triumph that has helped to foster a
belief in the mechanical body and the heart as a strictly mechanical pump.
Most people in our society see themselves as two people: as minds and as
bodies. We believe that the extracorporeal mind influences the machine
body, and that we can replace human hearts with mechanical hearts that and

not affect this delicate system. Of course, this view is difficult to accept when it is stated explicitly, but it is the way we conceive the human body. What I want to suggest is quite a different perspective, one that includes the view that our bodies are inextricably bound up in the most peculiar of all human functions—communication. Unfortunately, the dichotomy between mind and body has helped to obscure the vital links between speaking and the cardiovascular system. We cannot communicate extracorporally, as if we could speak outside of our bodies. Though it might at first sound obvious, this idea is far more subtle than it appears on the surface.

THE BROKEN HEART

From the quiet comforting of a dying person, to the cuddling of an infant, in single, widowed, divorced, or married people, in neurotic, schizophrenic, or normal people, one factor unites all of us—dialogue. Dialogue is the essential element of all social interactions. In its most general meaning, dialogue consists of reciprocal communication between two or more living creatures. It involves the sharing of thoughts, physical sensations, ideas, ideals, hopes, and feelings. In total, dialogue involves a reciprocal sharing of any and all life experiences.

There is, however, a widespread belief in our modern culture that words such as "love" have no meaning, that such feelings have no effect on our health. A whole generation of detached, independent, self-sufficient, non-committed individuals believes that no one needs to get hurt in modern human relationships, that it is possible to be intimate with someone and then leave, and nothing bad will happen. Yet scientific data suggest that this may not be true.

The rhythm of the heart beat of a patient in a coronary care unit can be altered when the patient is touched by another human being. This occurs in patients in deep coma as well as in those who are fully conscious. I first noticed this when I worked in a coronary care unit studying the effects of human contact on the heart rates and heart rhythms of cardiac patients. Being a somewhat detached observer in the coronary care unit—that is, someone not clinically responsible for the health of the patients—gave me the advantage of being able to see things that were being glossed over.

One of the phenomena made clear by health statistics in the past decade was that the nature of disease and premature death had changed in this country, in a very short period, from a system in which hospitals were dealing with infectious disease and communicable disease, essentially struggling against forces of nature that were attacking us, to a system where much of the disease appeared to involve human behavior. For many of the young people coming into hospitals, it was their own behavior or someone else's behavior that brought them there. Several generations ago, young people died primarily of infectious diseases. Today, three of every four deaths among American males between the ages of 15 and 25 are caused by accidents, suicide, or homicide (Lynch, 1977).

Since 1950 the leading causes of premature death in the United States of men between 24 and 65 have been, in order of frequency: heart disease; cancer, especially lung cancer in men under 70; cirrhosis of the liver; accidents; influenza and pneumonia; motor vehicle accidents; suicide; and homicide. All these causes of death have a great deal to do with human feelings and human behavior.

One of the factors that appears to cause people to behave in ways that puts their own health at risk is loneliness. There is no cause of death that does not kill people who are lonely at significantly higher rates than those who had satisfying lives with others. At all ages, for both sexes and all races in the United States, the single, widowed, and divorced die at rates from two to ten times higher than do married people before age 70. Obviously, not all who are single, divorced, or widowed will die prematurely because of loneliness. What seems to make the difference is the ability to adjust to the condition of living alone.

Examining the death rates of white U.S. males between the ages of 15 and 64 reveals that divorced men die of heart disease at a rate more than twice that of married men. Widowed men seem most vulnerable to motor vehicle accidents. Divorced men die of cirrhosis of the liver at a rate more than seven times higher than married men. Divorced men lead all categories as victims of homicide. Tuberculosis strikes more than five times as many single men as married men, six times more widowed men than married ones, and ten times as many divorced men as married ones. The death rate comparisons for penumonia are similar to those for tuberculosis. Death by accidental fire of explosion for single men is three times more frequent than for married men, for divorced men is eight times higher, and for widowed men is nine times higher.

While these statistics focus on white males, similar statistics hold true for nonwhite males. For example, in terms of coronary heart disease mortality, single nonwhite men between the ages of 25 and 34 die at a rate 2.24 times that of married men. Divorced nonwhite men die at a ratio of 2.64 to one married man. Nonwhite widowed men die at a rate more than four times that of married men.

Among women, 34% more widows die of heart disease than married women; 46% more die of cancer of the cervix; 55% more die because of cirrhosis of the liver. The suicide rate of widows is double that of married women. More than four times as many widows die in motor vehicle accidents. Death by accidental fire or explosion is six times more frequent for widows than for married women. Divorced women have even worse odds than widows; 25% more divorced women die of cirrhosis of the liver than do widows. Cancer of the cervix kills 28% more divorced women than widows, and divorced women commit suicide 43% more frequently than widows.

A closer examination of heart disease by geographic distribution shows even more. Heart disease is the leading cause of premature death in the United States. Looking at the death rates for white men and women between the ages of 25 and 64 in the United States by states for the period 1959 through 1961 reveals that Nevada had the highest death rates. For the same age range, Nevada also had the second highest income level, an average number of physicians and hospitals per population, and one of the lowest population densities in the United States.

Neighboring Utah, however, had one of the lowest death rates. In 1960, Nevada and Utah had identical education rates for white adults, 12.2 years, among the highest average rates in the country. Average income in Nevada was about 20% higher than in Utah, and lower income is usually correlated with higher death rates from heart disease. The number of people living in urban areas in the two states was practically identical. Can the difference in death from cardiovascular disease be attributed to air, water, nutrition, exercise, or obesity? It seems unlikely. However, there are important differences between the states.

Utah is a very religious state, with the Mormon religion the dominant influence. Mormons neither drink nor smoke. They maintain very stable lives. Marriages are generally secure. Family ties remain strong. Most of the state's inhabitants stay in Utah. Nevada is quite the opposite.

In 1960 twenty per cent of Nevada's men between 55 and 64 years of age were either single, widowed, divorced, or not living with their spouses. Figures from Utah were about half these. Of those married in the state of Nevada, one third had previously been widowed or divorced. Perhaps even more shocking was the fact that 90% of Nevadans of middle age were born somewhere else, while 63% of the residents of Utah over the age of 20 were born there. There is thus tremendous social instability, mobility, and uprootedness within the state of Nevada. The mortality statistics show the consequences of this.

Nevada in the early 1960s was a foretaste of current acceptable middle-class norms throughout the United States: divorce, mobility, living alone, and uprootedness have become widespread in every region of the United States. Consequently, the health of our infants, young people, and elderly will probably look more like Nevada's and less like Utah's for decades to come.

Almost every segment of our society seems to be deeply afflicted by one of the major diseases of our age—loneliness. The divorce rate in the United States has accelerated over the past two decades at a truly stunning rate. In 1975, more than one million marriages ended in divorce, an all-time record up to that date. The number of children under 18 who must now endure the loss of a parent through divorce has grown even more rapidly than the rate of divorce itself. During the last two decades, the number of children caught in parental divorce has more than tripled, from 330,000 children in 1953, to more than one million children in 1973.

If divorce, as is clearly reflected in the epidemiological statistics, increases the incidence of premature death in adults, then it seems clear that children who are caught in divorce also run the same types of risks. If human loss is a contributor to disease and death, then children who lose their parents may be as much at risk as adults who lose love.

The mortality statistics appear to lead to one inevitable conclusion: People truly need each other. As a society, we are more and more becoming victims of the popular notion that being independent of others equals strength and success. We seem to be moving away from rituals, cultural traditions, and religious ceremonies that have evolved over the course of centuries to provide generalized sources of human contact and friendship for the lonely and for those who have suffered human loss. No nation spends more money on biomedical research than the United States. Total war has been declared on heart disease and on cancer, but the health statistics appear to suggest that we may be working feverishly to control diseases that we ourselves are causing. The U.S. government has never declared war on loneliness.

CARDIOVASCULAR DISEASE AND ISOLATION

It is estimated that between 35 and 50 million Americans are hypertensive. Definitions vary, but systolic blood pressures higher than 155 mm Hg or diastolic pressures higher than 95 mm Hg on two or three successive readings are frequently used to classify a person as hypertensive. Risk for stroke is about four times higher in hypertensive persons than in those with normal blood pressure, and risk for myocardial infarction is about two to three times higher.

The American Heart Association warns our citizens about the dangers of hypertension in a way that frequently leads them to overlook the links between social existence and vulnerability to this disease. Commercials on television solemnly warn, "If you have hypertension, see a doctor." They do not speak in terms of *being* hypertensive, but of having "it." The language makes it appear as though hypertension is a disease like other infectious diseases. Patients who come to our clinic speak about their disease similarly. Few patients describe themselves as hypertensive; instead they assert that they "have" hypertension. I ask patients where they got "it." Because we have accepted the hydraulic model of the human cardiovascular system, we have disconnected blood pressure from any sense of personal involvement. So if you have hypertension and the disease is an object, it makes perfect sense to take "something" for "it."

Thus we are dealing with deep metaphorical problems in society that have to do with the way we look at disease. Although no one will dispute that isolation and loneliness increase the risk of disease and contribute to premature death, such problems will not be advertised on television. Diseases are portrayed on television as victimizing people, not as phenomena we ourselves cause. This is a problem of societal definitions.

However, new computerized methods of taking blood pressure may lead to a biomedical as well as to a cultural revolution in the way we think about heart disease. The Korotkoff method of measuring blood pressure with a stethoscope is discontinuous and discrete. The Korotkoff method can only yield a pressure for one heart cycle. More importantly, silence was built into the measurement of blood pressure in human beings. If communication has something to do with blood pressure, then physicians who have taken billions of blood pressures in silence may be forced to reexamine the meaning of the numbers they obtain.

The recent availability of computer technology has permitted us to observe that the simple act of speaking can have a truly profound effect on blood pressure. Thirty seconds of human talk can cause blood pressure to rise 50%. Virtually every physician and nurse recognizes that emotions can affect a patient's blood pressure. They know that if the patient is anxious, it is important to calm the patient down and take several measures of blood pressure. They are generally familiar with Cannon's emergency reaction, involving a rise in blood pressure and heart rate as animals prepare to fight or run away. This understanding of the role of the emotions, however, also helped to obscure the vital role of human communication in the entire process.

Franz Alexander wrote a series of papers in the 1930s on psychoanalytic psychotherapy with hypertensive patients. Building on Cannon's theory of fight or flight, he sought to help hypertensive patients reduce their blood pressure with the help of psychotherapy. His are extraordinarily important clinical observations of the personality of hypertensive patients.

Alexander was limited in part by having a stethoscope rather than a computer to measure blood pressure. The equipment limited the way the relationships between therapy and blood pressure could be observed. However, even though the patients he treated developed considerable insight, they were still as hypertensive at the end of treatment as at the beginning. These findings were replicated by a number of other investigators, and it was generally accepted that hypertension could not be treated with psychotherapy.

Following Alexander, Stewart Wolf showed that when hypertensive patients were deliberately given stress interviews, they exhibited marked increases in blood pressure. Wolf also recognized that a stethoscope was not the proper way to examine blood pressure, and he devised an instrument to measure blood pressure directly. Based on his work, and that of Morton Reiser and Harold Wolff, it became accepted that stress can significantly influence blood pressure.

Yet in all of these studies it was not who was talking, but what they were talking about that was considered important in the interviews. Stress was considered the key ingredient. Before 1965, a dominant perspective in psychology was that Pavlovian classical conditioning influenced the cardio-vascular system and other smooth musculature, while operant conditioning influenced the skeletal muscular system. In 1965, Neal Miller challenged that idea with a series of experiments that appeared to demonstrate that the autonomic nervous system and smooth musculature could be voluntarily controlled. His observations helped to found the field called biofeedback. Although Miller's experiments later proved to be nonreplicable, clinical investigators began to apply his techniques to successfully treat migraine and other problems.

This field was called biofeedback because it accepted the idea that a person could sit in front of a machine and learn to control his or her own body. I thought this method of bodily control was simplistic from the beginning. Thinking about my own experiences with blushing, it seemed to me that even if I could control my facial vasodilation while sitting in front of a biofeedback machine, it would be irrelevant. The simple fact is that I never blushed in front of a computer; blushing was essentially an interpersonal phenomenon, one that occurred only in the presence of another human being. The real stressors of life seemed to me to be of this ilk, somewhat akin to the stressors that led to blushing.

Sue Ann Thomas and I, and others who work with us, noticed an analogous phenomenon when we attached a computerized blood pressure device to patients. Every time the patient spoke, his or her blood pressure went up, and every time I spoke, the blood pressure went down. We attached the machine to me, and every time I spoke, my blood pressure went up, and every time the patient spoke, my blood pressure went down. We observed that we were on a dialogue seesaw and that human dialogue has a mirror image in the vasculature.

We subsequently completed over 50 research studies on this phenomenon. It is highly replicable. Virtually all persons elevate their blood pressure when they speak.

What makes the phenomenon clinically important is the additional observation that the higher a person's resting blood pressure, the more it rises when he or she speaks. The magnitude of the elevations was quite startling, with blood pressure rising 10%–50% on the average within 30 seconds after a person began to speak. Rapid speaking led to greater elevations than slow speaking. In addition, many hypertensive patients did not appear to breathe when they spoke, a physiological phenomenon that led to major increases in their blood pressure. Also of great interest to us was the surprising fact that no antihypertensive medications seemed to block these rises. Blood pressure increased dramatically in patients who were taking antihypertensive medications even though their baseline quiet blood pressure appeared to be well regulated.

These observations of the direct relationship between speaking and blood pressure gradually led to the development of a new approach to the treatment of hypertension. The approach not only emphasizes the minute-to-minute digital feedback of blood pressure and heart rate but also links these changes to shifts in dialogue within the context of human verbal interactions. It became obvious that an approach similar to, yet fundamentally different from, that originally employed by Alexander might help bridge the gap between the vascular consequences of loneliness and the hypertensive patient's needs for social distancing. Since the magnitude of blood pressure increases during speech was significantly correlated with baseline pressure, it appeared likely that efforts aimed at lowering baseline pressure would have the corresponding effect of lowering the magnitude of pressure rises when hypertensive persons spoke. In addition, the computerized feedback of pressure could be used by the patient and therapist to titrate the magnitude of pressured rises that could be tolerated before the patient should pause and be instructed to relax and be quiet. The type of approach used by Alexander, in which a patient was monitored only at the beginning and end of therapy, would not be sensitive to the marked shifts in blood pressure when the patient spoke. It also became clear that hypertensive patients with very high pressures would not be able to tolerate insight-oriented psychotherapy, since the physiological concomitants of their ongoing dialogue could be lethal. Since a number of relaxation, meditation, and biofeedback approaches rely on deep breathing and relaxation, it seemed appropriate to incorporate these techniques into periods of quiet during the therapeutic dialogue.

Beyond the technical orientation of titrating human dialogue, it occurred to us that blood pressure rises while speaking could be looked at as a hidden bodily communication, a form of internal blushing, which therapists could use as a psychophysiological signal to alter ongoing dialogue. We also began to recognize that the patient and the therapist share a fundamental problem: Neither can afford to ignore the important vascular consequences of their ongoing dialogue. Consequently, the therapeutic approach we developed—an approach called transactional psychophysiology, or TP therapy—was based on the fundamental idea that every bodily response in human dialogue is a communicative transaction that must be attended to and understood. Although a person's cardiovascular responses can be psychophysiological, like blushing, they can also be viewed as vascular responses that are essentially interpersonal. This notion of blood pressure elevations as a form of hidden internal blushing helped crystallise a way to make therapeutic use of the hypertensive patient's needs to maintain a comfortable distance at the beginning of therapy. By devising computerized feedback mechanisms that allowed us to titrate the magnitude of pressure rises during speech, we were in fact both detecting and respecting the social-distancing defense mechanisms of patients. Attempts to break through such defenses would only cause a patient's blood pressure to rise even higher—up to dangerously high and possibly physiologically intolerable levels—so that further dialogue would become virtually impossible.

The primary goal of TP therapy therefore centers on lowering the cardiovascular component of the fight or flight response in hypertensive dialogue. Although patients cannot directly control blood pressure elevations during stressful communications, they can be made aware of such reactions and taught not to ignore them when they speak. They can also be taught to slow their rate of speech, breathe more deeply, relax their muscles, and, if necessary, withdraw periodically for brief periods of quiet relaxation. All these maneuvers should help patients lower their blood pressure transiently.

The overall goal of lowering the cardiovascular component of the fight or flight response in hypertensive dialogue is accomplished through a series of steps. Although each of these steps involves a number of theoretical constructs that space limitations preclude us from discussing here, a brief outline may provide enough detail to give some sense of our approach.

The first step in this treatment is an intake interview done by a nurse who is a Masters-level clinical specialist. A nurse was chosen, and the general medical orientation of the therapy emphasized, in order to support the hypertensive patient's defense mechanisms. That is, these patients are generally quite resistant to psychological interpretations of their cardiovascular problems. Thus, the more the therapeutic approach resembles the traditional medical model, the more willing hypertensive patients appear to be to accept treatment. In the hour-long interview, the patient's medical history is obtained—including onset, duration, and precipitating, aggravating, and alleviating factors of the disease. Also included are questions about associated symptoms and relevant medical problems, such as the presence of diabetes, heart failure, depressed kidney function, or eye damage; the major risk factors of hypertension and cardiovascular disease, such as family history of hypertension, obesity, increased levels of blood sugar, cholesterol, other lipids, and smoking; current medications; and previous hospitalizations, surgery, and medications. The patient's social, psychological, family, and occupational history also is obtained by the nurse. The patient is then evaluated with a battery of computerized psychological and psychophysiological tests, including the Minnesota Multiphasic Personality Inventory (MMPI), the Life Change Index, and the Cornell Medical Index. Patients whose completed medical workup and psychological profile suggest that they have the capacity to undergo this treatment (those with severe elevations on the Psychotic scale of the MMPI are not accepted for TP therapy) are then admitted for therapy.

In the first phase of TP therapy, the patient is shown various maneuvers that can be used to regulate the cardiovascular system. As an initial step, he/she is taught to observe changes in his/her own blood pressure as he/she engages the therapist in dialogue. This process introduces the patient to the notion that major blood pressure changes occur frequently in the body and that human dialogue can have a significant impact on pressure. The idea is then gradually introduced that major changes in blood pressure reflect previously undetected changes in emotional arousal. The patient is taught that he/she must recognize his/her own feelings so that he/she can begin to differentiate hypertensive from relaxing dialogue and pleasant from unpleasant social interactions.

After these initial ideas have been taught, the patient is then introduced to the idea of dysfunctional dialogue. While this dysfunction has various components, one of the most important is the discrepancy between one's internal vascular system and one's external demeanor. Many hypertensive patients appear quite peaceful when their blood pressure surges out of control, a fact that would confuse anyone who attempts to communicate with these patients without computer feedback. Since these dysfunctional communications are an essential part of hypertension, it is important that those persons centrally linked to the patient's communicative life be involved in the therapeutic process. Thus, TP therapy necessarily involves teaching the spouse to understand and decode the patient's confusing vascular communications. Both the hypertensive patient and the spouse are exposed to each other's physiological changes when they speak to one another. In this way the spouse and the hypertensive patient learn some of the mechanical and behavioral cues that accompany previously undetected surges in blood pressure. Computer feedback permits the patient and the spouse to see the minute-to-minute changes in their pressures and heart rates as they communicate. They learn that blood pressure is not a static number but an ever-changing bodily process that is influenced by a variety of bodily mechanisms that they can control. Both the patient and the spouse are then shown various mechanisms that cause pressure elevations and various maneuvers (such as deep breathing) that can be used to lower blood pressure when they communicate.

As part of the overall therapeutic approach, patients are also instructed to record pressure at home both before and after 5 minutes of deep breathing. In addition, they are instructed to identify how they feel just before they take their own pressures. This instruction is given in order to reinforce continuously the idea that human feelings are linked to changes in human pressure.

As patients begin to observe themselves and their blood pressure, they learn to link changes in pressure with changes in their everyday lives. They also watch their mates communicate and see the concomitant changes in their pressures and heart rates. Thus, the initial step in TP therapy includes observation of self and significant others and linking the changes in pressure to the social world in which the patient lives.

During this initial phase of TP therapy, emphasis is placed on supporting the patient while giving as much didactic information about links between human communication and blood pressure as the patient can absorb. No efforts are made during this phase to "invade" the patient therapeutically or to provide him/her with dynamic insights about hidden psychological or interpersonal conflicts. This process is entered into only after the patient has some sense of mastery over blood pressure and the capacity to feel changes in pressure when he/she is emotionally upset.

The computerized displays of blood pressure and heart rate graphically emphasize that specific circumstances, people, and situations cause blood pressure to rise. As the individual sees his/her blood pressure and heart rate react, he/she begins to explore the meaning of these changes with his/her therapist and spouse. Thus, he/she gradually proceeds to the second phase, or what would be recognized as more conventional psychodynamically oriented psychotherapy, in which these changes can be linked specifically to interactions between the patient, spouse, and therapist. The crucial difference between conventional therapy and TP therapy during this phase is that emphasis remains focused on blood pressure. That is, whenever the patient's pressure begins to rise into hypertensive ranges, ongoing conversations are interrupted, and the patient is instructed to breathe deeply and relax. In TP therapy blood pressure is viewed as a dynamic response as well as a dynamic communication that must be attended to as carefully as a patient's verbal comunications.

By using blood pressure as a barometric indicator of potential hidden emotional storms, the therapist can titrate the dynamic course of therapy. In addition, both the patient and his or her mate begin to learn that their hidden vascular communications are as important to listen to and decode as their ongoing verbal dialogue. The therapist also emphasizes that continuing to engage in a dialogue with a person whose blood pressure is rising higher and higher is to participate unwillingly in a dialogue that at best is counterproductive and at worst potentially murderous.

The last phase in therapy involves teaching the patient and his/her spouse that, since blood pressure and heart rate changes are an inextricable component of all human dialogue, the process must be attended to throughout life. The hypertensive patient is taught that pressure will always tend to rise while discussing an emotional or difficult interpersonal issue because he/she has a genetically determined predisposition to respond to anxiety by altering blood pressure.

Patients usually learn to lower blood pressure after about 12 to 20 sessions, generally in a 6-month period. As is true in psychodynamic therapy, a longer period is required before the patient is able to handle deeper dynamic issues without becoming acutely hypertensive. Decisions about probing into deeper dynamic conflicts are usually negotiated during the therapy itself. Certain patients either cannot tolerate such probing or choose to focus specifically on mechanisms controlling blood pressure.

Systematic empirical evaluation of this therapeutic approach is in progress, and firm conclusions regarding its efficacy cannot as yet be reached. We are, nonetheless, as clinicians remarkably impressed with the results that have emerged, and we feel that transactional psychophysiology offers the hope of integrating a wealth of psychodynamic insights, developed over decades, with recent technological advances, as well as with findings emerging from behavioral medicine.

BIBLIOGRAPHY

Friedmann, E., Thomas, A. A., Kulick-Ciuffo, D., Lynch, J. J., & Suginohara, M. (1982). The effects of normal and rapid speech on blood pressure. *Psychosomatic Medicine, 44*(6), 545–553.

Katcher, A. H., Friedmann, E., Bech, A. M., & Lynch, J. J. (1983). Talking, looking and blood pressure: Physiological consequences of interaction with the living environment. In A. H. Katcher & A. M. Beck (Eds.), *New perspectives on our lives with animal companions.* Philadelphia: University of Pennsylvania Press.

Lynch, J. J. (1977). *The broken heart: The medical consequences of loneliness.* New York: Basic Books.

Lynch, J. J. (1981). Hypertension and dysfunctional communication. *Hyptertension Highlights,4,* 1.

Lynch, J. J. (1985). *The language of the heart: The human body in dialogue.* New York: Basic Books.

Lynch, J. J. (1988). *In search of the heart of reason: From pavlovian conditioning to the effect of person.* New York: Irvington Press.

Lynch, J. J., Long, J. M., Thomas, S. A., Malinow, K., & Katcher, A. H. (1981). The effects of talking on the blood pressure of hypertensive and normotensive individuals. *Psychosomatic Medicine, 43*(1), 25–33.

Lynch, J. J., & Thomas, S. A. (1985). Hypertension: Controlling blood pressure. In A. M. Razin (Ed.), *Helping cardiac patients: Behavioral and psychotherapeutic approaches.* San Francisco: Jossey-Bass.

Lynch, J. J., Thomas, S. A., & Hall, P. S. (1982). Blushing on the inside: A new look at hypertension. *RN, 45*(2), 40–41.

Lynch, J. J., Thomas, S. A., Long, J. M., Malinow, K., Friedmann, E., & Katcher, A. H. (1982). Blood pressure changes while talking. *Israeli Journal of Medical Science, 18*(5), 575-579.

Lynch, J. J., Thomas, S. A., Paskewitz, D. A., Malinow, K. L., & Long, J. M. (1982). Interpersonal aspects of blood pressure control. *Journal of Nervous and Mental Disease, 170*(3), 143-153.

Malinow, K. L., Lynch, J. J., Foreman, P. J., Friedmann, E., & Thomas, S. A. (1986). Blood pressure increases while signing in a deaf population. *Psychosomatic Medicine, 48*(1/2), 95-101.

Malinow, K. L., Lynch, J. J., Thomas, S. A., Friedmann, E., & Long, J. M. (1982). Automated blood pressure recording: The phenomenon of blood pressure elevations during speech. *Angiology, 33*(7), 474-479.

Thomas, S. A., Friedmann, E., Lottes, L. S., Gresty, S., Miller, C., & Lynch, J. J. (1984). Changes in nurses' blood pressure and heart rate while communicating. *Journal of Research in Nursing and Health, 7,* 119-126.

Thomas, S. A., Friedmann, E., Noctor, M., Sappington, E., Gross, H., & Lynch, J. J. (1982). Patients' cardiac responses to nursing interviews in a CCU. *Dimensions of Critical Care Nursing, 1*(4) 198-205.

Thomas, S. A., Lynch, J. J. Friedmann, E., Suginohara, M., Hall, P. S., & Peterson, C. (1984). Blood pressure and heart rate changes in children when they read aloud in school. *Journal of Public Health Reports, 99,* 77-84.

Thomas, S. A., Lynch, J. J., Gross, H. S., & Rosch, P. (1988). *Healing dialogue: A manual on the use of transactional psychophysiology (TP) therapy for stress related diseases.* New York: Basic Books.

Wimbush, F. B., Thomas, S. A., Friedmann, E., Sappington, E., & Lynch, J. J. (1986). Cardiovascular responses to communication during catheterization. *Dimensions of Critical Care Nursing, 114,* 244-250.

·8·

People Need People:
Social Support and Health

MEREDITH MINKLER

Epidemiologist Leonard Syme relates that when he was a child and used to complain to his mother about feeling ill, her almost constant reply was "go out and play with friends" (Syme, 1989). After years of studying coronary heart disease and the risk factors associated with mortality and morbidity, he has concluded that his mother was right, that somehow "playing with one's friends," or in today's terminology, forming and maintaining social support networks, is very important to our health.

The current rediscovery of the relationship of the mind and the body, while tremendously important, remains an incomplete focus of attention unless it is placed in a broader social context. A growing body of theoretical and empirical data suggest that supportive ties play a critical role in decreasing illness susceptibility and maintaining health—a role at least as important and probably more important than many of the traditional risk factors medical science has been concerned with thus far.

Few people question the fact that people do need people to be healthy. Sidney Cobb (1976) points out that there is nothing new in the conclusion that supportive interactions among people are important. What is new is that assembling of hard evidence that adequate social support can protect people in crises from a wide variety of pathological states: from low birth weight to death, from arthritis through tuberculosis to depression, alcoholism, and other psychiatric illnesses. It is also clear that social support can reduce the amount of medication required and can accelerate recovery.

Far more difficult than simply documenting the relationship between social support and health has been finding a precise mechanism of action that would help explain just how and why social support exerts so powerful an influence on health. While a number of hypotheses have been put forward in this regard, most fall within one of two broad conceptual categories.

The first of these, termed the "stress buffering hypothesis," argues that social support works by protecting the individual from the harmful psychological or physiological effects of stressful life events. Social support, viewed from this perspective, plays an important mediating role in helping to short circuit the illness response that so often follows traumatic life changes.

The second theoretical position, labeled the direct or "main effects hypothesis" suggests that social support plays a health promoting role in its own right, regardless of the level of stress that an individual may be experiencing. The evidence for and against these two alternative hypotheses is presented below.

THE BUFFERING ROLE OF SOCIAL SUPPORT

Early, albeit indirect support for the stress buffering effects of social support was provided in a study by Gore (1978) in which the protective effects of social support were examined for men who were unemployed because of a plant closing. The 110 men in this study were examined at several different points before and after the closing for levels of serum cholesterol, symptoms of illness and depression, and degree of social support. Gore found that men with higher levels of support from their families and friends and with more opportunity for social interaction were significantly less likely to exhibit mental and physical health problems than those who perceived themselves as having less social support during this critical period.

That social support may be important in relation to life changes of a positive nature also has been demonstrated. Nuckolls, Cassel, and Kaplan (1972) examined pregnancy outcomes for 170 women in relation to stressful life events experienced before and during the pregnancy and to psychosocial assets, including social support. Among the women who experienced substantial stressful life events and who had few psychosocial assets, including little perceived social support, 91% had complications in pregnancy, compared with only 33% of those who experienced stressful events but had strong psychosocial assets. While the small sample size in this study and the difficulty in separating out social support from other psychosocial assets limited the usefulness of the findings, subsequent and more rigorous research on pregnancy and social support has provided results highly consistent with those of the Nuckolls study.

The pregnancy and job loss studies described are among a number of investigations illuminating the role of social support in buffering the potential negative health consequences of a stressful life change. The evidence they provide tends to be indirect, however, and one cannot determine from studies like these what kind of support was available and whether or not it was clearly related to coping.

THE DIRECT ROLE OF SOCIAL SUPPORT

As noted earlier, the direct or main effects hypothesis suggests that social support plays a health promoting role regardless of the stress level an individual may be experiencing. Yet just what that direct support effect consists of has been open to debate. An early attempt to explain the social support and health relationship suggested that members of a person's supportive network may be encouraging that person to engage in healthier behaviors, to seek needed medical treatment, and to in other ways adopt a health promoting life style. These direct and positive influences, it was argued, might help explain why married people have lower morbidity and mortality rates from almost all causes than single, widowed, or divorced persons. Yet while some early evidence was put forward in support of this hypothesis (e.g., Langlie, 1977, showing that people with more frequent interactions with neighbors and friends scored significantly higher on the degree to which they engaged in preventive health behaviors), the research had serious methodological flaws and provided at best only indirect support.

Moreover, several large and well-designed epidemiological studies have demonstrated that the powerful influence of social support on health appears to be largely independent of the role that members of one's family or friendship network may have in influencing personal health habits or behaviors. Perhaps the best known of these is Berkman and Syme's (1979) study in which the mortality experience of a random sample of 7,000 residents of Alameda County, California, was examined over a 9-year period. Sample members were all part of a population that had been studied extensively in 1965, so that baseline data were available on many aspects of these people's lives, their health, and their behavior. A very simple index of social ties was constructed that looked at whether or not sample members were married, the number of close friends and relatives they had, and how often they were in contact, church attendance, and involvement in informal and formal group associations.

Disease morbidity and mortality rates from all causes appeared to be related to this simple index of social ties. Study subjects with few ties to other people thus had mortality rates two to five times higher than those with more ties. These mortality differences were independent of self-reported health status and of such traditional risk factors as smoking, drinking, exercise, and obesity. The strong link found between social ties and mortality rates appeared for both sexes, for all ethnic groups, and across socioeconomic lines. Moreover, a recent 17-year follow-up of this same sample by Seeman, Kaplan,

Knudsen, Cohen, and Guralnik (1987) has revealed that the relationship between social ties and health continues into old age.

Regardless of whether one's friends and relatives encourage healthy life styles then, there is something about having significant other people in one's life that appears to be health promoting. But one is still left with the fundamental question: "What *is* it about social support that gives it so powerful a role in influencing our health status?"

One promising line of reasoning within the direct or main effects hypothesis suggests that over time, people's perceived sense of support from others may lead them to a more generalized sense of control. From this perspective, it is perhaps this more global feeling of what Antonovsky (1979) described as "sense of coherence" or what Syme (1989) has labeled "control over destiny" that serves as the missing link explaining why social support might be among the factors critically related to health. Consistent with this hypothesis, Schultz (1980) has reviewed an impressive array of studies suggesting that lack of personal autonomy, often including decreased opportunities for social interaction and involvement, frequently has negative psychological and physical health consequences in the elderly. One such study, conducted by Langer and Rodin (1976), was designed to determine whether patients who were given more responsibility and control would exhibit better physical and mental health than those who remained in a more typical dependency-producing nursing home environment.

Two groups of nursing home residents were selected and matched for socioeconomic level, and for physical and psychological health status. Members of each group were then given a plant. Residents assigned to the treatment or "responsibility enhanced" group were told that the plant was theirs to take care of and that how it fared would depend largely on whether they remembered to water it and care for it appropriately. At the same time, they were told that they were competent men and women who should be making more decisions for themselves and participating more actively in their own care. Members of the control group were also given a plant, but they were told that the staff would take care of it just as the staff would continue to take care of them and serve them, since they were in the home to be cared for.

Within several weeks, the investigators found a noticeable difference between the two groups. The responsibility enhanced group exhibited significant improvement on a variety of measures of physical and mental well-being and further showed a visible increase in activity level. Even more dramatic was the finding that 18 months following the intervention, the responsibility enhanced group had a mortality rate only half that of the control group (15% versus 30%).

Data on how the plants fared in this experiment unfortunately are not available, but the findings concerning the residents are significant. As Langer

(1981) has pointed out, it may well be that many so-called aging problems result from an environmentally and socially induced loss of control. Furthermore, it is perhaps a perceived sense of "support exchange"—not just feeling that one can count on others, but also that others depend to some extent on one—that helps people develop and maintain this more general sense of responsibility and control.

In our own research (Minkler, Satariano, & Langhauser, 1983) we examined this hypothesis by studying one dimension of supportive exchange—the giving and seeking of advice—among 700 elderly residents of Alameda County, California. Contrary to expectation, however, we found advice-seeking to be far more important than the giving of advice in terms of its overall association with health status: Elderly people in better health were far more likely to be seekers of advice and assistance than were their counterparts in poorer health.

Recent research by Seeman and Syme (1987) sheds light on this finding by suggesting the importance of viewing social support instrumentally, as a powerful means of increasing one's sense of control. Their study of different components of social support among people undergoing angiography revealed that, in terms of predictive power, the strongest social support variable was not the number of close friends one had or one's satisfaction with personal relationships, but rather the instrumental dimension of support. People who could count on others for specific and tangible aid (advice, loans, assistance with household repairs, etc.) had less coronary atherosclerosis than others undergoing angiography.

As Syme (1989) has reasoned, social support viewed in this instrumental vein may be seen as an important contributor to control. And it is this larger, transcendent concept of control that may dramatically affect our health.

In sum, promising research on both the direct or main effects hypothesis and the buffering hypothesis is under way, and some evidence has been found for each. As Cohen and Syme (1985) have suggested, moreover, while the two hypotheses frequently are put forward as mutually exclusive attempts to explain the relationship between social support and health, it is likely that both types of effects are taking place.

SOCIAL SUPPORT AND RECOVERY FROM ILLNESS

The hypotheses and studies described above all suggest that social support may play a critical health promoting role in helping individuals cope with stressful life events or in contributing to a general sense of coherence and control over destiny that appears to be connected with health and well-being.

Yet social support is also known to play a key role in helping those who are already ill cope with and recover from illness.

Strauss (see Neal, 1978) thus has observed that patients in burn units do better in shared rooms than in private ones, since the former provide a natural helping environment in which they can observe others getting well. Early research by Hoebel (1976) revealed significant improvement in risk-factor modification among previously noncompliant post-myocardial-infarction patients when their spouses received training in improving inter-familial communication and interaction. Similarly, Berle, Pinsky, Wolf, and Wolff (1952) have shown that the emotional support provided by parents and spouses to patients with asthma, migraine headaches, and essential hypertension is among the key factors associated with clinical appraisal of symptom change. In the case of intrinsic asthma, social support has been found to be among the major correlates of the amount of prednisone needed to control an attack.

Social support also has been shown to constitute an important predictor of success in coping with AIDS, mastectomy, and chronic renal disease, and in recovery rate from stroke. Finally, among terminal cancer patients, higher quality supportive relationships with others have been found in several studies to increase life expectancy and to facilitate emotional adjustment to impending death.

While the above findings have defined support in human terms, the emotional resources for coping with illness need not come solely from people. Studies by Erika Friedman (1980) and her associates revealed that patients with chronic heart disease lived longer if they had pets than if they did not. The importance of pets, particularly among the elderly living alone, has been well documented, with one study finding that pets serve as confi-dants to a third of their owners. In light of such evidence, Lazarus (personal communication, September 17, 1988) has suggested that the "death of a pet" be added to scales measuring stressful life events in the elderly—and that it be placed high on the list of such stressors. In a more positive vein, increased attention to the presence or absence of pets among elderly patients and promising experiments placing pets in nursing homes and pediatric wards are among the indications of a growing appreciation of the importance of even nonhuman forms of support for health and recovery from illness.

WHAT SORT OF PATIENT HAS THE DISEASE?

While it is interesting and important to examine the many ways in which social support appears to facilitate recovery from illness, an even more basic question involves the role of social support in influencing who gets sick in the first place. Cassel's (1974) basic theoretical position in this regard is that while disrupted social ties affect the body's defense system so that people become more susceptible to disease in general, the specific disease they get seems to be a function of other risk factors. More succinctly, in the words of Sir William Osler, "It is much more important to know what sort of patient has the disease than what sort of disease the patient has."

We can hypothesize that the sort of patient who has the disease is likely to be the one who is not enmeshed in a strong social network, or is one who recently has experienced a disruption in his or her traditional sources of support. However, it is well documented that the poor have higher morbidity and mortality from all causes than their wealthier counterparts. Does this single fact belie the notion that lack of social support may be a principal risk factor in becoming ill?

The evidence seems to argue to the contrary. While it is an undisputed fact that the poor have higher rates of illness and death related to a host of problems, including inadequate nutrition, housing, and medical care, much of the excess morbidity and mortality found among the poor cannot be accounted for by looking simply at differences in smoking rates, nutrition, access to medical care, and other factors. In fact, in a recent study in Oakland, California, Haan, Kaplan, and Camacho (1987) discovered that after adjusting for differences in income, baseline health status, unemployment, race, and a host of health behavior variables among residents of a poverty and an adjacent nonpoverty area, a 47% difference in mortality rates between the two groups remained. These investigators argued that an underlying characteristic of low socioeconomic status, namely the combination of high environmental demands (both social and physical) and low resources for dealing with these demands (e.g., money, social support, and access to health care) may help account for the greater vulnerability to illness found among the poor.

Social marginality, often characterized by weak and impermanent ties with one's community, clearly fits within the demands/resources conceptualization. For people at the low end of the socioeconomic ladder, social marginality thus may translate into both greater demands from a hostile environment and fewer resources for coping, key among them social support and particularly the above-mentioned instrumental forms of support important to achieving a generalized sense of control. The problem of social marginality has been found to underlie diverse physical and mental health problems particularly prevalent among the poor, including tuberculosis, schizophrenia, psychiatric hospitalization for all causes, and frequently including suicide, alcoholism, multiple accidents, and hypertension.

Another view of the problem of social marginality and its relation to health involves the finding that people who are not socially marginal often nevertheless find themselves at high risk for illness at those times when they experience a disruption in their traditional sources of social support. People who experience a major geographic move or other sort of uprooting have high rates of illness and absenteeism. That this may be a function of a sudden disruption in ties, rather than the move per se, is suggested in several studies, probably the best known of which is the Japanese American Study.

This major cross-cultural study was geared at finding an explanation for the fact that while Japan has the lowest coronary heart disease rate in the world, the rate is considerably higher among Japanese who have migrated to Hawaii, and highest of all among those who have emigrated to California, where the rate corresponds to the United States rate. This gradient in coronary heart disease mortality among Japanese in three different environments cannot be accounted for by differences in diet, cholesterol, smoking, or blood pressure levels, and consequently has been hard to explain. Epidemiologists Marmot and Syme (1976) studied a group of Japanese emigrants to the San Francisco Bay Area who had very low rates of coronary heart disease and compared them with another group of Japanese emigrants in the same area who had rates of heart disease that were five times higher. They observed that members of the group with very low heart disease rates were characterized by what they termed traditional Japanese life styles. As children they had lived in Japanese neighborhoods and attended Japanese language schools. As adults their friends were Japanese and they remained highly identified with the Japanese community, visiting Japanese doctors and in other ways demonstrating this very strong cultural allegiance.

This group of transplanted Japanese men with very low heart disease rates had what Pilisuk (1982) describes as a sort of "social inoculation," which helps decrease vulnerability to illnesses that major life changes in the absence of social support seem more likely to trigger. Again, we don't know quite how social inoculation works, but we do know that it does, that people with strong supportive ties somehow remain healthier and live longer than those who are socially marginal or experience a breakdown of social ties.

IMPLICATIONS FOR PRACTICE

If social marginality is itself a major contributor to illness, can we intervene and in Pilisuk's words "reweave the social fabric" (Pilisuk, Chandler, & D'Onofrio, 1982) in ways that might increase resistance to disease? A number of studies have suggested that such reweaving may have positive effects. Kraus and Lilienfeld (1959) and Raphael (1977), as well as others, have demonstrated that recently bereaved widows with weak social ties may experience positive health benefits from involvement in a support group of similarly isolated persons. And studies among Viet Nam veterans have shown that veterans with post-traumatic stress syndrome made a better recovery if they had veteran friends to talk to than if they had access simply to formal professional help.

Finally, a 10-year-old project among isolated elderly residents of San Franciso's Tenderloin hotels has demonstrated the often dramatic physical and mental health outcomes of building supportive ties among the socially marginal. The Tenderloin Senior Outreach Project (TSOP) was initiated in 1979 by graduate students and faculty at the School of Public Health of the University of California at Berkeley who formed weekly support groups for elderly tenants of several low-priced, single-room-occupancy hotels. Facilitated initially by the students, the hotel groups soon were developing their own agendas for identifying and addressing such shared problems as high neighborhood crime rates, poor food access, and deteriorating housing.

Together, the residents of several TSOP hotels initiated the widely publicized Safehouse Project, through which more than 80 stores and agencies in the neighborhood began serving as places of refuge where residents could go for help in times of emergency. Residents of four of the hotels started minimarkets in their lobbies one day a week to provide tenants access to fresh fruits and vegetables. Others worked together to produce a "no cook cookbook" that was published and widely distributed by the City's Department of Public Health.

TSOP recently was renamed the Tenderloin Senior Organizing Project in recognition of its increasing focus on community organizing and empowerment. Current efforts have included successful campaigns to block illegal rent increases, improve local transportation access, and restore food service in some of the hotels. These various activities have had important tangible effects. A dramatic 26% decrease in the crime rate in the 18 months following the initiation of TSOP's multifaceted anticrime project has been recognized by local police as in part a consequence of TSOP's effective local organizing. Improvements in nutritional status and in other dimensions of physical health also have been witnessed as residents take increasing control over their health and the health of their community.

Yet by far the most significant effects of this project have been on the mental and emotional health of residents. Many of these elderly men and women had histories of mental health problems including alcoholism, depression, and previous institutionalization. For many, involvement with TSOP led to increased self-esteem, the "sense of control" Syme talks about, and a sense of connection with others that previously had been missing. One elderly tenant, a former resident of a state mental hospital, captured this change succinctly. Norris had been in the habit of making monthly visits to the state mental hospital for "reality orientation" but after 2 years' involvement with TSOP, the visits stopped altogether. When asked about this he replied, "I'm a co-leader of my hotel support group, a founder of (the anticrime project), and a member of the Mayor's Task Force on Aging. I don't have time for reality!"

While it is difficult to translate experiences like Norris's into statistics, the implications of hundreds of such anecdotes are clear: Being meaningfully involved with others, deriving the support that comes from giving and seeking assistance, and feeling increased control as a consequence can have powerful health effects. And where such human connections are lacking (as in the case of the isolated low-income elderly), intentional network building can sometimes play an important role in reweaving the social fabric that is so vital to our health.

CONCLUSION

An impressive body of evidence now supports the contention that social support plays a major role in promoting health, decreasing susceptibility to disease, and recovery from illness. This evidence in turn has been used as an empirical base of support for practice and policy interventions designed to strengthen and utilize preexisting networks and build new networks (self-help groups, intentional families, etc.) where the absence of support has been problematic.

Initial promising research findings regarding the role of social support in health promotion, however, provide a far from complete understanding of the social support and health relationship. Moreover, recent work by Syme (1989) and others suggests that the importance of social support may be primarily of an indirect nature, feeding into a more generalized sense of coherence or control over one's destiny, which in turn affects health.

Extensive research is needed to clarify many as yet unresolved questions regarding the relationship between social support and health. However, health care providers and the lay public alike can benefit from putting existing knowledge in this area into practice. People *do* need people to be healthy, and the strengthening of supportive interpersonal bonds is an important means of recognizing this basic fact of life.

BIBLIOGRAPHY

Antonovsky, A. (1979). *Health, stress, and coping: New perspectives on mental and physical well-being.* San Francisco: Jossey-Bass.

Berkman, L., & Syme, S. (1979). Social networks, host resistance, and mortality: A nine-year follow-up study of Alameda County residents. *American Journal of Epidemiology, 109,* 186–204.

Berle, B., Pinsky, R., Wolf, S., & Wolff, H. (1952). A clinical guide to prognosis in stress diseases. *Journal of the American Medical Association, 149,* 1624–1628.

Broadhead, W., Kaplan, B., James, S., et al. (1983). The epidemiological evidence for a relationship between social support and health. *American Journal of Epidemiology, 117*, 521–537.

Cassel, J. (1974). An epidemiological perspective of psychosocial factors in disease etiology. *American Journal of Public Health, 64*, 1040–1043.

Cobb, S. (1976). Social support as a moderator of life stress. *Psychosomatic Medicine, 38*, 300–313.

Cohen, S., & Syme, S. (Eds.). (1985). *Social support and health*. New York: Academic Press.

DeAravjo, G., Van Orsdel, P., Holmes, T., & Dudley, D. (1973). Life change, coping ability and chronic intrinsic asthma. *Journal of Psychosomatic Research, 17*, 359–363.

Friedmann, E., Katcher, A. H., Lynch, J. J., & Thomas, S. A. (1980). Animal companions and one year survival after discharge from a coronary care unit. *Public Health Reports, 95* (July–August), 307–312.

Gore, S. (1978). The effect of social support in moderating the health consequences of unemployment. *Journal of Health and Social Behavior, 19*, 157–165.

Haan, M., Kaplan, G. A., & Camacho, T. (1987). Poverty and health. In R. W. Amler & H. B. Dull (Eds.), *Closing the gap: The burden of unnecessary illness*. New York: Oxford University Press.

Hoebel, F. C. (1976). Family interactional therapy in the management of cardiac-related high risk behavior. *Journal of Family Practice, 3*(6), 613–618.

Kraus, A., & Lilienfeld, A. (1959). Some epidemiologic aspects of the high mortality rate in the young widowed group. *Journal of Chronic Diseases, 10*, 207–217.

Langer, E. (1981). Old age: An artifact? In J. McGough & S. Kiesler (Eds.), *Aging: Biology and behavior*. New York: Academic Press.

Langer, E., & Rodin, J. (1976). The effects of choice and enhanced personal responsibility for the aged: A field experiment in an institutional setting. *Journal of Personality and Social Psychology, 34*, 191–198, 1976.

Langlie, J. (1977). Social networks, health beliefs and preventive behavior. *Journal of Health and Social Behavior, 18*, 244–260.

Marmot, M., & Syme, S. (1976). Acculturation and coronary heart disease in Japanese Americans. *American Journal of Epidemiology, 104*, 225–247.

Minkler, M. (1986). The social component of health. *American Journal of Health Promotion, 1*(2), 33–38.

Minkler, M., Satariano, W., & Langhauser, C. (1983). Supportive exchange: An exploration of the relationship between social contacts and perceived health status in the elderly. *Archives of Gerontology and Geriatrics, 2*, 211–220.

Neal, H. (1978). *The politics of pain*. New York: McGraw Hill.

Nuckolls, K., Cassel, J., & Kaplan, B. (1972). Psychosocial assets, life crisis and the prognosis of pregnancy. *American Journal of Epidemiology, 5*, 431–441.

Pilisuk, M. (1982). Delivery of social support: The social inoculation. *American Journal of Orthopsychiatry, 52*, 20–31.

Pilisuk, M., Chandler, S., & D'Onofrio, C. N. (1982). Reweaving the social fabric: A model for immunizing against stress-induced illness, *International Quarterly of Health Education, 3*(1), 45–66.

Pilisuk, M., & Minkler, M. (1985). Social support: Economic and political considerations, *Social Policy, 15,* 6–11.

Raphael, B. (1977). Preventive intervention with the recent bereaved. *Archives of General Psychiatry, 34,* 1450–1454.

Schultz, R. (1980). Aging and control. In J. Garber & M. Seligman (Eds.), *Human helplessness: theory and applications.* New York: Academic Press.

Seeman, T. E., & Syme, S. L. (1987). Social networks and coronary artery disease: A comparison of the structure and function of social relations as predictors of disease, *Psychosomatic Medicine, 49,* 341–354.

Seeman, T. E., Kaplan, G. A., Knudsen, L., Cohen, R., & Guralnik, J. (1987). Social network ties and mortality among the elderly in the Alameda County Study. *American Journal of Epidemiology, 126*(4), 714–723.

Syme, S. L. (1989). Control and health: A personal perspective. In A. Steptoe & A. Appels (Eds.), *Stress, personal control and health.* New York: John Wiley.

·III·

ENVIRONMENTAL INFLUENCES

·9·

Air Ions and Brain Chemistry

MARIAN C. DIAMOND

In addition to our work on the effects of experience on cortical structure (see "How the Brain Grows in Response to Experience," Chapter 2, this volume), we have examined the effects of negative air ions on the cerebral cortex. It appeared that negative air ions increased cortical dimensions. Previously, during his years of working with negative ions, Albert Krueger had shown a respiratory ciliary response (Krueger & Reed, 1976). The cilia that line the respiratory system increase in activity in the presence of negative air ions. Therefore, some persons with respiratory difficulties have found it beneficial to breathe air rich in negative ions.

IONIZED AIR AND CORTICAL THICKNESS

Our first series of experiments were concerned with the effects of ionized air on cortical thickness. In this research, each cage with animals in the treated condition had a negative ionizer at the top that liberated 10^5 negative ions per cubic centimeter. A fan blew air slowly through the cage to be certain that the measurement of ion concentration was equal for the animals living in this condition. The animals receiving high concentrations of negative air ions lived in either enriched or impoverished experimental conditions, as described in Chapter 2.

In a second room adjacent to the one used for ion studies, we had an identical condition except that the animals were exposed to the regular air in the Life Sciences Building. (This regular air is such that at 5:00 P.M. it is fun to watch people come out of the building. The breath of outside air is truly refreshing.)

In the first experiment we exposed the treated animals to 20 days of ionized air before sacrificing them and weighing samples from the cerebral cortex. In order to take uniform samples, we used a calibrated plastic T-square that was put over the surface of the cortex. Somesthetic and visual cortex samples were similarly removed in each animal. In both the environmentally enriched and the impoverished groups, the animals exposed to negative air ions had a heavier sample than those exposed to normal atmospheric conditions. The differences were slightly greater for those animals in the enriched condition than for those in the impoverished condition.

IONIZATION AND NEUROTRANSMITTERS

Negative ions, according to the literature, make people feel better. Serotonin, a neurotransmitter, is decreased in the presence of negative air ions. We were curious whether our animals would show changes in their serotonin content as well as in brain structure if we exposed them to negative air ions when they were living in enriched and impoverished environments.

Negative air ions in nature are created around falling water. We may wonder why poets like to sit by waterfalls to write. Is it because they have altered transmitter levels so that they feel more romantic? We know that emotions are chemically induced, but we do not yet understand the mechanisms. Our study presented an opportunity to try to relate a subtle change in the air with brain chemistry.

Examining the serotonin in the somatosensory cortex and in the occipital cortex showed that negative ions did decrease the serotonin in the enriched animals. Serotonin is one of numerous neurotransmitters. We are not certain why we have so many. Cyclic AMP was also measured and a similar pattern was found, that is, a lower level in the animals exposed to negative ions. We can conclude from our studies that something as subtle as the ion content of the air can modify both the structure and the chemistry of the cerebral cortex. We might not associate specific behavior with changing one or another neurotransmitter, but the integration of action among many transmitters in different neural circuits creates behavioral patterns.

IONIZATION AND AGING

Increased ciliary motility and increased cortical thickness were found to be related to negative ion concentrations. These relationships suggest the possibility that negative air ions might increase the rate of maturation, and we therefore wondered what effect negative air ions might have on aging.

But how does one measure aging? Lipofuscin is an aging pigment. Its presence is not well understood, but we know that cells in our bodies that do not divide, such as most nerve cells and heart muscle cells, accumulate this pigment as they age. We think it is a degradation product. We were curious to know what happened to lipofuscin in animals exposed to negative air ions.

We compared concentrations of lipofuscin in the brains of environmentally enriched and impoverished animals and in the brains of negative ion enriched and impoverished animals. On comparing lipofuscin concentrations in our enriched and impoverished environment rats, we found a greater concentration of this aging pigment in the impoverished rats. We also noted 9% to 16% less aging pigment in the ion-exposed rats than in those exposed to normal air after a 7-month exposure. If anything, negative ions thus seem to be protective against aging, rather than promoting maturity, at least as indicated by the lipofuscin studies.

BIBLIOGRAPHY

Diamond, M. C. (1978). The aging brain: Some enlightening and optimistic results. *American Scientist, 66*, 66–71.

Connor, J. R., Diamond, M. C., & Johnson, R. E. (1980). Occipital cortical morphology of the rat: Alterations with age and environment. *Experimental Neurology, 68*, 158–170.

Diamond, M. C., Connor, J. R., Orenberg, E. K., Bissell, M., Yost, M., & Krueger, A. (1980). Environmental influences on serotonin and cyclic nucleotides in rat cerebral cortex. *Science, 210*, 652–654.

Diamond, M. C., (1980, June). Environment, air ions, and brain chemistry, *Psychology Today*.

Diamond, M. C., & Connor, J. R. (1981). A search for the potential of the aging brain. In S. J. Enna, T. Samorajski, & R. Beer (Eds.), *Aging: Vol. 17. Brain neurotransmitters and receptors in aging and age-related disorders*. New York: Raven Press.

Krueger, A. P., & Reed, E. J. (1976). Biological impact of small air ions. *Science, 193*, 1209–1213.

·10·

Ways That Foods Can Affect the Brain

RICHARD J. WURTMAN

The mechanism by which brain neurons send signals to other cells involves the release of particular chemicals, neurotransmitters, that are produced in and released from each neuron's myriad terminals. About 30 or 40 compounds have been identified that seem to function as neurotransmitters somewhere in the brain. In general, each of these compounds can be released from many distinct groups of brain neurons, which are distinguished by the locations of their cell bodies and terminals, and which subserve different functions. It appears that the rates at which some of the neurotransmitters are synthesized, and the quantities of them that are released, normally vary in nonmalnourished individuals, depending upon the composition of the food that has most recently been eaten. These changes in neurotransmitter release can also be associated with functional and behavioral consequences, thereby allowing one's nutritional state to affect one's behavior. This paper discusses the particular transmitters that are nutrient-dependent; the processes that couple food consumption to neurotransmitter synthesis; and some of the consequences of this coupling.

NUTRITIONAL CONTROL OF SEROTONIN SYNTHESIS

The synthesis of serotonin, 5-hydroxytryptamine (5-HT), in neurons is initiated by the hydroxylation of the essential amino acid tryptophan. The enzyme that catalyzes this reaction, tryptophan hydroxylase, has a poor

This chapter originally appeared in *Nutrition Reviews*, 1986, *44* (Suppl.), 2–5. It is reprinted here with permission from the International Life Sciences Institute—Nutrition Foundation.

affinity for its amino acid substrate. Hence, treatments that raise or lower brain tryptophan levels can, by changing the enzyme's substrate saturation, rapidly alter the rate at which tryptophan is hydroxylated and the rate at which its product (5-hydroxytryptophan) is converted to serotonin (Fernstrom & Wurtman, 1971a). Brain tryptophan levels in rats, and probably in human beings, normally undergo pronounced variations when plasma amino acid patterns change, for example, when foods are being digested and absorbed. A high-carbohydrate, protein-poor meal elevates brain tryptophan, accelerating serotonin synthesis (Fernstrom & Wurtman, 1971b). In contrast a high-protein meal depresses serotonin synthesis (Fernstrom & Wurtman, 1972). The plasma parameter that couples food composition to brain tryptophan level is the ratio of the plasma tryptophan concentration to the summed concentrations of such other large neutral amino acids (LNAA) as tyrosine, phenylalanine, and the branched-chain amino acids leucine, isoleucine and valine (Fernstrom & Wurtman, 1972, 1974; Wurtman, 1974; Wurtman, Hefti, & Melamed, 1980). This parameter is important because the transport macromolecules (within the capillary endothelia comprising the blood-brain barrier) that carry circulating tryptophan into the brain also transport the other LNAA with almost equal efficiency, so circulating tryptophan must compete with the other LNAA for transport sites (Pardridge, 1977). A carbohydrate-rich meal raises the plasma tryptophan ratio (Fernstrom et al., 1979) by eliciting the secretion of insulin, which has little effect on plasma tryptophan but greatly lowers plasma levels of the other LNAA, largely by facilitating their uptake into skeletal muscle. A protein-rich meal depresses the ratio by contributing very large quantities of the branched-chain amino acids to the systemic circulation but only small amounts of tryptophan (which is the least abundant amino acid in proteins and also is destroyed in the liver). This coupling of food composition to serotonin release allows serotoninergic neurons to function as variable ratio sensors, informing the rest of the brain about the proportions of protein and carbohydrate in the most recent meal or snack. The brain can then use this information in deciding what to eat at the next meal or snack.

Serotonin release from brain neurons can also be increased by ingesting pure tryptophan, especially by taking it along with an insulin-releasing carbohydrate (to lower the levels of the other plasma LNAA, thereby facilitating tryptophan's uptake into the brain) (Pan, Mauron, Glaeser, & Wurtman, 1982). Conversely, serotonin release can be depressed by ingesting large doses of any other LNAA, including both the amino acids that are naturally present in protein and synthetic compounds, like L-dopa or α-methyldopa, which are used therapeutically (Markowitz & Fernstrom, 1977). Tryptophan's efficacy—and that of any other natural or synthetic LNAA—is diminished if it consumed along with protein; the LNAA in the protein suppress its uptake into the brain.

BRAIN SEROTONIN AND APPETITE CONTROL

If animals are allowed to choose concurrently from among two or more diets (unfortunately an unusual circumstance in most research on appetite control) each containing different proportions of carbohydrates or protein or both, their behavior indicates that they are able to regulate not only the total quantities of food and of calories that they consume, but also the proportions of protein (Ashley & Anderson, 1975) and carbohydrates (Wurtman & Wurtman, 1979). Administration of a small carbohydrate-rich pre-meal before exposure to the test diets (Wurtman, Moses, & Wurtman, 1983) or administration of drugs (e.g., D-fenfluramine or fluoxetine [Wurtman & Wurtman, 1977] that enhance serotonin's release or suppress its inactivation causes the animal to adjust its food choices so as to increase the proportion of protein to carbohydrate in the next meal. Similar observations have been made in people given D-fenfluramine (or, to a lesser extent, tryptophan) and allowed to choose among snacks (Wurtman et al., 1981) or meal constituents containing varying proportions of protein and carbohydrate. All who responded to D-fenfluramine by reducing total calorie intake also significantly decreased the proportion of calorie intake supplied by carbohydrate and increased the proportion supplied by protein. Fat consumption was not significantly affected. Most of the decline in carbohydrate intake in such experiments is related to reduced consumption of snack foods (Wurtman et al., 1985) and not of mealtime carbohydrates. These observations imply that the brain mechanisms regulating protein and carbohydrate appetites involve, among others, serotonin-releasing neurons. A carbohydrate-rich, protein-poor meal that increases brain serotonin levels reduces the likelihood that the next meal will be of similar composition. Conversely, consumption of carbohydrate-poor, protein-rich meals (like those often used for weight reduction) diminishes brain serotonin synthesis and sometimes increases the subject's desire for carbohydrate to the point of carbohydrate-craving (Wurtman, 1983). Prolonged consumption of such meals may exacerbate the lowering of brain serotonin and the carbohydrate craving by diminishing the quantities of insulin secreted after meals. This would be expected to further increase plasma levels of the competing branched-chain LNAA. If an obese subject also happened to be insulin-resistant, this might further raise plasma LNAA and depress brain serotonin release.

We observe that a sizable proportion of obese subjects seeking assistance in weight reduction consume as much as half of their total daily intake as carbohydrate-rich snacks, and that this behavior is often associated with strong feelings of carbohydrate craving. Conceivably, this appetite disorder reflects an abnormality in the process that couples carbohydrate consumption to the release of brain serotonin. Many patients describe themselves as feeling anxious, tense, or depressed before consuming the carbohydrate snack and peaceful or relaxed afterwards. It may be more than a coincidence that dietary carbohydrates and both major classes of antidepressant drugs, the monoamine-oxidase inhibitors and the tricyclic-uptake blockers, are thought to increase the quantities of serotonin present within brain synapses. Perhaps the subjects snacking on carbohydrates are unknowingly self-medicating.

Carbohydrate consumption or tryptophan administration can also modulate other normal behaviors, increasing subjective fatigue and sleepiness, accelerating sleep onset in people with prolonged sleep latencies (Hartmann, Spinweber, & Ware, 1976), diminishing sensitivity to mild pain, and (in people over 40) increasing the likelihood of errors in performance tests (Spring, Maller, Wurtman, Digman, Cozolino, 1982, 1983). At present, no information is available on the relative potencies of sugars and starches in producing such effects. It might be expected that a carbohydrate's potency would depend upon its speed of absorption and its ability to stimulate insulin secretion.

NUTRIENTS AND CONTROL OF THE SYNTHESIS
OF CATECHOLAMINES AND ACETYLCHOLINE

The rates at which the enzymes tyrosine hydroxylase and choline acetyltransferase convert tyrosine to dopa (Wurtman, Larin, Mostafapour, & Fernstrom, 1974; Carlsson & Lindquist, 1978) and choline to acetylcholine (Cohen & Wurtman, 1975; Haubrich, Wang, Clody, & Wedeking, 1975), respectively, can be modulated by treatments that change brain levels of tyrosine or choline. Brain tyrosine levels are most conveniently increased by ingesting pure tyrosine alone or with a carbohydrate (to lower plasma levels of the competing LNAA). Consumption of a high-protein meal also increases the plasma tyrosine ratio and brain tyrosine levels slightly, but probably not enough to have major effects on catecholamine synthesis. Brain choline levels are increased by consumption of pure choline or of phosphatidylcholine (lecithin) (Hirsch & Wurtman, 1978), the substance providing most of the choline in the diet. Choline uptake into the brain is also catalyzed by a transport macromolecule within the endothelia of brain capillaries (Pardridge, 1977); apparently, choline is the only important circulating ligand for this transport mechanism.

Under basal conditions, when a particular catecholaminergic or cholinergic neuron is not firing frequently, it will respond poorly if at all to an increase in available tyrosine (Scally, Ulusn, & Wurtmann, 1977; Fuller & Snoddy, 1982) or choline (BierKamper & Goldberg, 1980). However, when the neurons are physiologically active, they concurrently become highly responsive to increases in precursor levels, synthesizing and releasing more dopamine, for example, when brain tyrosine levels are raised (Wurtman et al., 1980; Melamed, Hefti, & Wurtman, 1980) and more acetylcholine after choline (Wecker, Dettbarn, & Schmidt, 1978) or lecithin (Wurtman, Hirsch, & Growdon, 1977) is eaten. The biochemical mechanism that couples neuronal firing frequency to tyrosine-responsiveness apparently involves the activation (by phosphorylation) of tyrosine hydroxylase. This process greatly increases the enzyme's affinity for, and saturation with, its tetrahydrobio-pterin cofactor, causing its activity to become limited by the extent to which it is saturated with its amino acid substrate, tyrosine (Levine, Miller, & Lovenberg, 1981). Phosphorylation of the enzyme also diminishes its sensitivity to end-product inhibition by catecholamine, further increasing the rate at which the neuron converts tyrosine to dopamine or noradrenaline. The biochemical mechanism that couples a cholinergic neuron's firing frequency to its ability to synthesize more acetylcholine when given more choline remains unknown.

The fact that catecholaminergic and cholinergic neurons must be exhibiting sustained physiological activity in order to display precursor-responsiveness (a relationship that is not typical of serotoninergic neurons [Jacoby, Colmenares, & Wurtman, 1975]) imparts considerable specificity to the functional consequences of giving patients tyrosine or choline. The brain apparently can choose which particular catecholaminergic or cholinergic neurons will be allowed to respond to having more precursor simply by doing what brains normally do, that is modulating the firing frequencies of each group of neurons that releases these transmitters. This ability probably explains the paucity of side effects observed when people are given even very large doses of tyrosine (Melamed, Glaeser, Growdon, & Wurtman, 1980; Growdon, Melamed, Logue, Hefti, & Wurtman, 1982) or of choline-containing compounds (Growdon, Hirsch, Wurtman, & Wiener, 1977; Barbeau, Growdon, & Wurtman, 1979). It also explains why a particular dose of tyrosine can be used either to reduce blood pressure in hypertension (Sved, Fernstrom, & Wurtman, 1979) (by enhancing noradrenaline release from the brainstem noradrenergic neurons that reduce sympathetic outflow) or to raise blood pressure in hemorrhagic shock (Conlay, Maher, & Wurtman, 1981) (by increasing catecholamine secretion from the physiologically active sympathoadrenal cells).

Attempts to use tyrosine or choline-containing compounds to treat diseases of catecholamine or acetylcholine deficiency are in their infancy. Progress has been retarded by the unusual regulatory status of these compounds (foods or drugs?) and by the unavailability, until recently, of pure and palatable lecithin preparations. Tyrosine has been reported to help some patients with depression (Gelenberg & Wurtman, 1980) or mild Parkinson disease (Growden et al., 1982). Choline or lecithin have been used successfully to treat tardive dyskinesia (Growden et al., 1977; Davis, Berger, & Hollister, 1975; Growdon, Gelenberg, Doller, Hirsch, & Wurtman, 1978), mania (Cohen, Lipinski, & Altesman, 1982), and ataxias (Barbeau et al., 1979). Administration of choline or lecithin alone for short periods has not led to reproducible improvement in patients with advanced Alzheimer disease (Corkin, Davis, Growdon, Usdin, & Wurtman, 1982). However administration of high doses of nearly pure lecithin for longer periods (20 to 25 g daily for 6 months) apparently improved learning-memory and self-care indicies in older patients who had a milder form of the disease (R. Levy, personal communication, September 30, 1984).

SUMMARY

Numerous food constituents can affect the synthesis of brain neurotransmitters, and thereby modify brain functions mediated by the transmitters. This article describes the effects of dietary carbohydrate or protein on brain serotonin synthesis, and the involvement of serotonin-releasing neurons in control of appetite. Finally, it also mentions the changes in brain acetylcholine or catecholamine levels that can be induced by giving a dietary choline source or pure tyrosine.

Acknowledgments

These studies were supported, in part, by grants from the National Aeronautics and Space Administration, the U.S. Air Force, and the National Institutes of Health.

REFERENCES

Ashley, D. V., & Anderson, G. H. (1975). *Journal of Nutrition, 105*, 1405–1411.

Barbeau, A., Growdon, J. H., & Wurtman, R. J. (1979). In R. J. Wurtman & J. J. Wurtman (Eds.), *Nutrition and the brain* (Vol. 5). New York: Raven Press.

Bierkamper, G. G., & Goldberg, A. M. (1980). *Brain Research, 202*, 234–237.

Carlsson, A., & Lindqvist, M. (1978). *Naunyn-Schmiedeberg Archiv fuer Pharmakologie und Experimentelle Pathologie, 303*, 157–164.

Cohen, B. M., Lipinski, J. F., & Altesman, R. I. (1982). *American Journal of Psychiatry, 139*, 1162–1164.

Cohen, E. L., & Wurtman, R. J. (1975). *Life Sciences, 16*, 1095–1102.

Conlay, L. A., Maher, T. J., & Wurtman, R. J. (1981). *Science, 212*, 559–560.

Corkin, S., Davis, K., Growdon, J. H., Usdin, E., & Wurtman, R. J. (Eds.). (1982). *Alzheimer's disease: A report of progress in reseach*. New York: Raven Press.

Davis, K. L., Berger, P. A., & Hollister, L. E. (1975). *New England Journal of Medicine, 293,* 152.
Fernstrom, J. D., & Wurtman, R. J. (1971a). *Science, 173,* 149–152.
Fernstrom, J. D., & Wurtman, R. J. (1971b). *Science, 174,* 1023–1025.
Fernstrom, J. D., & Wurtman, R. J. (1972). *Science, 178,* 414–416.
Fernstrom, J. D., & Wurtman, R. J. (1974). *Scientific American, 230,* 84–91.
Fernstrom, J. D., Wurtman, R. J., Hammarstrom-Wiklund, B., Rand, W. M., Munro, H. N., & Davidson, C. S. (1979). *American Journal of Clinical Nutrition, 32,* 1912–1922.
Fuller, R. W., & Snoddy, H. D. (1982). *Journal of Pharmacy and Pharmacology, 34,* 117–118.
Gelenberg, A., & Wurtman, R. J. (1980). *Lancet, ii,* 863–864.
Growdon, J. H., Gelenberg, A. J., Doller, J., Hirsch, M. J., & Wurtman, R. J. (1978). *New England Journal of Medicine, 298,* 1029–1030.
Growdon, J. H., Hirsh, M. J., Wurtman, R. J., & Wiener, W. (1977). *New England Journal of Medicine, 297,* 524–527.
Growdon, J. H., Melamed, E., Logue, M., Hefti, F., & Wurtman, R. J. (1982). *Life Sciences, 30,* 827–832.
Hartmann, E., Spinweber, C. L., & Ware, C. (1976). *Sleep Research, 5,* 57–66.
Haubrich, D. R., Wang, P. F., Clody, D. E., & Wedeking, P. W. (1975). *Life Sciences, 17,* 975–980.
Hirsch, M. J., & Wurtman, R. J. (1978). *Science, 202,* 223–225.
Jacoby, J., Colmenares, J. L., & Wurtman, R. J. (1975). *Journal of Neural Transmission, 37,* 15–32.
Levine, R. A., Miller, L. P., & Lovenberg, W. (1981). *Science, 214,* 919–921.
Markowitz, D. C., & Fernstrom, J. D. (1977). *Science, 197,* 1014–1015.
Melamed, E., Glaeser, B., Growdon, J. H., & Wurtman, R. J. (1980). *Journal of Neural Transmission, 47,* 299–306.
Melamed, E., Hefti, F., & Wurtman, R. J. (1980). *Proceedings of the National Academy of Sciences of the United States of America, 77,* 4305–4309.
Pan, R. M., Mauron, C., Glaeser, B., & Wurtman, R. J. (1982). *Metabolism, 31,* 937–943.
Pardridge, W. M. (1977). In R. J. Wurtman & J. J. Wurtman (Eds.), *Nutrition and the brain* (Vol. 1), (pp. 141–204). New York: Raven Press.
Scally, M. C., Ulus, I., & Wurtman, R. J. (1977). *Journal of Neural Transmission, 41,* 1–6.
Spring, B., Maller, O., Wurtman, J., Digman, L., & Cozolino, L. (1982/1983). *Journal of Psychiatric Research, 17,* 155–167.
Sved, A. F., Fernstrom, J. D., & Wurtman, R. J. (1979). *Proceedings of the National Academy of Sciences of the United States of America, 76,* 3511–3514.
Wecker, L., Dettbarn, W. D., & Schmidt, D. E. (1978). *Science, 199,* 86–87.
Wurtman, J. J. (1983). *The carbohydrate craver's diet.* Boston: Houghton-Mifflin.
Wurtman, J. J., Moses, P. L., & Wurtman, R. J. (1983). *Journal of Nutrition, 113,* 70–78.
Wurtman, J. J., & Wurtman, R. J. (1977). *Science, 198,* 1178–1180.
Wurtman, J. J., & Wurtman, R. J. (1979). *Life Sciences, 24,* 895–903.
Wurtman, J. J., Wurtman, R. J., Growdon, J. H., Henry, P., Lipscomb, A., & Ziesel, S. H. (1981). *International Journal of Eating Disorders, 1,* 2–15.

Wurtman, J. J., Wurtman, R. J., Mark, S., Tsay, R., Gilbert, W., & Growdon, J. H. (1985). *International Journal of Eating Disorders, 4,* 89–99.

Wurtman, R. J. (1974). *Scientific American, 247,* 42–51.

Wurtman, R. J., Hefti, F., & Melamed, E. (1980). *Pharmacological Reviews, 32,* 315–335.

Wurtman, R. J., Hirsch, M. J., & Growdon, J. H. (1977). *Lancet, ii,* 68–69.

Wurtman, R. J., Larin, F., Mostafapour, S., & Fernstrom, J. D. (1974). *Science, 185,* 183–184.

·11·

Behavior and Nutrition: Strategies Used in Studies of Amino Acids, Protein, Carbohydrates, and Caffeine

HARRIS R. LIEBERMAN
BONNIE J. SPRING

INTRODUCTION

Investigation of the behavioral effects of foods and food constituents is a relatively new area of study. However, in spite of the comparatively small number of studies that have been conducted in this area, it is apparent that certain foods can affect behavior. Our studies have focused on the behavioral effects that certain food constituents can have on healthy adults. We have evaluated the effects of a variety of dietary constituents including the amino acids tryptophan and tyrosine, protein and carbohydrates, and low and moderate doses of caffeine. The results of these studies are discussed and related to research findings from other laboratories in the context of a discussion of strategies for detecting the effects of food constituents on healthy adults.

An earlier version of this chapter originally appeared in *Nutrition Reviews*, 1986, 44 (Suppl.), 61-70. It is reprinted here with permission from the International Life Sciences Institute—Nutrition Foundation.

METHODOLOGICAL ISSUES

Although the study of the behavioral effects of foods, at least as a discrete area of investigation, is itself quite new, a number of methods have been adapted from related fields. Many standard and widely used techniques, such as the double-blinding of experimental treatments and the use of placebos, have been employed. In addition, the use of specific testing methods selected from other disciplines is often possible. In our own studies we have used methods, often with certain appropriate modifications, drawn predominantly from experimental psychology, neuropsychology, and psychopharmacology. Such methods have been, at least in our experience, sensitive to the effects of the nutritional treatments we have administered (Lieberman, Corkin, Spring, Growdon, & Wurtman, 1983; Lieberman, Wurtman, Emde, Roberts, & Coviella, 1987; Lieberman, Wurtman, Garfield, & Coviella, 1987; Spring, Maller, Wurtman, Digman, & Cozolino, 1983). Since virtually all of the behavioral effects of foods that have been documented are subtle and therefore difficult to detect, very sensitive tests must be employed when such studies are conducted.

With the possible exception of certain beverages that contain caffeine (e.g., coffee), there are probably no foods that are generally considered, either by laymen or by scientists, to affect behavior. Even for caffeine, there is little agreement in the scientific literature regarding its behavioral effects at the doses present in foods (Dews, 1984; Sawyer, Julian & Turin, 1982). Based on currently available research, it seems unlikely that, under normal circumstances, any common food, when consumed in normal quantities, will dramatically affect human behavior. Virtually all of the behavioral effects of foods that have been well documented, are in fact, subtle and difficult to detect. Occasionally, claims have been made that sugar or certain food additives can cause major alterations in the behavior of children (Feingold, 1975); however these have not been substantiated by controlled studies (Behar, Rapoport, Adams, Berg, & Cornblath, 1984; Rapoport, 1983). Therefore, if the effects of foods on behavior are to be demonstrated, then highly sensitive techniques must be developed as well as adapted from other fields.

As noted above, psychopharmacological tests have often proved to be sensitive to the changes in behavior induced by food constituents, at least when foods are administered in greater than physiological quantities (Lieberman et al., 1983). However, even when food constituents are administered in high doses and in pure form they are not the same as drugs. Foods and food constituents (again with the possible exception of caffeine), unlike drugs, do not, to the best of our knowledge, interact directly with synaptic macromolecules or accumulate *in vivo* (Wurtman, Hefti, & Melamed, 1981). Therefore, they may generally be less potent than drugs with similar psychotropic properties (Lieberman et al., 1983). For example, although the essential amino acid tryptophan has hypnotic-like properties (Hartmann, 1983; Hartmann & Elion, 1977), it is not likely to be as potent a hypnotic as a barbiturate or benzodiazepine (Lieberman et al., 1983). It is likely to be especially difficult to detect the effects of foods administered as mixtures of different components. Unfortunately no field of psychology, psychiatry, or other behavioral science has developed standard methods for detecting relatively subtle effects of various acute or chronic treatments. The likely effects of foods, administered in the usual quantities, on the parameters typically measured in psychopharmacological experiments, might often be equivalent in magnitude to minor side effects of drugs and would go undetected using standard methods. We have, for example, found that demonstrating the effects of protein versus carbohydrate meals requires, when using standard experimental methods, much larger numbers of subjects than typically participate in laboratory studies (Lieberman, Spring, & Garfield, 1986; Spring et al., 1983).

Given the expected subtlety of the effects to be studied, the selection of the correct behavioral tasks to use is critical. The most carefully designed and conducted study that uses inappropriate or insensitive tests will fail to detect effects that are present. Even assuming the investigator knows which behavioral parameters are likely to be affected by a certain food or food constituent, there is still little agreement as to the most sensitive test to use to detect a change in any specific parameter; such as alertness, memory, or sensory sensitivity. Since there are many behavioral tests for most parameters likely to be selected for study, and the sensitivities of the tests have not been formally compared, test selection is not only critical but also a somewhat subjective task.

FOODS AND FOOD CONSTITUENTS
THAT ARE LIKELY TO AFFECT BEHAVIOR

Selection of Foods and Food Constituents for Testing

Another obvious issue in this emerging field is the selection of appropriate foods and food constituents for testing. We have attempted to approach this question from a physiological perspective. That is, we have studied substances for which a biochemical basis exists for hypothesizing that their administration will have behavioral consequences. For example, we have examined the effects of two neurotransmitter precursors, tryptophan and tyrosine, in certain aspects of human behavior (Lieberman et al., 1983). Tryptophan and tyrosine are both large neutral amino acids (LNAA) found in most foods that contain protein. They are transported across the blood-brain barrier, as are the other LNAA, by a single carrier mechanism and therefore they compete with each other and all of the other LNAA for uptake into the brain (Fernstrom, 1983; Wurtman et al., 1981). Tryptophan is the precursor of serotonin, a neurotransmitter that has been implicated in the regulation of sleep, pain sensitivity, and mood state (Hartmann, 1983; Hartmann & Elion, 1977; Hartmann & Spinweber, 1979; Lieberman et al., 1983; Seltzer, Dewart, Pollack, & Jackson, 1983; Seltzer, Stock, Marcus, & Jackson, 1982). Tyrosine is the precursor of several brain catecholamines including dopamine and norepinephrine. Dopamine is believed to modulate certain aspects of mood as well as various components of motor performance (Cotzias, Papavasiliou, & Gellent, 1969; Schildkraut, 1965). Another metabolite of tyrosine, norepinephrine, seems to play an important role in various aspects of the behavioral response to stress as well as other aspects of mood and emotion (Lehnert, Reinstein, Strowbridge; & Wurtman, 1984; McGeer, Eccles, & McGeer, 1978; Schildkraut, 1965). Because tryptophan and tyrosine are neurotransmitter precursors does not necessarily mean that changes in their systemic availability will alter the synthesis and release of their neurotransmitter products. In fact, it has been demonstrated experimentally that ingestion of tryptophan in pure form increases brain tryptophan and elevates brain serotonin in a dose-dependent fashion (Fernstrom & Wurtman, 1971). Tyrosine levels also increase in the brain after its systemic administration but it is more difficult to demonstrate that catecholaminergic neurons are precursor dependent. However, it does appear that when these neurons are highly active, precursor availability can be rate limiting (Wurtman et al., 1981; Lehnert et al., 1984). All of these findings indicate that these food constituents might have effects on normal human mood and performance. We therefore examined the behavioral effects of tryptophan and tyrosine. The selection of appropriate behavioral parameters to evaluate was governed by the literature on the functions of the neurotransmitter systems they may modulate.

Rationale for Studies with Pure Food Constituents

In a recent study we examined the effects of tryptophan and tyrosine on human mood and performance (Lieberman et al., 1983). These neurotransmitter precursors were administered in pure form, in quantities that were roughly equivalent to those that might be consumed by humans during the course of a single day. However, these amino acids are normally found in foods along with other amino acids that compete with them for transport across the blood-brain barrier. Therefore, a pure LNAA will have greater effects on the brain than the same amino acid consumed in a food that contains other LNAA. In part, we administered greater than physiological doses of these amino acids because of certain methodological considerations. If foods themselves are, as was discussed above, likely to have only subtle effects on behavior, then such effects are certain to be difficult to detect. It may therefore be appropriate to initially study higher doses of specific food constituents in pure form. This permits initial studies to be conducted with small population samples and provides important information about which behavioral tests are or are not sensitive to the effects of the pure foods. If treatment effects are not detected under these optimal conditions, it would indicate that similar effects will not be detectable when ordinary foods are given, since their administration results in qualitatively similar but reduced biochemical consequences compared with the pure substances. Additionally, if the effects of pure food constituents on human behavior are consistent with the predictions of particular neurochemically-based hypotheses (e.g., Wurtman et al., 1981), then these hypotheses can guide additional studies with foods themselves. Our initial study with tryptophan and tyrosine and a subsequent study we conducted with protein and carbohydrate foods provide an example of this process.

Studies with Foods: Background

Surprisingly, the neurochemical consequences of ingesting pure tryptophan or tyrosine resemble, respectively, those of eating a high carbohydrate or a high protein meal. In 1971 Fernstrom and Wurtman first demonstrated, in the rat, that protein and carbohydrate meals have different effects on the brain concentration of tryptophan and its neurotransmitter product serotonin (Fernstrom & Wurtman, 1971, 1972). Because both tryptophan and tyrosine are present in protein but not in carbohydrate foods, one might assume ingestion of protein would elevate the levels of both amino acids in the plasma and therefore in the brain. This is not the case, however. Protein meals do elevate plasma concentrations of both tryptophan and tyrosine, but these amino acids compete with each other as well as with the other LNAA at the blood-brain barrier for access to the brain. The parameter determining the access of each LNAA to the brain is thus the ratio of its plasma concentration to the other large neutral amino acids, not its absolute plasma concentration. Since tryptophan is the rarest of the LNAA in most protein foods, its plasma *ratio* (as opposed to absolute concentration) *declines* after such foods are ingested (see Figure 11.1). Protein meals increase the plasma tyrosine ratio and decrease the plasma tryptophan ratio (Glaeser, Maher, & Wurtman, 1983; Lieberman, Caballero, & Finer, 1986). Therefore, less tryptophan enters the brain and is available for serotonin synthesis, but more tyrosine is available for dopamine and norepinephrine synthesis.

It might also be anticipated that a pure carbohydrate meal would have little effect on either plasma tryptophan or tyrosine concentration since these

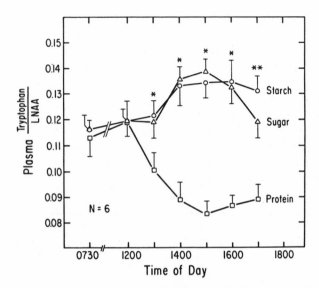

FIGURE 11.1. Effects of isocaloric lunch meals on ratios of human tryptophan to other large neutral amino acids (LNAA). Meals containing 120 grams of starch (circles) or 120 grams of sucrose (triangles) or 80 grams of animal protein (squares) were administered at noon to six healthy adults. One asterisk indicates a $p < .01$ difference between protein and the other meals, and two asterisks indicate a difference significant at $p < .05$ between all meals. Changes in the plasma tryptophan:LNAA ratio predict brain tryptophan concentration (Lieberman, Caballero, & Finer, 1986).

amino acids are not present in such foods. However, carbohydrate meals do significantly affect the ratio of tryptophan to the other LNAA, as a result of the secretion of insulin such meals elicit. Insulin lowers the plasma levels of the other large neutral amino acids relative to tryptophan. Carbohydrate meals thus have an effect opposite to that of protein meals on the plasma tryptophan ratio—such meals increase the tryptophan/LNAA ratio regardless of the type of carbohydrate tested, as shown in Figure 11.1. Therefore, more tryptophan is available for transport into the brain and thus carbohydrate meals increase brain serotonin (Fernstrom & Wurtman, 1971). The effect of a carbohydrate meal therefore resembles, with regard to the changes that occur in the plasma LNAA, administration of pure tryptophan, while a protein meal will resemble, in certain respects, the effects of pure tyrosine. A detailed explanation of these effects can be found in Wurtman et al. (1981) and Fernstrom (1983).

Effects of Tryptophan and Tyrosine on Mood and Performance

We administered, in pill form, 50 mg/kg of tryptophan, 100 mg/kg of tyrosine, and matched placebos to 20 healthy male volunteers aged 18–45. A double-blind crossover design was used (i.e., each subject received every substance on a different occasion). The four substances were administered in a counterbalanced order at the same time on four mornings. Testing began 2 hours later. Various aspects of mood and performance were measured with self-report questionnaires and tests of reaction time and motor performance. We selected tests that we believed would be sensitive to alterations in serotoninergic and catecholaminergic neurotransmission. Self-report mood questionnaires are standardized tests that have been used in a variety of settings to quantify certain aspects of mood states. They are simple to administer, consisting of a series of adjectives, each of which is rated individually. In addition to the self-report mood questionnaires, we also administered four tests of performance. Two were reaction-time tasks and two were tests of motor performance.

We found that tryptophan significantly altered alertness as measured by both of the self-report mood questionnaires administered. The two relevant scales of the Profile of Mood States (POMS) test (McNair, Lorr, & Doppelman, 1971), the Vigor scale and the Fatigue scale, as well as the Alert scale of Visual Analog Mood Scales (VAMS) test (Spring et al., 1983) all detected a significant sedative-like effect of tryptophan (Figures 11.2 and 11.3). These effects are consistent with the sleep-inducing and maintaining role of serotonin, the neurotransmitter synthesized from tryptophan. Hartmann and colleagues have previously reported that tryptophan has hypnotic properties when it is administered to humans (Hartmann, 1983; Hartmann & Elion, 1977).

We detected no significant effects of tryptophan or tyrosine when compared with their respective placebos on any of the performance tests we administered. However, there was a significant difference between the two amino acids in terms of the Simple Auditory Reaction Time test (Figure 11.4). This effect, although not large, was in the direction expected. On the day subjects received tryptophan, their reaction times were slower than on the day they received tyrosine. We had hoped to find some indication that these substances had antagonistic properties based on the functions of the neurotransmitters each is associated with and on the fact that they compete for uptake into the brain. Serotonin, synthesized from tryptophan, may act as a sleep-promoting neurotransmitter (Jouvet, 1973), and dopamine and perhaps norepinephrine, two of the transmitters that are products of tyrosine, may facilitate various types of motor and cognitive performance (Cotzias et al., 1969; Lehnert et al., 1984). Recent studies have indicated that tyrosine is most likely to affect behavior when animals and humans are subjected to some form of acute stress.

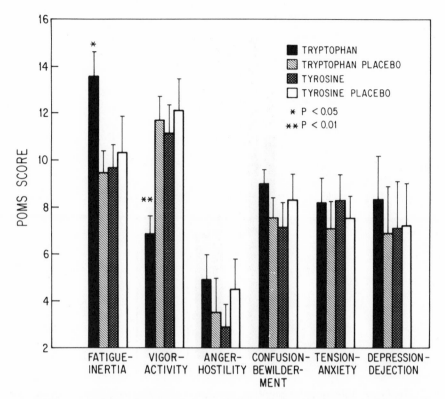

FIGURE 11.2.   Effects of tryptophan, tyrosine, and their respective placebos on the six subscales of the Profile of Mood States (POMS) self-report mood questionnaire (Lieberman, Corkin, Spring, Growdon, & Wurtman, 1983).

Effects of Protein and Carbohydrates

As discussed above, administration of protein as opposed to carbohydrate foods resembles, with regard to some of their effects on plasma amino acids, administration of tyrosine versus tryptophan (Glaeser et al., 1983). Since we were able to demonstrate that these pure amino acids affected certain aspects of behavior, it seemed appropriate to test the foods themselves. However, given the modest size of the effects that we found when pure amino acids were administered, we recognized that the effects of such foods would be very difficult to demonstrate. Also, at about the time we completed the tryptophan and tyrosine study, a very large ($n = 184$), parallel-design study with protein and carbohydrate foods was completed at the U. S. Army Laboratories in Natick, Massachusetts (Spring et al., 1983). The results of this study indicated that protein versus carbohydrate foods had behavioral ef-

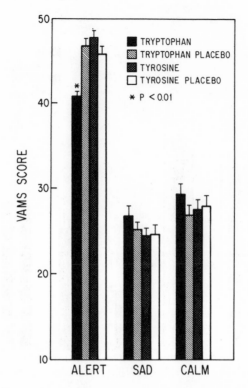

FIGURE 11.3.   Effects of tryptophan, tyrosine, and their respective placebos on mood as measured by the Visual Analog Mood Scales (VAMS) self-report mood questionnaire (Lieberman, Corkin, Spring, Growdon, & Wurtman, 1983).

fects, but they were not large and varied as a function of age and sex. The effects of protein (57 grams) versus carbohydrates (57 grams) detected in the study were consistent with the hypothesis that protein would resemble tyrosine in its behavioral effects and carbohydrate would have effects like those of tryptophan. We therefore designed an experiment (Lieberman, Spring, & Garfield, 1986) based on the findings of the tryptophan–tyrosine and Natick studies to further examine the effects of protein and carbohy-drates on mood and performance.

Forty young, healthy males aged 18–28 participated in this study. At noon they ingested either 80 grams of protein (turkey salad) or 120 grams of carbohydrate (wheat starch in the form of a bread-like food). Although much more like actual foods than pure amino acids, these are not typical balanced meals containing varying amounts of protein and carbohydrate. Based on the results of the Natick study (Spring et al., 1983), we determined, by perform-ing the appropriate statistical analysis, that an unreasonably large sample would be necessary to demonstrate the effects of more typical foods. The variability in the measures of mood and performance (even when a crossover design is used) and the size of the effects we expected are such that many more than 40 subjects would be required. We therefore administered pure protein and carbohydrate foods rather than more conventional lunches.

Throughout the afternoon we administered various mood and performance tests to the subjects. We used a large battery of such tests, particularly those that had been sensitive to tryptophan and tyrosine in our previous study and to protein versus carbohydrates in the Natick study.

The results of this study were consistent with the hypothesis that carbohydrate foods cause more sleepiness postprandially than protein meals. Although not statistically significant, perhaps as a result of the premeal baseline differences, the Vigor scale scores of the POMS and the Stanford Sleepiness Scale (SSS) scores (Hoddes, Dement, & Zarcone, 1972) were in the predicted direction. From approximately 1 to 3 hours after ingestion of the meals, subjects reported more sleepiness and less vigor on the day they had a carbohydrate meal even when the baseline differences were accounted for, although the differences were small. Moreover, the results of two of the performance tests administered at this time detected significant effects of the meals. At 1.75, 2.75, and 3.75 hours after administration of the foods the

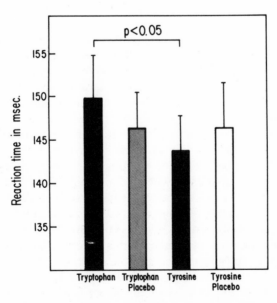

FIGURE 11.4. Effect. of tryptophan, tyrosine, and their respective placebos on auditory reaction time latency (Lieberman, Spring, & Garfield, 1986).

subjects were, on average, significantly slower on the Simple Auditory Reaction Time test if they had ingested the carbohydrate meal that day (Figure 11.5). This difference was statistically significant only at 1.75 hours. The Digit Symbol Substitution Test (DSST) devised by Wechsler (1955) also detected a small, but statistically significant, degree of impairment 3.5 hours after the carbohydrate meal was eaten. The DSST is a complex test of timed coding performance. It is interesting to note that of the various performance tests we administered in this study, our version of Simple Auditory Reaction Time test, which was sensitive to tryptophan versus tyrosine, was also sensitive to protein versus carbohydrate (Lieberman et al., 1983). Two important characteristics of our Simple Reaction Time test could be the relatively large number of trials administered (125) and the comparatively short anticipatory intervals used (less than 3 seconds).

Although it cannot as yet be stated conclusively, the evidence that protein versus carbohydrate meals have opposite behavioral effects continues to accumulate. It seems likely, based on the results of the studies discussed above, that carbohydrates, relative to protein, decrease arousal level and improve performance. However, the effects, as we expected, are subtle and difficult to detect.

CAFFEINE: BEHAVIORAL EFFECTS OF LOW AND MODERATE DOSES

Another food constituent we have been investigating, caffeine, also has been considered to have subtle and even capricious effects on behavior (Dews, Grice, Neims, Wilson, & Wurtman, 1984; Sawyer et al., 1982). Caffeine, and similar compounds that are found in foods, have behavioral and pharmacological effects in high doses. These effects may be mediated by a compound found in the brain, the nucleotide adenosine, which may be an inhibitory neurotransmitter. Since caffeine antagonizes the effects of adenosine, this would explain its stimulant-like properties (Snyder, 1984; von Borstel & Wurtman, 1984). Although caffeine has pharmacological properties when it is administered in high doses, when administered in the doses found in single servings of foods, behavioral effects have not been definitively demonstrated (Dews et al., 1984; Sawyer et al., 1982). About three-quarters of the caffeine consumed in the United States is taken in coffee (Roberts & Barone, 1983). However, the caffeine content of this beverage varies greatly depending on the type of coffee bean used and the method of brewing. Of the types of coffee regularly consumed in the United States, drip-method coffee usually contains the highest amounts of caffeine, about 110 mg per cup, and instant coffee the least, about 60 mg per cup; a cup of tea (made with a tea bag)

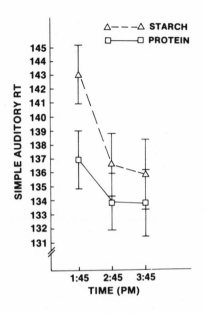

FIGURE 11.5. Mean results of Simple Auditory Reaction Time test at three different intervals following administration of an isocaloric protein (squares) or carbohydrate (triangles) meal at noon. Reactions of the 40 subjects were significantly slower ($p < .05$) at 1:45 P.M. on the day they consumed the carbohydrate meal (Lieberman, Spring, & Garfield, 1986).

contains about 42 mg; and a typical 12-ounce serving of a cola beverage about 38 mg (Roberts & Barone, 1984).

We examined the behavioral effects of caffeine by conducting a dose-response study using 32, 64, 128, and 256 mg doses of methylxanthine (Lieberman, Wurtman, Emde, Roberts, & Coviella, 1987). Our subjects were 20 healthy males aged 18–47. They ingested the caffeine in pill form at 8:00 A.M. after a 12-hour fast; the fast also served as a caffeine washout period. Only low and moderate consumers of caffeine (less than 400 mg per day) were included in the study. The protocol was double-blind, placebo controlled, and a counterbalanced crossover design was used. As in our other studies we used a series of mood and performance tests. With a few exceptions, the tests administered could be divided into three categories: self-report mood questionnaires, vigilance tests, and tests of motor performance. We selected tests based on various behavioral studies with other food constituents and our own previous studies. In our first study caffeine's detectable effects were limited to the vigilance tests we administered—of the three such tests used, two detected significant effects of all doses of caffeine relative to placebo. A modified version of the Wilkinson auditory vigilance test (Lieberman, Waldhauser, Garfield, Lynch, & Wurtman, 1984; Wilkinson, 1968, 1970) was the most sensitive (Figure 11.6). This test is 1 hour in duration and during it the subject must detect 40 signal tones embedded in 1,800 slightly longer background tones. Caffeine substantially improved per-

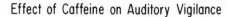

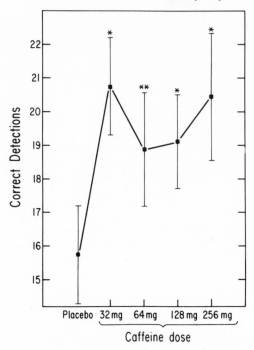

FIGURE 11.6.   Effects of various doses of caffeine and placebo on the mean number of correct detections on the Wilkinson auditory vigilance test. One and two asterisks indicate differences from placebo significant of $p < .01$ and $p < .05$, respectively (Lieberman, Spring, & Garfield, 1987).

formance even when only 32 mg was administered. Response speed on a four-choice visual reaction-time task (Wilkinson & Houghton, 1975) was also significantly facilitated by all four doses of caffeine. The Continuous Performance Test (CPT) devised by Buchsbaum and Sostek (1980), another test of visual vigilance, detected no effects of caffeine. Error rates on these vigilance tests, as well as the various motor performance tests administered, were not increased by caffeine. It appears therefore, at least for men who are not heavy caffeine consumers, that low and moderate doses of caffeine can improve vigilance performance (Lieberman, Wurtman, Emde, et al., 1987).

Since completing this initial study we have conducted other studies that have replicated and extended these findings. In particular, the modified Wilkinson vigilance test has consistently detected positive effects of caffeine, and we have seen beneficial effects on moods such as alertness and fatigue (Lieberman, Wurtman, Garfield, et al., 1987).

REPLICABILITY OF RESULTS: SOME GENERAL COMMENTS

Although we were able to detect significant and consistent effects of caffeine at all doses tested and have repeatedly replicated our findings (Lieberman, Wurtman, Emde, et al., 1987; Lieberman, Wurtman, Garfield, et al., 1987), other investigators have reported varied findings using tests of vigilance. Some have also reported improved vigilance performance (Clubley, Bye, Henson, Peck, & Riddington, 1979) while others have failed to detect any effects of caffeine. For example, in one study, Loke and Meliska (1984), using a visual vigilance task of their own design, were unable to detect effects of caffeine administered in doses of 195 and 325 mg. They controlled for caffeine use by selecting only the 24 lowest and highest users from a group of 36 volunteers. There were, however, at least three critical differences between their study and ours. First, the test of vigilance they employed had a relatively large percentage of signal trials—22.2% as opposed to 2.2% in the Wilkinson vigilance test. This may have increased the attention subjects allocated to the task, a critical parameter for vigilance tests. In fact, the subjects in the Loke and Meliska (1984) study were operating at a very high level of correct detections. Their performance was, on average, at about the 90% correct level, as opposed to the typical 50% correct in the Wilkinson vigilance task (Wilkinson, 1968, 1970). This could have resulted in a ceiling effect (the performance was so good, there was no room for improvement), leaving little chance to detect improved performance. Another problem in the Loke and Meliska (1984) study was its small, heterogenous population sample. They tested each of their 24 subjects only once (they used a parallel design). Every subject was assigned to one of three experimental groups and within each group they were stratified by sex and caffeine use. Each group therefore contained only eight subjects and each block of subjects per group consisted of two individuals. This might have been sufficient for a crossover study, but in a parallel design where subjects are tested on only one occasion, this is a rather small sample. There was one other serious problem with this study— there was only a 2-hour caffeine washout period before testing. Caffeine's half-life in humans is 5.2 hours, so a washout of 2 hours is insufficient and will result in considerable individual differences in plasma caffeine level, depending on how much caffeine the subject consumed that day (Bonati & Garattini, 1984). It should be noted, to the credit of Loke and Meliska (1984), that they did not conclude that caffeine does not affect vigilance.

The apparent differences in results between our caffeine study and that of Loke and Meliska (1984) illustrate a number of important methodological considerations. First is the question of test sensitivity and comparability. All tests of visual vigilance are not equivalent. Although similar in certain respects to other tests, the Wilkinson vigilance test appears more sensitive to the effects of caffeine. In our study it was the most sensitive of the three such tests we used. Had we used only the CPT vigilance test, we would have failed to detect any significant effect of caffeine even given the fact we used a crossover design with 20 subjects. Given the considerable differences between vigilance tests, it is to be expected that some will detect treatment effects and others will not. Even in studies employing independent variables that are more potent than food constituents, such as psychoactive drugs, long periods of sleep deprivation, or severe environmental alterations, the results vary greatly with subtle characteristics of the tests employed (Johnson & Chernik, 1982; Wilkinson, 1968, 1970).

In addition to the important question of test sensitivity, one must also consider the sensitivity of the experimental design to the variable of interest. There are statistical methods for measuring the probability of incorrectly concluding that a treatment has no significant effect. This is Type II error and can be computed given information on the variability of the behavioral test being used, sample size, and a criterion for the size of the effect sought (Young, Bresnitz, & Strom, 1983).

It would be helpful if more use were made of this statistic, especially in the case of negative findings. It is certainly likely considering the magnitude of effects we have seen after administration of foods, the inherent variability of the behavioral parameters assessed, and the failure of most investigators to use a measure of Type II error, that there will be numerous *apparently* contradictory findings reported as more investigators begin to study the behavioral effects of foods.

CONCLUSION

Detecting the effects of foods and food constituents on behavior is difficult, due, in part, to the subtlety of the effects and the lack of standardized and sensitive tests of human mood and performance. However, as more studies are conducted by different groups of investigators, it will become apparent that certain tests are usually most sensitive and that certain changes are reliably present after specific foods are administered. For example, of the various tests we have used, Simple Auditory Reaction Time has often been sensitive to the effects of foods and food constituents. Vigilance tests, particularly our version of the Wilkinson auditory vigilance task, also seem to detect relatively subtle changes in behavior. It should be noted, however, that relatively minor details of these tests may be critical in determining their sensitivity. It is therefore certainly appropriate to include a variety of tests in any behavioral study of foods. With regard to the other side of the equation, that is, what foods to test, progress also is being made. It seems certain that tryptophan has sedative-like properties (Hartmann, 1983; Hartmann & Elion, 1977; Lieberman et al., 1983) and carbohydrate foods relative to protein foods also may have similar effects. Eventually it may be agreed that caffeine, in the low doses found in foods, also affects behavior.

Acknowledgments

We wish to thank the staff of the Clinical Research Center, Massachusetts Institute of Technology, for their assistance. The following agencies provided support. U.S. Air Force Office of Scientific Research (AFOSR-87-04029) and the NIH (RR00088).

REFERENCES

Behar, D., Rapoport, J. L., Adams, A. J., Berg, C. J., & Cornblath, M. (1984). Sugar challenge testing with children considered behaviorally "sugar reactive." *Nutrition and Behavior, 1,* 277–288.

Bonati, M., & Garattini, S. (1984). Interspecies comparison of caffeine disposition. In P. B. Dews (Ed.), *Caffeine* (pp. 48–56). New York: Springer-Verlag.

Buchsbaum, M. S., & Sostek, A. J. (1980). An adaptive-rate continuous performance test: Vigilance characteristics and reliability for 400 male students. *Perceptual and Motor Skills, 51,* 707–713.

Clubley, M., Bye, C. E., Henson, T. A., Peck, A. W., & Riddington, C. J. (1979). *British Journal of Pharmacology, 7,* 157.

Cotzias, G. C., Papavasiliou, P. S., & Gellent, R. (1969). Modification of Parkinsonism: Chronic treatment with L-dopa. *New England Journal of Medicine, 280,* 337–345.

Dews, P. (1984). Behavioral effects of caffeine. In P. B. Dews (Ed.), *Caffeine* (pp. 86–103). New York: Springer-Verlag.

Dews, P., Grice, H. C., Neims, A., Wilson, J., & Wurtman, R. (1984). Report of fourth international caffeine workshop, Athens, 1982. *Food and Chemical Toxicology, 22*(2), 163–169.

Feingold, B. F. (1975). *Why is your child hyperactive?* New York: Random House.

Fernstrom, J. D. (1983). Role of precursor availability in control of monoamine biosynthesis in brain. *Physiological Review, 63,* 484–546.

Fernstrom, J. D., & Wurtman, R. J. (1971). Brain serotonin content: Increase following ingestion of carbohydrate diet. *Science, 174,* 1023–1025.

Fernstrom, J. D., & Wurtman, R. J. (1972). Brain serotonin content: Physiological regulation by plasma neutral amino acids. *Science, 178,* 414–416.

Glaeser, B. S., Maher, T. J., & Wurtman, R. J. (1983). Changes in brain levels of acidic, basic, and neutral amino acids after consumption of single meals containing various proportions of protein. *Journal of Neurochemistry, 83,* 1016–1021.

Hartmann, E. (1983). Effects of L-tryptophan on sleepiness and on sleep. *Journal of Psychiatric Research, 17*(2), 107–113.

Hartmann, E., & Elion, R. (1977). The insomnia of sleeping in a strange place. *Psychopharmacology, 53,* 131–133.

Hartmann, E., & Spinweber, C. L. (1979). Sleep induced by L-tryptophan: Effect of dosages within the normal dietary intake. *Journal of Nervous Mental Disorders*, *167*, 497–499.

Hoddes, E., Dement, W., & Zarcone, V. (1972). The history and use of the Stanford Sleepiness Scale. *Psychophysiology, 9*, 150.

Johnson, L. C., & Chernik, D. A. (1982). Sedative-hypnotics and human performance. *Psychopharmacology, 76*, 101–113.

Jouvet, M. (1973). Serotonin and sleep in the cat. In J. Barchas & E. Usdin (Eds.), *Serotonin and behavior* (pp. 385–400). New York: Academic Press.

Lehnert, H., Reinstein, D. K., Strowbridge, B. W., & Wurtman, R. J. (1984). Neurochemical and behavioral consequences of acute, uncontrollable stress: Effects of dietary tyrosine. *Brain Research, 303*, 215–223.

Lieberman, H. R., Caballero, B., & Finer, N. (1986). The composition of lunch determines afternoon tryptophan ratios in humans. *Journal of Neural Transmission, 65*, 211–217.

Lieberman, H. R., Corkin, S., Spring, B. J., Growdon, J. H., & Wurtman, R. J. (1983). Mood, performance, and pain sensitivity: Changes induced by food constituents. *Journal of Psychiatric Research, 17*(2), 135–145.

Lieberman, H. R., Spring, B. J., & Garfield, G. S. (1986). The behavioral effects of food constituents: Strategies used in studies of amino acids, proteins, carbohydrate and caffeine. *Nutrition Reviews, 44*(Suppl.), 61–70.

Lieberman, H. R., Waldhauser, F., Garfield, G., Lynch, H. J., & Wurtman, R. J. (1984). Effects of melatonin on human mood and performance. *Brain Research, 323*(2), 201–207.

Lieberman, H. R., Wurtman, R. J., Emde, G. G., Roberts, C., & Coviella, I. L. G. (1987). The effects of low doses of caffeine on human performance and mood. *Psychopharmacology, 92*, 308–312.

Lieberman, H. R., Wurtman, R. J., Garfield, G. G., & Coviella, I. L. G. (1987). The effects of caffeine and aspirin on mood and performance. *Journal of Clinical Psychopharmacology, 7*(5), 315–320.

Loke, W. H., & Meliska, C. J. (1984). Effects of caffeine use and ingestion on a protracted visual vigilance test. *Psychopharmacology, 84*, 54–57.

McGeer, P. L., Eccles, J. C., & McGeer, E. G. (1978). *Molecular neurobiology of the mammalian brain.* New York: Plenum Press.

McNair, P. M., Lorr, M., & Dopplemen, L. F. (1971). *Profile Of Mood States Manual.* San Diego: Educational and Industrial Testing Service.

Rapoport, J. L. (1983). Effects of dietary substances in children. *Journal of Psychiatric Research, 17*(2), 187–191.

Roberts, H. R., & Barone, J. J. (1983). Caffeine: History and use. *Food Technology, 37*(9), 32.

Sawyer, D. A., Julia, H. L., & Turin, A. C. (1982). Caffeine and human behavior: Arousal, anxiety, and performance effects. *Journal of Behavioral Medicine, 5*(4), 415–439.

Schildkraut, J. J. (1965). The catecholamine hypothesis of affective disorders: A review of supportive evidence. *American Journal of Psychiatry, 122*, 509–522.

Seltzer, S., Dewart, D., Pollack, R. L., & Jackson, E. (1983). The effects of dietary tryptophan on chronic maxillofacial pain and experimental pain tolerance. *Journal of Psychiatric Research, 17*(2), 181–186.

Seltzer, S., Stoch, R., Marcus, R., & Jackson, E. (1982). Alteration of human pain thresholds by nutritional manipulation and L-tryptophan supplementation. *Pain, 13*, 385–393.

Snyder, S. H. (1984). Adenosine as a mediator of the behavioral effects of xanthines. In P. B. Dews (Ed.), *Caffeine* (pp. 129–141). New York: Springer-Verlag.

Spring, B., Maller, O., Wurtman, J. J., Digman, L., & Cozolino, L. (1983). Effects of protein and carbohydrate meals on mood and performance: Interactions with sex and age. *Journal of Psychiatric Research, 17*(2), 155–167.

von Borstel, W. R., & Wurtman, R. J. (1984). Caffeine and the cardiovascular effects of physiological levels of Adenosine. In P. B. Dews (Ed.), *Caffeine* (pp. 142–150). New York: Springer-Verlag.

Wechsler, D. (1955). *Wechsler Adult Intelligence Scale.* New York: Psychological Corporation.

Wilkinson, R. T. (1968). Sleep deprivation: Performance tests for partial and selective sleep deprivation. In B. F. Reiss & L. A. Abt (Eds.), *Progress in clinical psychology* New York: Grune and Stratton.

Wilkinson, R. T. (1970). Methods for research on sleep deprivation and sleep function. In E. Hartmann (Ed.), *Sleep and dreaming.* Boston: Little Brown.

Wilkinson, R. T., & Houghton, D. (1975). Portable four-choice reaction time test with magnetic tape memory. *Behavior Research Methods and Instrumentation, 7*, 441–446.

Wurtman, R. J., Hefti, F., & Melamed, E. (1981). Precursor control of neurotransmitter synthesis. *Pharmacology Review, 32*, 315–335.

Young, M. J., Bresnitz, E. A., & Strom, B. L. (1983). Sample size nomograms for interpreting negative clinical studies. *Annals of Internal Medicine, 99*, 248–251.

·IV·

PSYCHONEUROIMMUNOLOGY

· 12 ·

Self-Healing: A Personal History

RENÉ DUBOS

This article is concerned with general considerations about what keeps people from dying, but it is illustrated by two or three occasions during which I have been on the point of death. At age 8, I suffered from rheumatic fever and developed a very severe heart lesion. I have never been able to run or to play any physical game, but what I have done is to train myself to walk a great deal. I walk an enormous amount, progressively more and more, including the four flights of stairs to my office every day.

By the age of 70, I had become physically quite strong. But one day I noticed that I was becoming weaker and weaker and just thought it was old age. I went to see my physician, who immediately diagnosed that I had a very advanced case of bacterial endocarditis, which could have killed me. I recovered from bacterial endocarditis and as soon as I could I started walking again and engaged in as much physical training as I could.

I believe I reached the peak of my physical strength at age 78. But at age 78 I overexerted myself clearing land on my farm in the Hudson highlands. I went into an extreme case of atrial fibrillation and soon developed massive pulmonary edema with complete cardiac decompensation. I recovered from it, and once more I began to walk, although I have tried not to exert myself as much as I used to. I have had several other metabolic disorders. I'll mention only one, a duodenal ulcer I contracted at the age of 22. I believe this was because of my intense worry at that time concerning unemployment. This was in France during the depression immediately after the war, but I continued to function with it until sometime around 50, when I was immensely successful professionally—president of three societies and doing all sorts of things, many of which I did not care for especially. One day I fainted in the street, and it was discovered I was bleeding from my duodenal ulcer. I was taken to the hospital and recovered, but while I was in the hospital I tried to imagine how I could conduct my life in a more intelligent way. I have been only partly successful in that, in overcoming my tenseness, but nevertheless I am somewhat more relaxed than in the past.

The reason for telling these stories is to acknowledge the help I have received from very wise physicians, but I believe that I have been able to do what I have done because consciously I have taken decisions about the kind of behavior that I believe makes for a longer life.

I have discussed these problems with Howard Rusk, who knows this much better than I do, that rehabilitation from any disease requires the complete participation of the patient. Most ailments for which people seek the help of a physician are in reality diseases that are self-terminating, and the patient would recover without ever seeing a physician or getting the help of any healer. Many very sophisticated students of disease do not hestitate in stating that probably 90% to 95% of the ailments for which people seek medical attention would take care of themselves without any medical help. As a matter of fact when you think about it, you could almost guess this a priori. You could guess that in all living things, human beings included, there must be some mechanism for spontaneous recovery, because if there were not, no living thing could survive the constant insults from the environment. After making this a priori statement, I have amused myself by trying to see how far it can go. How far among living things does this ability to recover spontaneously from environmental insults go?

It occurred to me that it occurs even at the most minute level of life, for example, in the simplest cell; in all cells without exception there exist enzymatic mechanisms for gene repair. If a gene is damaged by any mechanism, by a poison or by radiation, there exist within the cell enzymatic processes for gene repair. So even the most primitive cell is equipped with mechanisms for self-healing.

Naturally, plants and animals in the wild commonly recover from even the most traumatic accidents. Everyone has had the chance to see a plant or animal in nature that has been badly wounded or poisoned and that has spontaneously recovered. Similarly, human beings can recover from wounds, from infections, from all shorts of shortages, from all the traumatic experiences of life. If they had not, they could not have survived throughout prehistory and history, and here we have very excellent anthropological evidence that human beings have recovered from the most painful experiences even during the Stone Age, long before there was any modern medicine.

It seems possible that all healing practices, whether it be the Navajo shaman or the most sophisticated physician practicing on Park Avenue, must be evaluated in the light of this very widespread capacity for healing that exists in all living things and in each and every human being. It would be very entertaining to see that in reality all they do is simply help the self-healing processes that operate naturally. This was my original title for this article, self-healing. But while thinking about it, I decided that I might convey a more useful point of view if I were to convey my view that when we speak of healing we speak of two very different things.

One kind of healing depends on the ability of the organism, of the patient, to return to the state of health in which that patient was before the disease. In other words, healing can be considered to be just clinically correcting the damage that had been done. In my opinion that does not happen very often.

There is another kind of healing that implies a very different mechanism, a kind of permanent change in the patient or in the organism, whatever the nature of the organism we consider, that makes that patient or organism better capable of coping with whatever new situation has happened, and this is what I call creative adaptation.

Throughout this article I will contrast at every step the return to the original state, which one usually calls cure, and the permanent lasting change that makes for greater ability to cope with the world, which I call creative adaptation. First, let me speak about the classical view of recovery from disease, the concept of cure. The belief that all organisms have in them, in their constitutions, the mechanisms for correcting any interference coming from the outside world in insult, has its origin in the concept of homeostasis. The concept of homeostasis was born about 150 years ago with Claude Bernard, who insisted that the characteristic of the healthy living organism is to be capable to maintain the constancy, the stability, of the internal environment. This theme was taken up at the turn of the century by Walter Cannon at Harvard, who restated it with the phrase that there exists in all organisms an ability for homeostatic response, namely the ability to return the organism to its original state after the internal environment had been disturbed by any kind of insult.

The great contribution of Cannon was to emphasize the role of hormones and of metabolic mechanisms, the control by the autonomic nervous system in maintaining the ability of the organism and in correcting the physiological disturbances brought about by environmental insults and by other forms of trauma.

Why has medical science continued developing the concept of disease and of recovery along the lines started by Cannon some 75 years ago? We do know now that there exist all sorts of mechanisms to bring about tissue repair, once the tissue has been damaged, scar tissue being a form of tissue repair. We do know that there are immunological mechanisms that enable the body to bring about immunological responses in the form of antibodies or in the form of cellular immunity, against infection or against toxins. Some infectious organism invades the tissue, a toxin is produced, and the organism gets rid of it through immunological mechanisms. One knows, of course, that there are also behavioral patterns that help to overcome whatever disturbances can come from certain human contacts. This is really the fundamental spirit of classical medicine during our century: the ability of the organism to get rid of whatever insult it has experienced, and to come back to its original state.

One used to assume that most of these self-correcting mechanisms, these homeostatic responses, operate almost or completely unconsciously. A change has begun to occur here. There is now overwhelming evidence, to which I shall return, that some of the homeostatic responses can be influenced by the mind. Nobody knows exactly how it happens, but nobody doubts that it happens. The homeostatic response of which Cannon spoke certainly is influenced by mind processes, even though it is difficult to establish exactly the precise link between the mind and the physiological processes, except to state that it occurs through this or that part of the autonomic nervous system. I think we can take for granted that practically all the rituals of healing with which we are familiar, ranging all the way from Transcendental Meditation to Zen processes and the laying on of hands, intervene in body processes through the autonomic nervous system, and that in some way they facilitate the reestablishment of homeostasis, the reestablishment of health.

So much for homeostatic response, so much for the view of cure that has dominated most of modern medicine. If you chance to read Cannon's book *The Wisdom of the Body*, which was immensely influential on all persons of my generation, you will see in it that Cannon was so much impressed by the effectiveness of the mechanisms involved in homeostasis that he barely mentions disease; he almost assumes, or he writes as if he did assume, that the wisdom of the body is such that it is usually capable of correcting physiological disturbances and therefore preventing the development of pathological processes.

This is where I am going to separate myself completely from Cannon. In my opinion, the outcome of the response of the organism to a disturbing influence is only very rarely homeostatic. My conviction now is that whatever happens to us, whatever we experience, we respond to it by changing. And if you think about yourself, you will see how true this is, and how this affects all of your life. There is not one experience that you have that does not become incorporated into your nature. You are never the same after having done something or having experienced something. For example, if you have had any kind of emotional disturbance, even though you may have overcome it, seem to do very well as if you had never suffered from it, nevertheless you know that you are marked by it for life. Now everybody accepts that, more or less, for emotional disturbances, but the fact is that any change that occurs in the body also leaves a mark.

For example, I mentioned as an example of homeostatic response, that if an infection takes place, the body can develop immunological mechanisms so that there is no trace left of the infection. But there is a trace left in your whole immunological mechanism, such that your immunological mechanism has been marked by that first experience. You will never from now on respond as if you had never had that first experience. So that I take it for granted now that there is nothing, hardly anything, that is completely homeostatic; everything we experience becomes incarnated, so to speak, in our physical and mental being.

Another difference that I have with Cannon is that many of those so-called homeostatic responses, instead of simply correcting the damage, often have long-range consequences that are deleterious. Many of the homeostatic responses are in reality the cause of disease. Let me give only three or four examples. Developing repair tissue, scarring, looks like a valuable homeostatic response to a wound, of course. But the same mechanism, if it happens somewhere else in the body, may result for example in fibrosis in the liver, glomerulonephritis in the kidney, and almost certainly accounts for the lesions of multiple sclerosis. So scar tissue, which is a homeostatic response, is probably responsible for an immense variety of diseases. Now the immune response, of course, can protect us against infection and against toxins, but in a very large number of cases, the immune mechanisms express themselves not in increased resistance, but in allergic reactions or in autoimmune disease.

Now let us take another of those homeostatic responses in which Cannon was much interested. Consider the case of traumatic shock. As a result of traumatic shock there is vasoconstriction, and there is no doubt vasoconstriction has protective effects because it preserves blood pressure, a perfect homeostatic response. But in so doing, the vasoconstriction may deprive the kidney and other organs of vital blood flow, with all sorts of untoward consequences. And I could, if you would be interested in it, illustrate how all sorts of behavioral responses that are supposed to be homeostatic in that they protect us from environmental insults, eventually become obsessive attitudes and all sorts of other pathological conditions. One can say without hesitation that these aberrations of the homeostatic response constitute the largest causation of disease. In fact, it is very likely that most diseases are the consequences of misguided homeostatic response.

Returning to healing, I want to emphasize that the response of the body, instead of attempting to restore the mind or the body to the condition in which it was before the insult, most commonly, practically always, brings about a lasting change. That change can be deleterious, as in the examples I gave before, but the change can be also adaptive, namely, it can be a change in the whole organism that makes that organism different from the way it was before, but much better able in the future to meet new conditions.

As soon as one makes this statement, one asks if this is something peculiar to human beings, the ability to undergo changes that will result in better adaptation. It is not peculiar to human beings; it happens at all levels of organization of living things. And once again, beginning with the smallest possible living unit, the cell, we can examine the gene. Recall that there exist in all cells enzymatic mechanisms that are capable of repairing a gene that has been damaged. But in reality, what probably happens in the largest percentage of cases is that, in the course of the repair of the gene, the gene is slightly changed. Indeed, many molecular biologists believe, most of them for all I know, that what we call mutation is the consequence of a repair of a damaged gene, but a repair that instead of returning the gene to exactly what it was before, reconstructs it in a slightly different form, and we have a mutation. And as you think of it, it is out of those mutations that the whole process of adaptation, of genetic adaptation, goes on in the living world. So I believe that the most elementary unit of life, namely the gene within the cell, the repair of the gene resulting in a mild change of it, is at the origin of all genetic adaptive processes.

Let me move now from such a simple organism to a more complex one. Go into the woods after a storm, see how a tree has lost several of its branches, has become completely disorganized, and then return a few years later, and you know very well what has happened. Other branches have grown, changing the shape of the tree, but reestablishing a harmonious structure, reestablishing a balance between the different components of the tree. And in reality, some of the most interesting, beautiful trees, with the most interesting shapes, are the trees that have suffered from such trauma.

In an animal that, for example, has lost a leg or has suffered some kind of accident, one knows very well that all sorts of changes occur in that animal that would make it move in a different way, strengthening certain muscles that could not have been developed otherwise, and soon enough the animal looks different from what it was, but functions essentially just as well. What about human beings? People who have lost their sight, at say, the age of 20, and I have known several, and therefore can no longer experience the world through the organ of sight undergo all sorts of changes that make them much better able to perceive the world through the other senses, through touch, smell, all sorts of feelings that otherwise were there but were not developed and that make that person become a different person in relation to other persons, but just as effective through the creative adaptations.

One could carry this concept of adaptation through creative changes in all living things, and I have amused myself doing that during the past 2 or 3 years. I shall mention only one of the applications to large social problems, namely the evolution of medicine during the past hundred years or so. I think it is very easy to demonstrate that historically medicine has evolved both from the scientific and the practical point of view by undergoing changes, very profound changes, which are due not only to new discoveries, but to the fact that new problems have emerged, that emphasis has been shifted from one thing to the other. I have amused myself making the prediction that the craze of interest during the past 10 to 20 years in all the paramedical ways of healing will certainly affect scientific medicine by bringing about an increase in the studies dealing with the mechanisms through which the body influences the mind, and in fact this is no longer a prediction, it has begun to happen. Anybody who travels a great deal sees that the interest of the public in the other ways of healing than so-called scientific medicine is compelling the reorientation of medical research and will certainly result in profound changes in the science and the practice of medicine.

What I want to convey through all these examples is that there are within the body and the mind, whatever the word "mind" means, all sorts of potentialities that may remain unexpressed if they are not used and that can deteriorate, after they are developed, if one does not use them. The famous phrase, "Use it or lose it," implies that the total organism has potentialities that become fully expressed only by use and that tend to undergo atrophy as a result of disuse. As soon as one takes this view, one will see how this affects the whole process of development in human beings.

Once more I am going to take some very obvious examples, but one can think of others. Just think of muscle development. All of us are born with more or less the same potentiality for muscular development, but see how we turn out to be very different persons physically in our muscle development depending on the kind of life we lead, the kind of sports we practice, the kind of professional activities we engage in. What we end up being is something that is not only the consequence of the potentialities we were born with, but also the expression of our ways of life on our latent potentialities, which either remain latent or develop completely.

Consider learning ability. Everybody practically is born with an immense range of learning ability, but the skills one acquires depend on how one exercises the body and the mind. One can enormously develop one's capacities for memory. If I may speak about myself, a number of years ago, I developed difficulties with my eyesight so that I cannot read a manuscript, so I trained myself to speak without a manuscript. I speak with a manuscript in front of me, so that audiences can see that I am a serious person, but I talk around it. I have trained myself to do all sorts of things that I would not have if I had not been compelled by some necessity.

It is extraordinary how one can develop one's sensory perception. Any one of you who has been in the woods with a real hunter knows how he can hear things that one will not hear if one has not cultivated that sense. Skills in relating to people—my heavens, the wide range of skills that one can develop by effort and by practice. So I do not hesitate in saying to you that all aspects of physical and mental development result in better adaptation if we cultivate the right kind of development to fit the circumstances under which we live.

The very broad conclusion of all this is that what we call natural development is not merely the unfolding of a pattern encoded in our genetic endowment. We must always keep in mind that genes do not determine what we become, do not determine how we change in the course of time. Genes provide only the instructions that govern the responses of each part of the organism to whatever conditions we experience. That presents the problem of education, of training, of forming people, in a very different light. This affirms that there is an immense diversity of potentialities in human beings, and there are possibilities of taking advantage of them for whatever purpose we have in mind.

The word purpose is used carefully here. As well as the correction of damage, creative adaptation always implies some kind of purpose, some kind of decision we make as to how we are going to behave toward developing this way or that way, toward correcting this or that deficiency. I am aware of the fact, that like the mechanisms that control homeostasis, many of the mechanisms that result in the kind of lasting change of which I have been writing are largely unconscious, of course, but on the other hand, the changes undergone by a person need not be passive, they need not be blind adjustments to environmental circumstances, they can be the consequences of deliberate choices, and choices based on anticipations of the future.

I am convinced that for the future of the science of healing, this is the most important statement I could make or that anybody could make. Namely, that whatever happens to us depends on deliberate choices based on anticipation of the future, based on what we want our future life to be. I know of course that a large percentage of our responses to environmental forces are carried out by instincts, which operate outside of consciousness, and it is plainly obvious that we, like animals, have instincts. Now these instincts are useful, often, but not always. They enable the organism to deal rapidly in a decisive and often successful manner with certain life situations, but they are useful only to deal with life situations that the organism has experienced repeatedly during the evolutionary past. In other words, our instincts are mechanisms that are useful if they help us to deal with the kind of situations that human life has experienced during evolution.

This is, by the way, why instincts are often very useful and effective in animals in the wild; they are practically always effective, because animals in the wild are still living essentially under the conditions under which they evolved. In other words, their instincts fit the situations of today because they are the same situations under which the instincts developed, perhaps a million years ago. But in the case of human beings, instincts are not flexible enough to meet adaptably the new and unpredictable complexities of life. In other words, instincts are of little use for adaptation to change.

For human beings adaptation to change cannot take place through instincts. It has to take place through something other. It has to take place through something called awareness, motivation, free will, and ability to anticipate the future. Those are the properties, the faculties, that are so peculiarly human, that account for the phenomenal creativity of adventurous liberty, and adventurous liberty is something that is so uniquely human.

I have always liked that phrase of John Dewey's, "The brain is primarily the organ of a certain type of chosen behavior, not an organ of knowing the world." This is one of those peculiar statements by a philosopher that has to be repeated over and over again in order to grasp the full meaning of it. Our brain, of course, helps us to know the world, but we don't know it so well, we don't apprehend it so very much better than an animal. But certainly our brain permits us all sorts of freedom in behavior, and this is essentially the basis of adaptation, because choices and free will help to give a direction to the adaptive responses we make to new conditions and even to conditions that have not yet occurred, but which we anticipate for the future.

I am convinced that the great adaptive process that is happening in society today is that almost for the first time we are capable of anticipating to a certain extent, often to a very large extent, what are the difficulties we are going to experience in the next century. And we begin to adapt ourselves today. Our societies are beginning to change themselves today to adapt themselves to something that they have not yet experienced, but they will experience only in the 21st century.

To return to human life today, instead of accepting the wisdom of the body, which is blind, and in any case, is often at fault, because that wisdom evolved under conditions that were very different from the ones under which we live now, we must practice a wisdom based on judgment of modern conditions, and on anticipation of the future and anticipation of consequences.

Once more a few trivial examples. If one lives in a very noisy place, one can make a blind adaptation to it, the hearing apparatus will change in such a way that one does not hear the noise as much as if one had never been exposed to it. But that happens by impairment of hearing, so that one becomes adapted to noise by losing the ability to hear some of the most pleasant sounds including music and some qualities of the human voice. That is an adaptation through impairment. Obviously, although that adaptation can happen biologically, we don't want it, so our kind of adaptation must be one where we keep ourselves away from noise, or try to change the kind of equipment we use so that we do not have the noise.

Everybody knows that one can become adapted to air pollution, but this occurs through changes in our respiratory tracts, an increase in secretion of mucus from certain cells, and that certainly protects us from certain pollutants, but the consequence is that 20 years later we suffer from some chronic respiratory disease. So there again biological adaptation is no good; we must engage in some social adaptation, which is either to remove ourselves from the polluted environment, or more properly, to change our industrial structure so that we do not produce those objectionable pollutants.

Similarly, we can become adapted to all sorts of unpleasant situations, to unpleasant forms of crowding. One can spend one's life at the corner of Broadway and 42nd Street, and if one spends all one's life there one won't suffer from it. But one will not suffer from it because one develops all sorts of ways of shielding oneself from the rest of human beings, one adapts by impairing one's potentialities for human relationship, one adapts by impoverishing one's emotional life, and obviously we don't want that kind of adaptation, and therefore we must change something in our lives. In other words, we must make choices concerning environmental circumstances and life styles. We must seek conditions and activities that favor the development of certain functions and attitudes that we regard as desirable, and we must seek conditions that prevent the development of biological adaptative changes that we do not find desirable.

All those prophecies of self-healing, whether achieved through homeostatic recovery or adaptive change depend in the final analysis on some form of control over our internal environment. That kind of control can be exerted through many different mechanisms. Naturally, we can carry it out by changing the environment in which we live, because we know how the external environment inevitably affects the composition of bodily tissues and fluids. But much more interestingly, the mind can play a role in changing the internal environment, because the mind affects in a profound manner the hormonal and physiological mechanisms that control the nutrition and the operation of each and every one of the body's components.

In our medical research establishment there is beginning to be an awareness that something can be done about it. Something can be done about it because there are beginning to be some really good observations. Not so long ago one used the word hypnosis and saw people do some queer things. Students of hypnosis are beginning to demonstrate that people under hypnosis are able to bring about all sorts of very pointed changes—the vascular bed in a certain part, the temperature in another part. In other words, it is plainly obvious that hypnosis has demonstrated that we are capable of changing our internal environment.

In a final example, the secretion by the brain of endorphins and other endogenous opiates is affected by outside influences. This has consequences for our behavior that are fascinating for the future.

In conclusion, choices concerning ways of life and mental attitudes concerning life situations influence most phases of normal development, and they also influence all phenomena of re-education, using the word re-education as all those processes through which one attempts to correct disabilities either innate or resulting from accidents or other pathological processes. But the most important point is that development implies more than the passive unfolding of genetically coded characteristics. And similarly, re-education involves more than passive training of the patient. Both normal development and re-education require participation of the organism as a whole, integrated through volition in a truly curative process of adaptive change.

But I started by stating, which I believe, that certain persons are capable of exerting, by themselves, a very high level of control over their organic and mental functions, as well as over their social environment. In other words, we are capable of doing that, we can govern the adaptive processes that enable us to cope with threatening life situations.

But I know also that most of us, probably all of us, require help and guidance to achieve this kind of self-healing. Why do we require guidance and help? Because self-healing processes are not likely to operate well when we are under stress. It seems to me that the various therapeutic practices are successful to the extent that they reinforce the self-healing mechanisms through a large variety of techniques. Naturally, there would be the orthodox methods of scientific medicine. But also, those mechanisms of self-healing can be reinforced by the mental support provided by the presence of a trusted person, for example, a healer or a physician whom one trusts. They can also be reinforced by a whole social group, for example by a Navajo chant. Or they can be reinforced by faith in a certain kind of procedure in a religion.

This brings me to a point that I realize is incorporated in everything I say. What is health? It seems obvious, but nothing is more obscure. Health does not mean so much absence of disease as the ability to conduct one's life according to certain acceptable patterns, social patterns, individual patterns. And it happens that all forms of disease, organic or mental, reduce the ability of the patient to conduct life as the patient would like to conduct it, reduce the ability of the patient to reach the goal that the patient would formulate for himself. And this is a deprivation that really amounts to a loss of freedom, and anyone who has dealt a great deal with patients knows that that loss of freedom is one of the most tragic aspects of disease.

I believe this is where the healer can intervene. Healers can often do a great deal toward the restoration of this freedom, even when they cannot do anything about curing the disease. Healers can help patients by restoring that sense of freedom even when it is not possible to cure the disease. One can help the patient to overcome pain, to function in a more normal way, through drugs, prosthetic measures. And one can help the patient through advice, based not only on medical technologies, but also on knowledge of human nature and of the total environment.

So that to heal does not necessarily imply to cure. To heal may simply mean helping the patient to make curative adaptations to any kind of organic deficiencies. This caring as against curing aspect of medicine aims at rehabilitating patients by helping them to achieve a way of life that the patient finds tolerable and productive even in the presence of continuing disease.

·13·

The Wisdom of the Receptors: Neuropeptides, the Emotions, and Body-Mind

CANDACE B. PERT

In this talk, I am going to describe an array of fascinating, mostly new findings about the chemical substances in the body called neuropeptides. Based on these findings, I am going to suggest that neuropeptides and their receptors form an information network within the body. Perhaps this suggestion sounds fairly innocuous, but its implications are far reaching. I believe that neuropeptides and their receptors are a key to understanding how mind and body are interconnected and how emotions can be manifested throughout the body. Indeed, the more we know about neuropeptides, the harder it is to think in the traditional terms of a mind and a body. It makes more and more sense to speak of a single integrated entity, a "body-mind."

Most of what I will describe are laboratory findings, hard science. But it is important to recall that the scientific study of psychology traditionally focuses on animal learning and cognition. This means that if you look in the index of recent textbooks on psychology, you are not likely to find "consciousness," "mind," or even "emotions." These subjects are basically not in the realm of traditional experimental psychology, which primarily studies behavior because it can be seen and measured. What goes on in the so-called black box of the brain/mind, B. F. Skinner has maintained, is not something to be speculated about. It cannot be observed, and so its study is not hard science.

This chapter originally appeared in *Advances*, 1986, 3(3), 8–16. It is reprinted here with permission from the Institute for the Advancement of Health.

One of the things I can report today is that the realm of laboratory research has widened enormously. My findings come from the domain of hard science, and I believe they are directly relevant to the comprehension of emotions and even open a window into the black box of the mind.

THE SPECIFICITY OF RECEPTORS

Now, there is one area where mind—at least consciousness—has been objectively studied for perhaps 20 years as a part of psychology, and that is the area of psychopharmacology. People have thought of highly rigorous ways to measure the effects of drugs and altered states of consciousness.

Pharmacology evolved talking about how no drug acts unless it is fixed—that is, somehow gets attached to the brain—and people imagined hypothetical tissue constituents that they called receptors. In this way, the notion of specific receptors became a central theory in pharmacology. It is a very old idea. In the past several years, the critical development for the study of receptors has been the invention of new technologies for actually binding drugs to these molecules and for studying both their distribution in the brain and body and their actual molecular structure.

My initial work in this area was in the laboratory of Solomon Snyder at Johns Hopkins, and we focused our attention on opium, a drug that obviously alters consciousness and that also is used medicinally, to alleviate pain. I worked long and hard, over many months of failure, to develop a technical system for measuring the material in the brain with which opium interacts to produce its effects. To make a long (and technical) story short, we used radioactive drug molecules, and with this technology were able to identify the receptor element in the brain. You can imagine a molecule of opium attaching itself to a receptor much as a key fits into a lock—and then from this small connection, large changes follow.

It next turned out that the whole class of drugs to which opium belongs—they are called opiates, as you probably know, and they include morphine, codeine, and heroin, as well as opium—attach to the *same* receptors. Further, we discovered that the receptors were scattered throughout not only the brain but also the body.

I might mention that each opiate is slightly different in its shape and binds more or less tightly to the receptor molecules. For instance, the reason a person does not get the tremendous rush from codeine that comes with heroin is that heroin has blobs of molecular matter that allow it to course into the brain while codeine first has to be transformed into morphine in the liver. Morphine, for its part, penetrates the brain, where euphoria receptors are located, very poorly.

After finding the receptor for the external opiates, our thinking took another step. If the brain and the other parts of the body have a receptor for something taken into the body—called an exogenous ligand—it makes sense to suppose that something produced inside the body—an endogenous ligand—also fits the receptor. Otherwise, why would the receptor be there? This perspective ultimately led to the identification of the brain's own form of opiates—or, rather, one of them. This is a chemical substance called beta endorphin. With beta endorphin we come to the first of the neuropeptides— which are simply peptide structures produced by nerve cells in the brain. Beta endorphin is created in nerve cells; it chemically consists of peptides, so it is a neuropeptide.

Perhaps I should explain that peptides are strings of amino acids, and as you know, there are sixteen amino acids and everything in the body is made out of these sixteen amino acids strung out and arranged in different sequences. You can think of the amino acids as 16 different colored beads, which provide an almost infinite number of sequences. Different sequences produce different chemicals, some of which are neuropeptides.

In the case of beta endorphin, we now know its precise sequence of amino acids. I want to mention in passing that beta endorphin is found in very large quantities in the human pituitary gland, which of course is part of the brain, and recently it has been shown to be in the gonads as well. Brain and body. We will come back to this point later.

Now, it is quite exciting that the endogenous ligands for the opiate receptors turned out to be peptides because peptides come directly from the DNA. There is no enzyme in between; they grow directly off the DNA, which stores the information to make our brains and bodies.

If you picture an ordinary nerve cell, you can visualize the general mechanism. In the center (as in any cell) is the DNA, and a direct printout of the DNA leads to the production of a neuropeptide, which then traverses down the axons of the nerve cell to be stored in little balls at the end waiting for the right electro-physical events that will release it. The DNA also has the information that codes for the receptors, which are made out of the same peptide material but are much bigger. Beta endorphin has 30 amino acids, but the opiate receptor for it turns out to have about 20,000 amino acids.

What has to be added to this picture is the fact that 50 to 60 neuropeptides have been identified, each of them as specific as the beta endorphin neuropeptide. In other words, the DNA produces all these neuropeptides, which all traverse down axons and all wait for the right electro-physical events. We have here an enormously complex system which is kept straight by the high specificity of the neuropeptides and their receptors.

Until quite recently, it had been thought that the information in the nervous system was distributed across the gap between two nerve cells called synapses. We all learned about synapses in high school biology. The notion was that one nerve cell communicated to another across a synapse, which meant that the proximity of the nerve cells determined what could be communicated. Now we realize that synapses are not as important as we thought. They help control some kinds of information flow, particularly muscle contraction. But the largest portion of information coming from the brain is kept straight not by the close physical juxtaposition of nerve cells, but by the specificity of the receptors. What was thought of as a highly rigid linear system appears to be one with far more complex patterns of distribution.

When a nerve cell squirts out opiate peptides, the peptides can act "miles" away at other nerve cells. The same is true of all neuropeptides. At any given moment, many neuropeptides may be floating along within the body, and what enables them to attach to the correct receptor molecules is, to repeat, the specificity of the receptors. Thus, the receptors serve as the mechanism that sorts out the information exchange in the body.

THE BIOCHEMISTRY OF THE EMOTIONS

What is this leading up to? To something very intriguing—the notion that the receptors for the neuropeptides are in fact the keys to the biochemistry of emotion. In the last 2 years, the workers in my lab have formalized this idea in a number of theoretical papers (Pert, Ruff, Weber, & Herkenham, 1985; see also Pert, 1985; Schmitt, 1984), and I am going to review briefly the evidence to support it.

I should say that some scientists might describe this idea as outrageous. It is not, in other words, part of the established wisdom. Indeed, coming from a tradition where the textbooks do not even contain the word "emotions" in the index, it was not without a little trepidation that we dared to start talking about the biochemical substrate of emotions.

I will begin by noting a fact that neuroscientists have agreed on for a long time: that emotions are mediated by the limbic system of the brain. The limbic system refers to a section of neuroanatomical parts of the brain which include the hypothalamus (which controls the homeostatic mechanisms of the body and is sometimes called the "brain" of the brain), the pituitary gland (which regulates the hormones in the body), and the amygdala. We will be talking mostly about the hypothalamus and the amygdala.

The experiments showing the connection between emotions and the limbic system were first done by Wilder Penfield and other neurologists who worked with conscious, awake individuals. The neurologists found that when they used electrodes to stimulate the cortex over the amygdala they could evoke a whole gamut of emotional displays—powerful reactions of grief, of pain, of pleasure associated with profound memories, and also the total somatic accompaniment of emotional states. The limbic system was first identified, then, by psychological experiments.

Now when we began to map the location of opiate receptors in the brain—by a method involving radioactive molecules, whose density, as they accumulate in the opiate receptors in different spots of the brain, can be transformed into a quantitative color scale—we found that the limbic system was highly enriched with opiate receptors (and with other receptors too we eventually learned). The amygdala and the hypothalamus, both classically considered to be the main components of the limbic system (the great physiologist, Walter B. Cannon, singled out the hypothalamus as the foremost area for emotions to hook up to the brain), are in fact blazing with opiate receptors—40-fold higher than in other areas in the brain. These hot spots correspond to very specific nuclei or cellular groups that physiological psychologists have identified as mediating such processes as sexual behavior, appetite, and water balance in the body. The main point is that our receptor-mapping confirmed and expanded in important ways the psychological experiments that defined the limbic system.

Let me backtrack a moment and bring in some other neuropeptides. I have already noted that 50 to 60 substances are now considered to be neuropeptides. Where do they come from? Many of them are the natural analogs of psychoactive drugs. But another major source—very unexpected—is hormones. Hormones historically have been conceived of as being produced by glands—in other words, not by nerve cells. A hormone presumably was stored in one place in the body, then travelled over to its receptors in other parts of the body. The prime hormone is insulin, which is secreted in the pancreas. But, now, it turns out that insulin is not just a hormone. In fact, insulin is a neuropeptide, made and stored in the brain, and there are insulin receptors in the brain. When we map insulin, we again find hot spots in the amygdala and hypothalamus. In short, it has become increasingly clear that the limbic system, the seat of emotions in the brain, is also the focal point of receptors for neuropeptides.

Another critical point: As we have studied the distribution of these receptors, we have found that the limbic system is not just in the forebrain, in the classical locations of the amygdala and the hypothalamus. It appears that the body has other places in which many different neuropeptide receptors are located—places where there is a lot of chemical action. We call these spots nodal points, and they are anatomically located at places that receive a lot of emotional modulation. On nodal point is the dorsal (back) horn of the spinal cord, which is the spot where sensory information comes in. This is the first synapse within the brain where touch–sensory information is processed. We have found that for virtually all the senses for which we know the entry area, the spot is always a nodal point for neuropeptide receptors.

I believe these findings have amazing implications for understanding and appreciating what emotions do and what they are about. Consider the chemical substance angiotensin, another classic hormone that is also a peptide and now shown to be a neuropeptide. When we map for angiotensin receptors in the brain, we again find little hot spots in the amygdala. It has long been known that angiotensin mediates thirst, so if one implants a tube in the area of a rat's brain that is rich with angiotensin receptors and drops a little angiotensin down the tube, within 10 seconds, the rat will start to drink water, even if it is totally sated with water. Chemically speaking, angiotensin translates as an altered state of consciousness, a state that makes animals (and humans) say, "I want water." In other words, neuropeptides bring us to states of consciousness and to alterations in those states.

To list another example, we have in the laboratory mapped the receptors for PCP (commonly referred to as "angel dust"), a drug of abuse that induces an altered state of consciousness. Using radioactive PCP, we have shown that the receptors tend to be in the brain cortex, and with rats as our subjects, we have been able to determine (using the technique of operant animal behavior) that we are in fact measuring the peptide molecules of PCP that are responsible for an altered state of consciousness.

Equally important is the fact that neuropeptide receptors are not just in the brain, they are also in the body. We have mapped and shown biochemically that there are angiotensin receptors in the kidney identical to those in the brain, and in a way that is not yet quite understood, the kidney-located receptors conserve water. We know that they play with the ion fluxes so that water is conserved. The point is that the release of the neuropeptide angiotensin leads both to the behavior of drinking and to the internal conservation of water. Here is an example of how a neuropeptide—which perhaps corresponds to a mood state—can integrate what happens in the body with what happens in the brain. (A further important point that I only mention here is that overall integration of behavior seems designed to be consistent with survival.)

My basic speculation here is that neuropeptides provide the physiological basis for the emotions. As my colleagues and I argued in a recent paper in the Journal of Immunology (Pert et al., 1985): The striking pattern of neuropeptide receptor distribution in mood-regulating areas of brain, as well as their role in mediating communication throughout the whole organism, makes neuropeptides the obvious candidates for the biochemical mediation of emotion. It may be too that each neuropeptide biases information processing uniquely when occupying receptors at nodal points with the brain and body. If so, then each neuropeptide may evoke a unique "tone" that is equivalent to a mood state.

In the beginning of my work, I matter-of-factly presumed that emotions were in the head or the brain. Now I would say they are really in the body as well. They are expressed in the body and are part of the body. I can no longer make a strong distinction between the brain and the body.

COMMUNICATING WITH THE IMMUNE SYSTEM

I now want to bring the immune system into this picture. I have already explained that the hormone system, which historically has been studied as being separate from the brain, is conceptually the same thing as the nervous system. Pockets of juices are released and diffuse very far away, acting via the specificity of receptors at sites far from where the juices are stored. So, endocrinology and neuroscience are two aspects of the same process. Now I am going to maintain that immunology is also part of this conceptual system and should not be considered a separate discipline.

A key property of the immune system is that its cells move. The brain of course is stable. It stays in one place. The cells of the immune system—although they are identical to the cells of the brain with their little nuclei, their cell membranes, and all of their receptors—move around. Monocytes, for example, which ingest foreign organisms, start life in your bone marrow, and they then diffuse out and travel through your veins and arteries, and decide where to go by following chemical cues. A monocyte travels along in the blood and at some point comes within "scenting" distance of a neuropeptide, and because the monocyte has receptors for that neuropeptide on its cell surface, it begins literally to chemotax, or crawl, toward that chemical. This is very well documented, and there are excellent ways of studying it in the laboratory.

Now, monocytes are responsible not just for recognizing and digesting foreign bodies but also for wound healing and tissue-repair mechanisms. For example, they have enzymes that produce and degrade collagen, an important structural material out of which the body is made. What we are talking about, then, are cells with vital, health-sustaining functions.

The new discovery I want to emphasize here is that *every* neuropeptide receptor that we have looked for (using an elegant and precise system developed by my colleague Michael Ruff) is also on human monocytes. Human monocytes have receptors for opiates, for PCP, for another peptide called bombasin, and so on. These emotion-affecting biochemicals actually appear to control the routing and migration of monocytes, which are so pivotal in the immune system. They communicate with B-cells and T-cells, interact in the whole system to fight disease and to distinguish between self and nonself, deciding, say, which part of the body is a tumor cell to be killed by natural killer cells, and which parts need to be restored. I hope the picture is clear to you. A monocyte is circulating—this health-sustaining element of the immune system is traveling in the blood—and then the presence of an opiate pulls it over, and it can connect with the neuropeptide because it has the receptor to do so. It has, in fact, many different receptors for different neuropeptides.

It turns out, moreover, that the cells of the immune system not only have receptors for these various neuropeptides, as is becoming clear, they also make the neuropeptides themselves. There are subsets of immune cells that make beta endorphins, for example, and the other opiate peptides. In other words, they are making the same chemicals that we conceive of as controlling mood in the brain. They control the tissue integrity of the body, and they also make chemicals that control mood. Once again, brain and body.

I want to emphasize the point that the same receptors are in the brain and in the immune system. CCK, another neuropeptide, was first sequenced and discovered by its action on the gut. In the pharmacological beginnings of the search for receptors, people would string up gut muscles in organ baths and study their contractions. Since the gut contained functional receptors, it was used to isolate and determine the chemical structures of the bioactivity in tissue extracts. It turns out the CCK is highly involved with food satiety. Doses of CCK make you not want to eat any more. We have recently shown that the brain and the spleen—which can be described as the brain of the immune system—contain receptors for CCK. So brain, gut, and immune system can all be affected by CCK.

What do these kinds of connections between brain and body mean? Ordinarily they are referred to as "the power of the mind over the body." As far as I am concerned, that phrase does not describe what we are talking about here. The body in these experiments is the outward manifestation of the mind. I would go further. When we document the key role that the emotions, expressed through neuropeptide molecules, play in affecting the body, it will become clear how emotions can be a key to the understanding of disease.

I want to expand on this speculation by returning to the example of the gut. The entire lining of the intestine, from the esophagus through the large intestine is lined with cells—nerve cells and other kinds of cells—that contain neuropeptides and neuropeptide receptors. It seems entirely possible to me that the richness of the receptors may be why a lot of people feel their emotions in their gut—why they have a "gut feeling."

We are all aware of the bias built into the Western idea that consciousness is totally in the head. I believe the research findings I have described indicate that we need to start thinking about how consciousness can be projected into various parts of the body. Unfortunately, people who think about these things do not usually work in a government laboratory.

Let me summarize the basic idea I have been developing. My argument is that the three classic areas of neuroscience, endocrinology, and immunology, with their various organs—the brain (which is the key organ that the neuroscientists study), the glands, and the immune system (consisting of the spleen, the bone marrow, the lymph nodes, and of course the cells circulating through the body)—that these three areas are actually joined to each other in a bidirectional network of communication and that the information "carriers" are the neuropeptides. There are well-studied physiological substrates showing that communication exists in both directions for every single one of these areas and their organs. Some of the research is old, some of it is new. We now know, for example, that peptide-producing neurons come from the brain and actually innervate the bone marrow.

The word I would stress in regard to this integrated system is "network," which comes from information theory. What we have been talking about all along is information. In thinking about these matters, then, it might make more sense to emphasize the perspective of psychology rather than of neuroscience. For "psycho" clearly conveys the study of mind, and perhaps mind is the information flowing among all of these bodily parts, and that may be what mind is. A mind is composed of information, and it has a physical substrate, which is the body and the brain, and it also has another immaterial substrate that has to do with information flowing around. Maybe mind is what holds the network together.

THE UNITY OF THE VARIETY

The last point I am going to make about the neuropeptides is an astounding one I think.

As we have seen, neuropeptides are signalling molecules. They send messages all over the body (including the brain). Of course, to have such a communications network, you need components that can talk to each other and listen to each other. In the situation we are discussing here, the components that "talk" are the neuropeptides, and the components that "hear" are the neuropeptide receptors. How can this be? How can 50 to 60 neuropeptides be produced, float around, and talk to 50 or 60 types of listening receptors that are on a variety of cells? Why does order rather than chaos reign?

The finding I am going to discuss is not totally accepted, but our experiments show that it is true. I have not published it yet, but I think that it is only a matter of time before everybody can confirm these observations.

There are thousands of scientists studying the opiate receptors and the opiate peptides, and they see great heterogeneity in the receptors. They have given a series of Greek names to the apparent heterogeneity. However, all the evidence from our lab suggests that in fact *there is actually only one type of molecule in the opiate receptors, one long polypeptide chain whose formula you can write*. This molecule is quite capable of changing its conformation within its membrane so that it can assume a number of shapes.

I note in passing that this interconversion can occur at a very rapid pace—so rapid that it is hard to tell whether it is one state or another at a given moment in time. In other words, receptors have both a wave-like and a particulate character, and it is important to note that information can be stored in the form of time spent in different states.

As I said, the molecular unity of the receptors is quite amazing. Consider the tetrahymena, a protozoan that is one of the simplest organisms. Despite its simplicity, the tetrahymena can do almost everything we can do—it can eat, have sex, and of course it makes the same neuropeptide components that I have been talking about. The tetrahymena makes insulin. It makes beta endorphins. We have taken tetrahymena membranes and in particular studied the opiate receptor molecules on them, and we have studied the opiate receptor in rat brains and on human monocytes. Receptors, as you know, are proteins consisting of a long sequence of amino acids, but the chain is all twisted up because of electrical and physical forces that cause it to assume a shape. It is possible to take receptors out of the membrane and put them in detergent, which takes away their tertiary structure—that is, makes them a straight line—and then you can determine their molecular weight and characteristics (by running them in an electrical field). Having done this for opiate receptors, we believe that we have shown that the molecular substance of *all* opiate receptors is the same. The actual molecule of the rat brain opiate receptor is identical to the human brain opiate receptor and is also identical to the opiate receptor components in that simplest of animals, the tetrahymena. I hope the force of this is clear. The opiate receptor in my brain and in your brains is, at root, made of the same molecular substance as the tetrahymena's.

This finding gets to the simplicity and the unity of life. It is comparable to the four DNA-based pairs that code for the production of all the proteins, which are the physical substrates of life. We now know that in this physical substrate there are only 60 or so signal molecules, the neuropetides, that account for the physiological manifestation of emotions—for enlivening emotions, if you will, or perhaps better yet, for flowing energy. The protozoan form of the tetrahymena indicates that the receptor molecules do not become more complex as an organism becomes more complex. The identical molecular components for information flow are conserved throughout evolution. The whole system is simple, elegant, and it may very well be complete.

IS THE MIND IN THE BRAIN?

We have been talking about mind, and the question arises: Where is it? In our own work, consciousness has come up in the context of studying pain and the role of opiate receptors and endorphins in modulating pain.

A lot of labs are measuring pain, and we would all agree that the area called periaqueductal gray, located around the third ventricle of the brain, is filled with opiate receptors, making it a kind of control area for pain. We have found that the periaqueductal gray is also loaded with receptors for virtually all the neuropeptides that have been studied.

Now, everyone knows that there are yogis who can train themselves so that they do or do not perceive pain, depending on how they structure their experience. There are other people, called mothers, who have done the same thing. What seems to be going on is that these sort of people are able to plug into their periaqueductal gray. Somehow they gain access to it—with their consciousness, I believe—and set pain thresholds. Note what is going on here. In these situations, a person has an experience that brings with it pain, but a part of the person consciously does something so that the pain is not felt. Where is this consciousness coming from—this conscious I that somehow plugs into the periaqueductal gray so that he or she does not feel a thing?

I want to go back to the idea of a network. A network is different from a hierarchical structure, which has one top place. You theoretically can plug into a network at any point and get to any other point. A concept like this seems to me valuable in thinking about the processes by which a consciousness can manage to reach the periaqueductal gray and use it to control pain.

The yogi and the laboring woman both use a similar technique to control pain, breathing. Athletes use it, too. Breathing is extremely powerful. I suggest that there is a physical substrate for these phenomena, the brainstem nuclei. I would say that we now must include the brainstem nuclei in the limbic system because they are nodal points, thickly encrusted with neuropeptide receptors and neuropeptides. The idea, then, goes like this: breathing has a physical substrate that is also a nodal point, this nodal point is part of an information network in which each part leads to all the other parts, and so, from the nodal points of the brainstem nuclei, the consciousness can, among other things, plug into the periaqueductal gray.

I think it is possible now to conceive of mind and consciousness as an emanation of emotional information processing, and as such, mind and consciousness would appear to be independent of brain and body. One little hint about how the mind might send its information through the brain and body is suggested by another astounding fact. It is well established in experimental work that some of the monocytes, which rise in the bone marrow and circulate around, actually enter the brain and are transformed and become glial cells. What are glial cells? They have been generally ignored by neuroscientists. They are ten times more plentiful in the brain than nerve cells. People say, "They're nutritive," or "They clean up." They have not been studied much because they do not have measurable electrical properties. (A lot of neuroscience has been based on the ability to measure electrical epiphenomena.) It is possible that glial cells have the potential to be pro-grammed in the brain and under the appropriate cues to leave the brain and go out into the body. Also, there is a precedent for monocyte-like cells, which contain information about the state of the body, to take up residence in—and talk directly to—the brain. Perhaps that is one mechanism of action by which the mind and body intercommunicate.

One last speculation, an outrageous one perhaps, but on the theme I was asked to consider for this symposium on "Survival and Consciousness." Can the mind survive the death of the physical brain? Perhaps here we have to recall how mathematics suggests that physical entities can suddenly collapse or infinitely expand. I think it is important to realize that information is stored in the brain, and it is conceivable to me that this information could transform itself into some other realm. The DNA molecules surely have the information that makes the brain and body, and the bodymind seems to share the information moleucles that enliven the organism. Where does the information go after the destruction of the molecules (the mass) that com-pose it? Matter can neither be created nor destroyed, and perhaps biological information flow cannot just disappear at death and be transformed into another realm. Who can rationally say "impossible"? No one has yet mathe-matically unified gravitational field theory with matter and energy. The mathematics of consciousness have not even been approached. The nature of the hypothetical "other realm" is currently in the religious or mystical dimension, where Western science is clearly forbidden to tread.

REFERENCES

Pert, C. B (1985). *Cybernetics, 1*, 1.
Pert, C. B., Ruff, M. R., Weber, R. J., & Herkenham, M. (1985). Neuropeptides and their receptors: A psychosomatic network. *Journal of Immunology, 35*, 2.
Schmitt, F. O. (1984). Molecular regulation of brain function: A new view. *Neuroscience, 13*, 991.

·14·

Possible Mechanisms of Psychoneuroimmunological Interaction

RUTH LLOYD

> There is no pure sorrow. Why? It is bedfellow to lungs, lights, bones, guts, and gall!
>
> DJUNA BARNES, *NIGHTWOOD*, 1937.

The biopsychosocial model of disease, as we currently understand it, has developed from two premises. The first premise holds that the healthful state in human beings is one of continuously adaptive homeostasis. The second premise, following logically from the first, proposes that habitually inappropriate emotional response to perceived stress, particularly when accompanied by potentially harmful physiological habit patterns, disrupts homeostatic balance, and so operates as an active agent in disease susceptibility. The model is an acknowledgment that emotion and subjective state can have an impelling influence on the psychological infrastructure of an individual, and is supported by an enormous body of research on the symptomatology of various diseases and on the life circumstances surrounding disease onset, exacerbation, and remission (Fox 1981; Levy, 1982; Weiner, Hofer, & Stunkard, 1980).

Most important, the model leads us, by inference, to ask *how* psychogenic stress can so alter physiological homeostasis over time that normal

This chapter originally appeared in *Advances*, 1984, *1*(2), 42–51. It is reprinted here with permission from the Institute for the Advancement of Health.

immunological response to pathogen is either compromised or altogether undermined (Weiner, 1977). When we frame the question in this way, we are asking whether the immune system itself may not be an element in what has been termed the "transducer chain" of events connecting conscious experience to the endocrine and neurochemical processes of the body (Bergmann et al., 1969). In other words, is it not reasonable to propose that the generally flawless communication network of immune effector cells fulfills an auxilliary role in transduction, or psychophysiological encoding, thereby abetting the process by which neuronal impulse translates into bloodborne hormonal discharge linking brain and peripheral organ, emotion and endocrine effect? By implication, we are asking whether the immune system is not also involved in adaptive response and in the protection of internal equilibrium.

I will explore this question of interconnection between brain, psyche, and immune mechanisms in three different ways, each approach necessarily providing only a partial answer. To begin, I will give examples of the interaction of nervous, endocrine, and immune systems, with emphasis on new data that are revealing functional overlap among these systems. Secondly, I will seek to illustrate ways in which brain chemistry, the secretory products of endocrine glands, and the activated constituents of the immune system complement and counteract one another in the behaving, adapting organism. To do so, I will cite studies that are providing an important new dimension to immunological research by documenting the potent influence of psychoendocrine factors on immune function in both humans and experimental animals. Thirdly, and as a logical extension of this last point, I will review a number of immune conditioning studies that may well have touched upon the underlying psychoneuroimmunological linkage in adaptation and also may have offered a promising experimental paradigm for examining the integration of systems and analyzing their interlocking segments. I will end with some speculations on what possible relevance the structural modification of sensory neurons (occurring as a result of sensitization, associative learning, etc.) might have to the immune system's capacity to be conditioned.

THE NERVOUS, NEUROENDOCRINE, AND IMMUNE SYSTEMS ARE ALL LINKED: BASIC FINDINGS

It is germane to my central thesis to mention, at the outset, the remarkable evolution of investigative technique in brain research, beginning with the axon degeneration studies (Navta & Gygax, 1954) and histochemical fluorometric and electomicroscopic work carried out in the 50s and 60s (Andén,

Dahlström, Fuxe, Larsson, & Olson, 1966; Falck & Hillarp, 1959), which has made possible the definition of a number of neurotransmitter systems in the brain, each originating from a relatively small number of neurons, each characterized by an extensive fiber distribution. Concurrently, the amino acid, monoamine, and cholinergic transmitter substances released from these fiber terminals—substances essential to neuronal activity—have been purified and chemically characterized.

More recently, the neuropolypeptides have been shown to represent still another idiosyncratic system of molecular organization in both the brain and body periphery, one that acts as the source for a number of potent "enabling" neurohormones (Kreiger, 1983; Kreiger & Martin, 1981a, 1981b). These substances include the hypothalamic releasing hormones, the pituitary tropic hormones, and a family of peptides, some of whose activities have particular relevance to this discussion—namely corticotropin (ACTH), α-melanocyte-stimulating hormone, β-lipotropin, and the opioid peptides, the enkephalins and endorphins.

The identification of the fine structure and pharmacology of central effector fiber tracts has been an impressive accomplishment in itself. Of particular interest, however, are recent findings that point to previously unsuspected anatomical, bioelectric, and biochemical relationships between and within the neuronal and neuropeptidergic systems. For example, the neurotransmitter serotonin and the polypeptide transmitter, substance P, have been found to occupy the same raphe neurons in the brain-stem medulla (Björkland, Emson, Gilber, & Skagerberg, 1979), a pairing that may reflect a general condition in the central nervous system (Hökfelt et al., 1980). Moreover, a recent report of combined serotoninergic and opioid peptide mediation of distress vocalization in experimental animals (Olivier & Bradford, 1983) suggests that pairings of this kind are also functional.

In the discussion of thymic peptides that is to follow, it is also important to keep in mind that a given neurotransmitter can perform as neurohormone, a neurohormone as neurotransmitter, and either as neuromodulator (Siggins, 1979), depending upon such factors as (1) the locus, speed, and duration of a given substance's biological action; (2) the intrinsic spontaneous activity and environmental matrix of the effector cell; and (3) the stable and dynamic characteristics of receptor sites (Baker, 1977; Rotsztejn, 1980). With regard to the polypeptides, investigators have maintained that "a particular peptide may exercise different effects at different sites by different mechanisms, doubtless in response to different stimuli" (Defendini & Zimmerman, 1978) and that the "cellular source of the peptide, the receptive cell and its receptor class, and . . . the manner of transmittal between the source and the response site" (Koob, Le Moal, & Bloom, 1981) are all to be considered critical variables in determining its biological role.

New research in immunochemistry now impels us to introduce still more complexity into the picture by calling attention to data demonstrating the neuromodulatory capability of the immune system. However, it would be well, by way of preamble, to take note of various sorts of evidence supporting the idea that the immune system is under a degree of central and peripheral neural control. First, transmitter- and peptide-specific binding sites (receptors) are present on the surface membranes of lymphocytes and accessory phagocytic leukocytes (Lopker, Abood, Hoss, & Lionetti, 1980; Maslincki, Grabozewska, & Ryzewski, 1980). Second, there is ample evidence that three principal structures of the immune system, the thymus gland, lymph nodes, and spleen, are innervated by the autonomic nervous system (Felten, Overhage, Felten, & Schmedtje, 1981; Felten, Malone, Madura, & Felten, 1983; Giron, Crutcher, & Davis, 1980; Sergeeva, 1974; Williams et al., 1981). Third, a preganglionic cholinergic pathway has been delineated from brainstem nuclei and spinal cord neurons to the thymus gland (Bulloch & Moore, 1981). And fourth, there have been a number of studies showing that lesions, ablation, and electrical stimulation of the hypothalamus can both activate (Dann, Wachtel, & Rubin, 1979) and (more commonly) suppress immune function (Cross, Markesbery, Brooks, & Roszman, 1980; Spector & Korneva, 1981; Stein, Schleifer, & Keller, 1981).

Now let us consider evidence for the converse: namely, that the immune system directly influences the activity of a critical neuroendocrine circuit involving the hypothalamus, pituitary, and adrenal glands. This influence appears to derive from the thymic peptides. Studies show the following: (1) thymosin β_4 (Hannappel, Xu, & Morgan, 1982) and thymosin α_1 (two components of the heterogeneous peptide preparation, thymosin fraction 5) are present in the brain, extensive thymosin α_1-like immunoreactivity having been detected in the tuberal region of the hypothalamus (specifically, in the arcuate nucleus and median eminence) (Hall et al., 1982); (2) thymosin β_4 will elicit the release of luteinizing hormone-releasing hormone from medial basal hypothalamic tissue, in vitro (Rebar, Miyake, Low, & Goldstein, 1981); (3) injection of thymic polypeptides into the cerebral ventricles can have marked effect upon the pituitary axis (when so injected in chronically cannulated mice, thymosin$_4$ will bring about a significant increase in luteinizing hormone serum levels (Hall et al., 1982), and thymosin$_1$ will stimulate increases in serum corticosterone [Hall, McGillis, & Goldstein, 1984]); (4) in prepubertal primates, intravenously administered doses of thymosin fraction 5 (but neither thymosin α_1 nor thymosin β_4) have been shown to elevate endogenous plasma levels of ACTH, β-endorphin, and cortisol (Healy et al., 1984). The point to emphasize with regard to the latter finding is that a corticotropin-releasing factor-like peptide may reside within the thymus itself, and may participate in the hypothalamic feedback-mediated control of pituitary ACTH secretion (Healy et al., 1984).

These findings, taken as a whole, indicate that thymic peptides, in a manner similar to the neuropeptides (Krieger, 1983), are capable of an indirect, facilitative (or inhibitory) role in neurotransmission by either amplifying or dampening synaptic events. The following two observations in support of this argument also point to their possible mode of action: first, the dendritic membranes of central neurons have been shown to be permeable to such small molecules as enzymes, nucleotides, amino acids, and glycoproteins (Griepp & Revel, 1977; Peracchin, 1977) (most secretory proteins, including the thymic peptides, are glycoproteins); second, neuropeptidergic systems have been shown to have the capability of utilizing local circuitry (Barker, Neale, Smith, & McDonald, 1978)—a special mode of cell-to-cell communication characterized by the relatively slow transmittal of graded, low-voltage electrotonic potentials across various membranous affiliations (including desmosomes, reciprocal synapses, unidirectional and bidirectional gap junctions) (Schmitt, Dev, & Smith, 1976; Sotelo, 1977). Conversely, given the proved junctional permability of the lymphocyte (Oliveira-Castro & Dos Reis, 1977; Resch, 1976), it is possible that this particular mode of stimulus transmittal might contribute to the neuroendocrine mediation of immune function.

In view of the close functional, as well as structural, associations that are seen to exist among the immune, neuroendocrine, and nervous systems, it would seem useful, at this point, to introduce a kind of organizing principle that might lend additional support to the proposition that these systems are in active relationship and that brain and psyche do in fact influence immune efficacy. It is an axiom in biology that the central source of efferent hormonal tropism is, in turn, modulated by peripheral end-organ hormone inhibitory feedback. Whereas this axiom may not apply to immune system responsivity in the conventional sense, it is nevertheless reasonable to surmise that the synthesis of thymic hormones is also feedback-controlled. In other words, it is not beyond the realm of possibility that a long-loop feedback connection exists between the brain and the primary and secondary tissues of immunity. In truth, there is speculation in the literature that primary, secondary, and even tertiary levels of feedback most probably do exist.

One such internal regulatory circuit has recently been suggested by experiments that have succeeded in demonstrating an afferent link between peripheral sites of humorally mediated (B cell-mediated) acute inflammatory response and specific nuclei in the hypothalamus (Besedovsky, Sorkin, Felix, & Haas, 1977). It has also been shown that a peripheral inflammatory response will increase the turnover rate of the neurotransmitter norepinephrine in the hypothalamus (Besedovsky et al., 1983), and that the injection of lymphokine-containing supernatant obtained from mitogen-activated rat spleen cells and human peripheral blood leukocytes will elicit two- to threefold increases in circulating corticosterone levels in the rat (Besedovsky,

Del Rey, & Sorkin, 1981). This finding indicates that by stimulating the production of an adrenal steroid, a soluble protein factor released by sensitized T (thymus-derived) lymphocytes can mimic the role of a tropic, feedback-controlled pituitary hormone (ACTH).

It is apparent, therefore that immunologic signals are not only transmitted to the adrenal gland and brain from distant tissue loci, but that these same signals are also capable of eliciting central nervous system activity, perhaps even capable of initiating a condition of positive feedback. As the authors of the above three studies have put it: "the immune system may . . . act as a peripheral receptor organ" for information relating to the "intrusion of antigenic macromolecules or modified self-antigens" (Besedovsky et al., 1983).

SYSTEMS INTERACT IN RESPONSE TO ENVIRONMENTAL STRESSORS: BEHAVIORAL STUDIES

With the foregoing material as background, I would like to turn now to a number of studies that appear to have presented unequivocal evidence that both disease susceptibility and the genesis of health are, to a considerable extent, affected by the social milieu, by the *symbolic* climate of everyday life. It will be seen, for example, that an organism's adaptive resources are dependent, in large part, upon its perception of control over environmental challenge, or threat; that loss of such control can represent a significant stressor; and that this particular experience of stress is likely to be associated with reduced immune competence.

The point that I will want to emphasize in this part of the discussion is that immunological response appears to be a silent partner in the psychoneuroendocrine reaction patterns that are known to characterize the stress response—a response, or set of responses, now documented in countless multidisciplinary studies. Preliminary research, of the sort that I will cite, suggests that immunological response is an inseverable part of these patterns and that, whenever possible, studies on the interplay of psyche and soma should necessarily and routinely include the monitoring of immunologic function.

It has been shown, for example, that unsatisfactory adjustment to "life-change stress" in young adults is directly correlated with significantly reduced activity of the immune system's natural killer (NK) cells (Locke & Kraus, 1982), which carry tumor and immunoglobulin (IgG)-specific receptors on their surface membranes. The immunological impact of this type of stressor has also been demonstrated in studies of immune function in the bereaved: for example, widowers show an immune suppression (as evaluated by T and B lymphocyte response to mitogen test) that may persist for as long as 2 months following initial bereavement (Schleifer, Keller, Camerino, Thornton, & Stein, 1983). In a third example taken from animal research, infant monkeys will show depressed cellular (T cell-mediated) immunity during and immediately following mother–infant and peer separation (Reite, Harbeck, & Hoffman, 1981).

The issue of subjective, psychological influence on immune system response has been more directly addressed in animal research that has documented an inverse relationship between degrees of coping and tumor susceptibility. In the "yoked" testing procedure, for example, in which both animal subjects receive identical electric shocks, adult male rats, subjected to random and inescapable shock, have been found to have a much-reduced capacity to reject tumor cell implantation (Visintainer, Volpicelli, & Seligman, 1982), and to show more rapid and exaggerated tumor development and reduced survival rate (Sklar & Anisman, 1981), compared with those animals given control over shock delivery. (In view of these data, it is not surprising that inescapable shock should also have been found to suppress cellular immune responsivity, as evaluated in vitro by mitogen assay [Lauderslager, Ryan, Drygan, Hyson, & Maier, 1983].)

Other recent work has shown not only how closely the immune system may be coupled to an organism's perception of control over aversive environmental events, but also how intimately the system may act in parallel with other neurochemical processes that are known to mediate adaptive response. By way of illustration, a virtually identical shock/stress experimental paradigm, again tested in the rat, will elicit amphetamine sulfate- and cocaine-induced behavioral stereotypy (repetitive, compulsive behavior) only in those animals that are unable to control the delivery of shock, with both groups, experimental and control, receiving identical shocks and identical doses of drug (MacLennan & Maier, 1983). We know, in addition, that concentrations of immunosuppressive norepinephrine metabolite in rat brain show considerable increase following a single exposure of an animal to inescapable shock (Cassens, Roffman, Kuruc, Orsulak, & Schildkraut, 1980). Most significantly (as we shall see when we turn to experiments on the conditioning of the immune response), a like increase will occur following re-exposure of an animal *solely to the environmental context associated with this one isolated experience of shock*. This alteration in brain chemistry is accompanied, by the way, by such behavioral indices of emotion as crouching and postural rigidity (Cassens et al., 1980).

The neurochemical and behavioral effects induced in experimental animals by the experience of vulnerability have been further illustrated by an experiment showing a pronounced analgesia (mediated by the endogenous opiate, β-endorphin) following the experience of defeat in laboratory mice, a condition induced by repeated and violent physical attack from animals of another strain (Miczek, Thompson, & Shuster, 1982). This same psychosocial condition of defeat, again tested in mice, again accompanied by submission and "appeasement gestures," has also been shown to be associated with pronounced elevations of serum corticosterone (Leshner, Merkle, & Mixon, 1981), an immunosuppressive adrenal steroid (Claman, 1975). Finally, in rats, β-endorphin-mediated analgesia, produced in reaction to shock, reportedly compromises normal immunological rejection of transplanted mammary tumors (Shavit, Lewis, Terman, Gale, & Liebeskind, 1983).

These data serve to illustrate the fact that the opioid peptide, β-endorphin, can exert a whole spectrum of effects that can be at once biochemical, behavioral, immunological, and opiate-related. Not surprisingly, research efforts are currently under way to differentiate these effects more precisely (Shavit et al., 1983).

CLASSICAL CONDITIONING CAN INFLUENCE THE IMMUNE RESPONSE

The conditioning of the immune response, through the use of classical conditioning techniques, has added still another facet to the study of central influence on immune function. This conditioning has proved to be a replicable, generalizable phenomenon in both adrenalectomized and intact animals (Ader, Cohen, & Grota, 1979), one that holds true for both humorally mediated (Ader & Cohen, 1981) and cellularly mediated immunity (Bovbjerg, Ader, & Cohen, 1982).

In this work, conditioned immunosuppression is initially established by the single pairing of an innocuous gustatory stimulus with illness-induced taste aversion. For example, presentation of sodium saccharin (innocuous stimulus), acting as conditional stimulus, is temporally associated with the intraperitoneal (i.p.) injection of an aversive, immunosuppressive drug (for instance, cyclophosphamide) acting as unconditional stimulus. The acquisition of conditioned immunosuppression is then demonstrated by a depressed hemagglutinin antibody titer serving as the measure of conditioned response to antigen (i.p. injection of sheep red blood cells) presented in association with the once innocuous, now behaviorally significant conditioned stimulus (in this case, saccharin).

In view of the fact that the significant pairing in the conditioning paradigm (that is, the pairing of a neutral stimulus with an unconditioned response) should, in theory, operate in both immune suppression and enhancement, the implications of this work are far-reaching. It has been shown, for example, that the onset of lethal symptoms (proteinuria and glomerulonephritis) in the autoimmune disease, systemic lupus erythrematoseus, can be significantly delayed by the application of this same taste aversion conditioning procedure in female New Zealand hybrid mice, a standard experimental model for the study of this immunological disorder (Ader & Cohen, 1982).

Furthermore, there is evidence to show the extent to which the immune response can be manipulated by conditioning. That is to say, the conditioned response of immunosuppression can be positively reinforced by the reintroduction of both the conditioned, behaviorally significant stimulus and the unconditioned, aversive stimulus; and can be attenuated by the reintroduction of the conditioned stimulus alone (Gorcznski, Macrae, & Kennedy, 1982). Taken as a whole, these experiments on the behavioral conditioning of immune reactions suggest, in the words of two pioneering investigators, "an intimate and virtually unexplored relationship between the central nervous system and immunologic processes . . . a mechanism that may be involved in the complex pathogenesis of psychosomatic disease" (Ader & Cohen, 1975, 338–339).

IMMUNOLOGICAL CONDITIONING MAY INVOLVE TRANSFORMATION AT THE MOLECULAR LEVEL: SPECULATIONS

In conclusion, I will briefly mention an area of research that, on its face, would seem to be totally unrelated to psychoneuroimmunology. I am referring to work that has succeeded in describing changes in the protein structure of the synapse which occur as a result of sensitization and aversive learning in invertebrates (the synaptic junction being the anatomically specialized region that mediates the electrochemical transmission of nerve impulse between pre- and postsynaptic nerve terminals). More specifically, four molecular events are now known to follow aversive conditioning of the withdrawal reflex in the gill and syphon of the mollusk *Aplysia*: an elevation in intraneuronal levels of cyclic AMP (Castellucci, Bernier, Schwartz, & Kandel, 1983) (a stimulant to the phosphorylation of protein); enlargement of the synaptic area; an increase in the number of so-called synaptic "active zones" in varicosities within the presynaptic terminals of sensory neurons (Bailey & Chen, 1983); and the insertion of new active zone material (Kandel, 1983). Moreover, it is thought that these alterations may be associated with changes within the genome itself (Kandel, 1983), that is, in the linear arrangement of nucleotides in the gene substance. In a word, by looking at the activity-dependent presynaptic facilitation of a "simple" reflex in a relatively "simple" organism, this field of research is helping to define the molecular substrate of the conditioned fear response, or learned fear (Hawkins, Abrams, Carew, & Kandel, 1983; Walters & Byrne, 1983), and, to quote a principal investigator, we seem to be on the threshold of defining the "molecular grammar to mentation" (Kandel, 1983).

To place these findings in a psychoneuroimmunological frame of reference is not as incongruous as it might seem, once we recognize that of all physiological systems, the nervous and immune systems *alone* have the capacity to learn and to remember. This realization leads, of course, to the next question: When we speak, for example, of conditioned immune suppression in an aversive stimulus context, what do we mean? Are there morphological and biochemical transformations in immune system microcomponents comparable to those found in neural tissue under like circumstances? Or, to suggest another comparison, if the memory for aversive experience is directly dependent upon the endogenous activation of opiate receptors within the brain, as recent research has shown (Gallagher & Kapp, 1981; Thompson, 1983), what of immunological memory for such experience?

Inasmuch as the immunosuppressive effects achieved through avoidance conditioning are most likely a by-product of nervous system conditioning, it is probably more to the point to ask what influence alterations in transmitter output (resulting from increased numbers of terminal active zones?) might have upon thymus gland, spleen, and lymph nodes, as well as upon transmitter- and peptide-specific ligand-receptor binding sites on immune effector cells. Perhaps one of the more generalized effects of modified neurotransmission might have to do with immune cell recruitment, or with the redistribution, or change in pattern, of circulating T cell subpopulations.

Answers to such questions are likely to come from investigations conducted at the boundary zone dividing the immune network, the endocrine system, and the nervous system. This area has been described as one encompassing the cell surface receptor and its complementary antireceptor structure, and it has been said that a better understanding of certain disease states should come about through the interdisciplinary application of techniques of molecular biology to this focal point of systems convergence (Köhler, 1980). Unquestionably, any analysis of the pathways through which psychological factors influence immunity must take into account how the psychological status of an organism can influence the complex series of energy transformations that are ultimately resolved at this most fundamental level of organization.

REFERENCES

Ader, R., & Cohen, N. (1975). Behaviorally conditioned immunosuppression. *Psychosomatic Medicine, 37,* 333–340.

Ader, R., & Cohen, N. (1981). Conditioned immunopharmacological responses. In R. Ader (Ed.), *Psychoneuroimmunology.* New York: Academic Press.

Ader, R., & Cohen, N. (1982). Behaviorally conditioned immunosuppression and murine systemic lupus erythematosus. *Science, 215,* 1523-1536.

Ader, R., Cohen, N., & Grota, L. J. (1979). Adrenal involvement in conditioned immunosuppression. *International Journal of Immunopharmacology, 1,* 141-145.

Andén, N. N., Dahlstrom, A., Fuxe, K., Larsson, K., & Olson, L. (1966). Ascending monoamine neurons to the telencephalon and diencephalon. *Acta Physciologica Scandivinaca, 67,* 313-326.

Bailey, C. H., & Chen, M. (1983). Morphological basis of long-term habituation and sensitization in Aplysia. *Science, 220,* 91-93.

Baker, J. L. (1977). Physiological roles of peptides in the nervous system. In H. Gainer (Ed.), *Peptides in neurobiology.* New York: Plenum Press.

Barker, J. L., Neale, J. H., Smith, T. J., & McDonald, R. L. (1978). Opiate peptide modulation in amino acids: Responses suggest novel form of neuronal communication. *Science, 199,* 1451-1453.

Bergmann, K., Burke, P. V., Cerda-Olmedo, E., David, C. N., Delbrück, M., et al. (1969). Phycomyles. *Bacteriology Review, 33,* 99-157.

Besedovsky, H. O., Del Rey, A., & Sorkin, E. (1981). Lymphokine-containing supernatants from Con A-stimulated cells increase corticosterone blood levels. *Journal of Immunology, 126,* 385-387.

Besedovsky, H. O., Del Rey, A., Sorkin, E., Da Prada, M., Burri, R., & Honnegger, C. (1983). The immune response evokes changes in brain noradrenergic neurons. *Science, 221,* 564-566.

Besedovsky, H. O., Sorkin, E., Felix, D., & Hass, H. (1977). Hypothalamic changes during the immune response. *European Journal of Immunology, 7,* 325-328.

Björkland, A., Emson, P. C., Gilbert, R. F. T., & Skagerberg, G. (1979). Further evidence for the possible co-existence of 5-hydroxytryptamine and substance P in medullary raphe neurons of rat brain. *British Journal of Pharmacology, 66,* 112-113.

Bovbjerg, D., Ader, R., & Cohen, N. (1982). Behaviorally conditioned suppression of a graft-vs-host response. *Proceedings of the National Academy of Sciences USA, 79,* 583-585.

Bulloch, K., & Moore, R. Y. (1981). Thymus gland innervation by brainstem and spinal cord in mouse and rate. *American Journal of Anatomy, 162,* 157-166.

Cassens, G., Roffman, M., Kuruc, A., Orsulak, P. J., & Schildkraut, J. (1980). Alterations in brain norepinephrine metabolism induced by environmental stimuli previously paired with escapable shock. *Science, 209,* 1138-1140.

Castellucci, V. F., Bernier, L., Schwartz, J. H., & Kandel, E. R. (1983). Persistent activation of adenylate cyclase underlies the time course of short-term sensitization in *Aplysia Society for Neuroscience Abstracts, 9,* 169. (*Abstract No. 51.9*)

Claman, H. N. (1975). How corticosteroids work. *Journal of Allergy and Clinical Immunology, 55,* 145-151.

Cross, R. J., Markesberry, W. R., Brooks, W. H., & Roszman, T. L. (1980). Hypothalamic-immune interaction. I. The acute effect of anterior hypothalamic lesions on the immune response. *Brain Research, 196,* 79-87.

Dann, J. A., Wachtel, S. S., & Rubin, A. L. (1979). Possible involvement of the central nervous system in graft rejection. *Transplantation, 27,* 223-226.

Defendini, R., & Zimmerman, E. A. (1978). The magnocellular neurosecretory system of the mammalian hypothalamus. In S. Reichlin, R. J. Baldessarini, & J. B. Martin (Eds.), *Research publications: Association for Research in Nervous and Mental Diseases: Vol. 56. The hypothalamus.* New York: Raven Press.

Falck, B., & Hillarp, N. A. (1959). On the cellular localization of catecholamines in the brain. *Acta Anatomica* (Basel), *38*, 277-279.

Felten, D. L., Overhage, J. M., Felten, S. Y., & Schmedtje, J. F. (1981). Noradrenergic sympathetic innervation of lymphoid tissue in the rabbit appendix: Further evidence for a link between the nervous and immune systems. *Brain Research Bulletin, 7*, 595-612.

Felten, S. Y., Malone, R. K., Madura, D. J., & Felten, D. L. (1983). Sympathetic innervation of the spleen. *Society of Neuroscience Abstracts, 9*, 116. (*Abstract No. 34.6*)

Fox, B. H. (1981). Psychosocial factors and the immune system in human cancer. In R. Adler (Ed.), *Psychoneuroimmunology.* New York: Academic Press.

Gallagher, M., & Kapp, B. S. (1981). Influence of amygdala opiate-sensitive mechanisms, fear-motivated response, and memory processes for aversive experiences. In J. L. Martinez, R. A. Jensen, R. B. Messing, H. Rigter, & J. L. McGaugh (Eds.), *Endogenous peptides and learning and memory processes.* New York: Academic Press.

Giron, L. T., Crutcher, K. A., & Davis, J. N. (1980). Lymph nodes: A possible site for sympathetic neuronal regulation of immune responses. *Annals of Neurology, 8*, 520-525.

Gorcznski, R. M., Macrae, S., & Kennedy, M. (1982). Conditioned immune response associated with allogeneic skin grafts in mice. *Journal of Immunology, 129*, 704-709.

Griepp, E. B., & Revel, J. P. (1977). Gap junctions in development. In W. E. de Mello (Ed.), *Intracellular communication.* New York: Plenum Press.

Hall, N. R., McGillis, J. P., & Goldstein, A. L. (1984). Activation of neuroendocrine pathways by thymosin peptides. In E. L. Cooper (Ed.), *Stress, immunity and aging.* New York: Marcel Dekker.

Hall, N. R., McGillis, J. P., Spangelo, B. L., Palaszynski, E., Moody, T., & Goldstein, A. L. (1982). Evidence for a neuroendocrinethymus axis mediated by thimosin polypeptide. In B. Serrou, C. Rosenfeld, J. C. Daniels, & J. P. Saunders (Eds.), *Current concepts in human immunology and cancer immunomodulation: Vol. 17. Developments in immunology.* New York: Elsevier North-Holland.

Hannappel, E., Xu, G., Morgan, J., Hempstead, J., & Horecker, B. L. (1982). Thymosin $\beta 4$: A ubiquitous peptide in rat and mouse tissues. *Proceedings of the National Academy of Sciences USA, 79*, 2172-2175.

Hawkins, R. D., Abrams, T. W., Carew, T. J., & Kandel, E. R. (1983). A cellular mechanism for classical conditioning in *Aplysia*: Activity-dependent amplification of presynaptic facilitation. *Science, 219*, 405-408.

Healy, D. L., Hall, N. R., Schulte, H. M., Chrousos, G. P., Goldstein, A. L., et al. (1984). Pituitary response to acute administration of thymosin and to thymectomy in prepubertal primates. In A. L. Goldstein (Ed.), *Thymic hormones and lymphokines: Basic chemistry and clinical applications.* New York: Plenum Press.

Hökfelt, T., Lundberg, J. M., Schultzberg, M., Johansson, O., Skirboll, L., et al. (1980). Cellular localization of peptides in neural structures. *Proceedings of the Royal Society (Biology)*, *210*, 63–77.

Kandel, E. R. (1983, March). *Invited address*. Paper presented at the American Psychosomatic Society meeting, New York, NY.

Köhler, H. (1980). Idiotypic network interactions. *Immunology*, *1*, 18–21.

Koob, G. F., Le Moal, M., & Bloom, F. E. (1981). Enkephalin and endorphin influences on appetitive and aversive conditioning. In J. L. Martinez, R. A. Jensen, R. B. Messing, H. Rigter, & J. L. McGaugh (Eds.), *Endogenous peptides and learning and memory processes*. New York: Academic Press.

Kreiger, D. T. (1983). Brain peptides: What, where, and why? *Science*, *222*, 975–985.

Kreiger, D. T., & Martin, J. B. (1981a). Brain peptides: Part I. *New England Journal of Medicine*, *304*, 876–885.

Kreiger, D. T., & Martin, J. B. (1981b). Brain peptides: Part II. *New England Journal of Medicine*, *304*, 944–951.

Lauderslager, M. L., Ryan, S. M., Drygan, R. C., Hyson, R. L., & Maier, S. F. (1983). Coping and immunosuppression: Inescapable but not escapable shock suppresses lymphocyte proliferation. *Science*, *221*, 568–570.

Leshner, A. I., Merkle, D. A., & Mixon, J. F. (1981). Pituitary—adrenocortical effects on learning and memory in social situations. In J. L. Martinez, R. A. Jensen, R. B. Messing, H. Rigter, & J. L. McGaugh (Eds.), *Endogenous peptides and learning and memory processes*. New York: Academic Press.

Levy, S. M. (Ed.). (1982). *Biological mediators of behavior and disease: Neoplasia*. New York: Elsevier Biomedical.

Locke, S. E., & Kraus, L. (1982). Modulation of natural killer cell activity by life stress and coping ability. In S. M. Levy (Ed.), *Biological mediators in behavior and disease: Neoplasia*. New York: Elsevier Biomedical.

Lopker, A., Abood, G., Hoss, W., & Lionetti, F. J. (1980). Stereospecific muscarinic acetylcholine and opiate receptors in human phagocytic leukocytes. *Biochemical Pharmacology*, *29*, 1361–1365.

MacLennan, A. J., & Maier, S. F. (1983). Coping and the stress-induced potentiation of stimulant stereotypy in the rat. *Science*, *219*, 1091–1093.

Maslincki, W., Grabozewska, E., & Ryzewski, J. (1980). Acetylcholine receptors in rat lymphocytes. *Biochimica et Biophysica Acta*, *633*, 269–273.

Miczek, K. A., Thompson, M. L., & Shuster, L. (1982). Opioid analgesia in defeated mice. *Science*, *215*, 1520–1522.

Nauta, W. J. H., & Gygax, P. A. (1954). Silver impregnation of degenerating axons in the central nervous system. *Stain Technology*, *29*, 91–93.

Oliveira-Castro, G. M., & Dos Reis, G. A. (1977). Cell communication in the immune response. In W. E. de Mello (Ed.), *Intercellular communication in the immune response*. New York: Plenum Press.

Olivier, B., & Bradford, L. D. (1983). Serotoninergic-opiate interactions in distress vocalization in juvenile guinea-pigs. *Society for Neuroscience Abstracts*, *9*, 714. (*Abstract No. 209.8*)

Peracchia, C. (1977). Gap junction structure and function. *Trends in Biochemistry*, *2*, 26–31.

Rebar, R. W., Miyake, A., Low, T. L. K., & Goldstein, A. L. (1981). Thymosin stimulates secretion of luteinizing hormone-releasing factor. *Science, 213,* 669-671.

Reite, M., Harbeck, R., & Hoffman, A. (1981). Altered cellular immune response following peer separation. *Life Sciences, 29,* 1133-1136.

Resch, K. (1976). Membrane-associated events in lymphocyte activation. In P. Cuatrecacas & M. F. Greaves (Eds.), *Receptors and recognition.* London: Chapman and Hall.

Rotsztejn, N. H. (1980). Neuromodulation in neuroendocrinology. *Trends in Neuroscience, 3,* 67-70.

Schleifer, S. J., Keller, S. J., Camerino, M., Thornton, J. C., & Stein, M. (1983). Suppression of lymphocyte stimulation following bereavement. *Journal of the American Medical Association, 250,* 374-377.

Schmitt, F. O., Dev, P., & Smith, B. H. (1976). Electrotonic processing of information by brain cells. *Science, 193,* 114-120.

Sergeeva, V. E. (1974). Histotopography of catecholamines in the mammalian thymus. *Bulletin of Experimental Biology and Medicine* (USSR), 77, 456-458.

Shavit, Y., Lewis, J. W., Terman, G. W., Gale, R. P., & Liebeskind, J. C. Endogenous opioids may mediate the effects of stress on tumor growth and function. *Proceedings of the Western Pharmacology Society, 26,* 53-56.

Sklar, L. S., & Anisman, H. (1981). Stress and cancer. *Psychological Bulletin, 89,* 369-406.

Siggins, G. R. (1979). Neurotransmitters and neuromodulators and their mediation by cyclic nucleotides. In Y. H. Ehrlich, J. Volavka, L. G. Davis, & E. G. Brungraber (Eds.), *Advances in experimental medicine and biology.* New York: Raven Press.

Sotelo, C. Electrical and chemical communication in the central nervous system. In R. R. Brinkley & K. R. Porter (Eds.), *International cell biology.* New York: Rockefeller University Press.

Spector, N. H., & Korneva, E. A. (1981). Neurophysiology, immunophysiology and neuroimmunodulation. In R. Ader (Ed.), *Psychoneuroimmunology.* New York: Academic Press.

Stein, M., Schleifer, S. J., & Keller, S. E. (1981). Hypothalamic influence on immune responses. In R. Ader (Ed.), *Psychoneuroimmunology.* New York: Academic Press.

Strom, T. B., Lane, M. A., & George, K. (1981). The parallel, time-dependent, bimodal change in lymphocyte cholinergic binding activity and cholinergic influence upon lymphocyte-mediated cytotoxicity after lymphocyte activation. *Journal of Immunology, 127,* 705-710.

Thompson, R. F. (1983). Neuronal substrates of simple associative learning: Classical conditioning. *Trends in Neuroscience, 6,* 270-275.

Visintainer, M., Volpicelli, J. R., & Seligman, M. E. P. (1982). Tumor rejection in rats after inescapable or escapable shock. *Science, 215,* 437-439.

Walters, E. T., & Byrne, J. H. (1983). Associative conditioning of single sensory neurons suggests a cellular mechanism for learning. *Science, 219,* 400-405.

Weiner, H. (1977). *Psychobiology and human disease.* New York: Elsevier North-Holland.

Weiner, H., Hofer, M., & Stunkard, A. J. (Eds.). (1980). *Brain, behavior and bodily disease.* New York: Raven Press.

Williams, J. M., Peterson, R. G., Shea, P. A., Schmedtje, F. J., Bauer, D. C., & Felten, D. L. (1981). Sympathetic innervation of murine thymus and spleen: Evidence for a functional link between the nervous and immune systems. *Brain Research Bulletin, 6,* 83–94.

Wybran, J., Appelboom, T., Family, J. P., & Govaerts, A. (1979). Suggestive evidence for receptors for morphine and methionine-enkephalin on normal human blood T-lymphocytes. *Journal of Immunology, 123,* 1068–1070.

·15·

Emotions, Stress, and Immunity

GEORGE F. SOLOMON

Because of the prevailing scientific dogma that the immune system is autonomous in its responses to stimulation by antigens, until relatively recently most people remained unaware that psychosocial factors in our lives might influence our immune systems and therefore play a significant role in the patterns of disease, even to the point of determining who gets ill. In the early 1960s Jonas Salk pointed out that all diseases are about genetic, behavioral, nervous, and immune system relationships. I would expand that to include the endocrine system. What we have now learned is not to be simplistic about our approach to disease, but to look on all disease as having numerous interrelated causes.

Mirsky (1960) showed that three factors must be present to cause peptic ulcer: a high pepsinogen level, a dependent personality, and stress. A dependent man who has a very high pepsinogen level does not need much stress to give him an ulcer, whereas the man who has a slightly lower level needs more stress before he ends up with his ulcer. Similarly, if one has very allergic tendencies, one needs only a relatively slight amount of stress to give one asthma, whereas slightly allergic people will not succumb until or even if they have a very high stress level. On the other hand, allergy itself also can be related to particular personality and coping patterns, as well as to genetic factors.

The immune system is highly complex and is designed to defend our bodies against foreign invaders such as bacteria, viruses, and noxious chemicals and also to act as a surveillance system pinpointing and then killing any mutant cells that could develop into cancer. To achieve all this, the immune system is divided into two main branches, each with different responsibilities and different subsystems and active agents.

The first branch is known as the humoral or antibody-mediated system. It operates via the blood stream by means of antibodies produced by white blood cells (lymphocytes) called B cells. When the B cells are activated by some foreign threat, they produce any of five known types of antibodies, known as immunoglobulins. The variety known as IgE is responsible for allergic reactions. IgM and IgG are suppressed by stress, whereas IgE tends to increase during stress. The action of B cells in the humoral immune system is influenced by cells called macrophages, which engulf things, and by T cells; both belong to the other branch of the immune system, the cell-mediated system. Both produce "messenger" substances called cytokines or lymphokines that influence other immune cells. A tumor cell can be attacked by macrophages after being coated in antibodies or can be killed directly by cytotoxic (killer) T cells. Other T cells, called helper cells and suppressor cells, serve to enhance or suppress the functions of the killer cells and B cells. Still other lymphocytes are called natural killer (NK) cells and are the first line of defense against tumor cells and virus-infected cells since they do not have to be "programmed" or to "learn" by prior exposure. Thus, both the humoral and the cell-mediated systems are in a complex interrelationship.

The humoral system is the one that provides an instant reaction against toxic, viral, and bacterial foreign proteins; is responsible for transfusion reactions against incompatible blood types when they occur; and is the cause of immediate kinds of allergic reactions. If, for instance, a small amount of house dust or pollen were injected into the skin of a person sensitive to those things, there might be an immediate reddening and swelling on the skin, caused by the humoral system going into action with its antibodies. If inhaled, sneezing or wheezing would occur as the result of release of histamine and other substances secondary to the antigen–antibody reaction.

The cell-mediated system is concerned with fighting virus-infected cells and foreign or abnormal cells. Transplant rejections are due, when they occur, to the cell-mediated immune response. Cell-mediated immunity is also responsible for delayed types of hypersensitivity or allergy. For example, a person sensitive to tuberculin as a result of exposure to tuberculosis will develop an area of reddening and hardness of the skin some 1 or 2 days after the injection within the skin.

Deficiency in the immune system may increase our susceptibility to infection or allow mutant cells to divide and grow and become malignant cancers. However, the correlation between a given degree of lowering of a specific immune function and disease is often not clear. An overactive immune system, on the other hand, may end up failing to distinguish between body cells and foreign cells and start attacking itself, giving rise to any of the so-called autoimmune diseases, such as rheumatoid arthritis, systemic lupus erythematosus, and Graves disease (hyperthyroidism). To illustrate the complexity of the immune system, such autoimmune "overactivity" may actually result from deficient functions of suppressor T cells. It now seems clear that immune deficiency or autoimmunity often can be linked with psychosocial stressors and with over- or underproduction of particular hormones. The development and function of T cells, for instance, has been found to be dependent on a family of hormones produced by the thymus gland. In addition, more and more is becoming known about regulation of immunity by small proteins produced in the nervous system and elsewhere, the neuropeptides, which John Morley and I have called "conductors of the immune orchestra" (Morley, Kay, Solomon, & Plotnikoff, 1987).

My involvement in the field of psychoimmunology arose from my interest in emotional and stress factors associated with the onset and course of rheumatoid arthritis and other autoimmune diseases. Some of my earliest patients had systemic lupus erythematosus, an often fatal disease associated with an autoimmune reaction to the nuclei of cells in major organs such as the kidneys and heart. Some of these patients also had a psychosis associated with the disease, a psychosis that can mimic schizophrenia, but is not schizophrenia. Lupus is treated with immunosuppressant drugs, or steroids. The similarity of the psychiatric features of lupus and schizophrenia, however, made me start to wonder whether schizophrenia might not also be a type of autoimmune disease. Both autoimmune diseases and schizophrenia appear to have predisposing genetic and personality factors and often are precipitated by stress.

Jeffrey Fessel and I began to look for antinuclear antibodies in schizophrenia and discovered that autoantibodies of all kinds are significantly higher in the blood of schizophrenics than in the general population (Fessell & Solomon, 1960). For instance, whereas the general population showed no antinuclear antibody, about 5% of schizophrenics did. Whereas 5% of the general population has the autoantibody associated with rheumatoid arthritis, 20% of schizophrenics showed it.

Work is still under way to discover the significance of all this. For example, perhaps an autoantibody could stimulate the receptor for dopamine, a neurotransmitter that has been implicated in schizophrenia. A fascinating but puzzling apparent fact is that autoimmune diseases and schizophrenia very rarely coexist. Both rheumatoid arthritis and schizophrenia, for instance, are relatively common diseases, each affecting about 1% of the population. Surveys of thousands of patients with schizophrenia did not reveal any who had rheumatoid arthritis. Other psychoses, such as manic-depressive illnesses and paranoid disorders, were found to exist at the same time as rheumatoid arthritis, but the paradox of why active schizophrenics have a high incidence of autoantibodies and yet virtually no autoimmune disease has not yet been explained.

It would make sense for the two systems, nervous and immune, to be linked. Both are concerned with adapting to and defending against the environment and relate the organism to the outside world. Some investigators now even believe that the immune system evolved before the nervous system and was initially only an internal regulating system, but that when the central nervous system evolved, it extended its functions to defense against outside attack. Two adaptive–defensive systems that respond to the environment ought to "talk" to each other, as actually appears to be the case.

Clearly, the two systems are similar in several ways. In both systems, defenses gone awry produce disease. In the immune system, inappropriate defenses are called allergies. Allergic individuals react to a substance such as pollen as if it were dangerous, when it is not. Similar overreaction to imaginary danger manifests itself in the nervous system as neuroses, such as phobias or extreme anxiety. When the immune system turns on itself, the result is autoimmune disease. When the nervous system does likewise, the result is depression, which psychoanalytic theory relates to aggression turned inward. Both systems are capable of learning by experience. Immunization can lead either to tolerance (acceptance of a foreign protein) or to immunity, and the experience of stress early in life can lead either to increased resistance against later stress or to a quicker breaking point. In the army, slum children were more resistant to the stresses of battle than drafted college boys because, in a sense, they had been through it before. Conversely, experience of a highly traumatic event may make some people hypersensitive to other, even if lesser, stressors. People who are prone to depression, for instance, often have lost a parent early in childhood. In the immune system of rodents, early infantile handling leads to enhanced adult immunity, whereas premature weaning leads to relative immune deficiency in the adult.

If, the immune and nervous systems truly are liked, certain hypotheses should hold true. First, emotional upset and distress should influence the incidence or severity of diseases resisted or mediated by the immune system such as cancer or autoimmune diseases. Second, severe emotional and mental disorders should be accompanied by abnormality in the immune system. Third, hormones regulated by the central nervous system, such as the neuroendocrines, should influence the workings of the immune system. Fourth, any experimental manipulation of relevant parts of the central nervous system should have immunological consequences. Fifth, events that affect behavior, such as stress, conditioning, or different types of childhood experience, should also have immunological consequences. Sixth, cells involved in the immune system should also be responsive to hormones connected with the nervous system and to the nervous system's chemical messengers. Seventh, any activation of the immune system should be reflected in activity by the central nervous system. As research continues, far more implications of bidirectional interactions between the central nervous and immune systems will be recognized.

All of these hypotheses have supporting evidence. The data are too lengthy to offer in full, but examples can be given for each. Personality and stress have been shown to play a significant role in the onset of a variety of allergic diseases. Guinea pigs, for instance, when injected with a mild dose of some foreign substance, do not develop an allergy to it. However, if they are put under stress first, that mild dose is sufficient to cause an allergic reaction. In humans it has been noted that asthma patients, while they have varied personalities, tend to share an unconscious trait of overdependency, caused by specific childhood experiences or parental attitudes. When the person is frustrated in his or her need for support, the asthma attack usually follows.

Persons with autoimmune diseases tend to have similar personality characteristics. They are generally quiet, introverted, reliable, conscientious, restricted in expression of emotions (particularly anger), conforming, self-sacrificing (tending to allow themselves to be imposed on), sensitive to criticism, distant, overactive and busy, stubborn, rigid, controlling, and pseudoindependent in an effort to deny to themselves the fact that they are really extremely dependent on others.

Autoimmune diseases usually become apparent after the person has undergone some severe psychological stress, such as the loss of a loved one, or when a pattern of life that has allowed him or her to avoid psychological distress is interrupted: the athlete, for instance, who is forced to retire because of age and so loses an allowed way by which to express aggression. The poorer the person's psychological defenses, the more rapid the progression of the disease, the more resistant to any kind of treatment, and the more severe the incapacitation.

In one study, we were able to show the link between physiological and psychological factors as it operates in healthy people. We tested a large group of relatives of people who had rheumatoid arthritis to see whether they too had the rheumatoid autoantibody in their blood. We found, as expected, that some did and some did not. What was interesting and revealing, however, was that those who did have the antibody were emotionally very healthy, whereas those who did not were a normal cross-section of the population, varying from the severely neurotic to the well adjusted. None of the people who had the autoantibody were in any significant way anxious, depressed, or alienated, which seemed to indicate that it was their emotional health that saved them from falling prey to the disease.

In another study, we found that among football players who might be expected more frequently to show autoimmune prone patterns, only those who were neurotic (when tested before the football season) developed a low level of autoantibodies after the stress of losing close matches with longstanding rival teams. The players who were not neurotic did not develop the antibodies. Goodman (1963) similarly found that emotional stress heightened some people's tendency to produce thyroid autoantibodies.

A large number of studies have related emotional and personality factors to the contracting of cancer. The rapidity of the progression of the cancer also has been related to unsuccessful psychological defenses and distress, such as inability to express hostile feelings, unresolved tension about a parent figure, loss of an important person before the development of the tumor, and, sometimes, sexual problems.

There are two infectious diseases that have a clear connection with stress. One is acute necrotizing ulcerative gingivitis, or trench mouth, which tends to occur after acute stress, such as that undergone by college students before taking their final examinations. In this disease, the invading bacteria are the very ones that are normally present, without any ill effects, in the mouth. It would seem that the stress must cause some alteration in the balance of the immune system, and it has in fact now been shown that IgA, the antibody found in saliva to protect the mouth from such bacteria, is reduced under stress.

Another infectious disease with a known stress component is herpes. In affected persons, the virus continues to live on in the tissues but is normally kept under control by T cells. Under conditions of physical or emotional stress, however, the virus is able to become active and cause another outbreak. Even in the absence of a frank outbreak of herpes, stress causes elevation of antibodies to herpes virus, indicating a breakdown of cellular immune control.

Another line of evidence to show that the central nervous system is related to immunity is that major disorders in the functioning of the nervous system are accompanied by malfunctioning in the immune system. Schizophrenics are found to have high levels of autoimmune antibodies, as mentioned, and other abnormalities occur in patients with other mental disorders. Work at Loma Linda in California suggests that schizophrenic patients have a deficiency of suppressor T cells, which could account for their high incidence of autoantibodies. Severe depressive mental illness is accompanied by significantly reduced function of T cells.

Soviet experiments have shown that destruction of certain areas of the hypothalamus can lead to suppression of all immune functions. Conversely, stimulation of the same areas can enhance the effectiveness of the immune system. The hypothalamus is rich in hormones, regulates the pituitary gland, and has a complex relationship with the limbic system, the area of the brain concerned with emotions. There is a known interaction between the pituitary and the thymus gland, on which the immune system's T cells are dependent: The hormones produced by each affect the working of the other. Another link between the hypothalamus and the immune system is shown by the fact that structures that respond to serotonin, a neurotransmitter found in the hypothalamus, appear to play a part in the regulation of antibody production. Moreover, nerve cells in the hypothalamus fire in a particular sequence following immunization.

The studies that have shown the effects of experience on immune function are too extensive to describe in full. Chronic stress may have very different effects on the immune system than acute stress. Also, the nature and the timing of the stressor is very relevant in its effect on the immune system. Controllability of the stressor may be critical. One of the best known immunosuppressive stressors is overcrowding. Could this perhaps have evolutionary significance in that, when populations of animals become very dense, nature's mechanism for reducing the population is a decrease in immune efficiency?

Evidence that conditioning can alter immune responses has been elegantly demonstrated by the psychologist Robert Ader and the immunologist Nicholas Cohen at the University of Rochester. They made their discovery accidentally, while engaged in another experiment, which entailed giving rats water sweetened with saccharin, which they love, and then teaching them an aversion to it by following the drink with the injection of a drug that causes an upset stomach. After about 40 days some of the animals died and the researchers realized that, as the drug they had used happened to be an immunosuppressant, perhaps they had conditioned a suppression of the immune system as well as an aversion to saccharin. When they tried the experiment again, they followed a period of giving saccharin and the drug by a period when they gave saccharin followed by a saline injection. The rats' immune systems were still suppressed, even when the drug was not given, because they had learned to associate saccharin with suppression of the immune response.

Another experiment showed the same effect in reverse in response to grafted skin tissue. Researchers at the Ontario Cancer Research Institute tested the immune response of mice to skin grafts. The automatic response of a healthy organism is to mobilize the immune system to fight any foreign tissue, such as grafted skin or a transplanted organ. After several skin grafts, the researchers succeeded in conditioning an association between all the paraphernalia of the operation (anesthetic, bandages, etc.) and a foreign piece of skin to be rejected, because when they repeated the procedure without a skin graft, the immune systems of the mice were still mobilized to fight the expected threat.

Studies of human experience on immune function are now being regularly reported. Marvin Stein and colleagues at Mount Sinai School of Medicine in New York tested the immune systems of men whose wives were dying of breast cancer. They found that in the 2 months after the wives' deaths, the husbands' immune systems were significantly depressed but usually returned to normal after about 4 months. The recovery seemed to be linked with expression of grief, that is, those who went through their mourning instead of putting on a brave front were more likely to recover their immune response more quickly. Inability to mourn, with a concomitant long-term suppression of immunity, may explain why bereaved people so often fall ill or get cancer later themselves. Recently, Janice Kiecolt-Glaser and Ronald

Glaser of Ohio State University have found decreased immune function under the stress of caretaking of a family member wth Alzheimer's disease and also in the context of conflicted marriages.

We may also have something to learn from the fact that elderly people have a higher incidence of autoimmune diseases as well as of cancer. Is this linked to an inevitable aging process of the immune system, or could it be due to the cumulative effects of stress over a lifetime and the fact that depressive emotions are relatively common in old age? My colleagues and I are finding that physically and mentally healthy elderly persons have remarkably intact, even superior immune function.

These are early days yet for psychoimmunology, but already it is clear that a fuller understanding of the mechanisms involved will help us encourage health and prevent disease. It is worth study to find out whether relaxation, a counter to stress, or other types of interventions can help to enhance the immune system, for instance. We may find, from our growing understanding of how the immune system works and communicates, that we may understand also more about the brain and how it works, since both operate in similar ways and clearly are interactive.

BIBLIOGRAPHY

Ader, R., & Cohen, N. (1975). Behaviorally conditioned immunosuppression. *Psychosomatic Medicine, 37,* 333–340.

Kiecolt-Glaser, J. K., Glaser, R., Shuttleworth, E. C., Dyer, C., Ogrocki, P., & Speichen, C. E. (1987). Chronic stress and immunity in family caregiver of Alzheimer's disease victims. *Psychosomatic Medicine, 49,* 523–555.

Fessel, W. J., & Solomon, G. F. (1960). Psychosis and systemic lupus erythematosus: A review of the literature and case reports. *California Medicine, 92,* 266–270.

Fessel, W. J. (1963). The "antibrain" factors in psychiatric patients' sera. *Archives of General Psychiatry, 8,* 614–621.

Goodman, M. (1963). Effect of age, sex, and schizophrenia on thyroid autoantibody production. *Archives of General Psychiatry, 8,* 114–122.

Mirsky, I. A. (1960). Physiologic, psychologic and social determinants of psychosomatic disorders. *Diseases of the Nervous System, 21,* 50–54.

Morley, J. E., Kay, N. E., Solomon, G. F., & Plotnikoff, N. P. (1987). Neuropeptides: Conductors of the immune orchestra. *Life Sciences, 41,* 527–544.

Solomon, G. F. (1987). Psychoneuroimmunology: Interactions between central nervous system and immune system. *Journal of Neuroscience Research, 18,* 1–9.

Solomon, G. F., & Moos, R. H. (1965). The relationship of personality to the presence of rheumatoid factor in asymptomatic relatives of patients with rheumatoid arthritis. *Psychosomatic Medicine, 27,* 350–360.

·16·

The Emerging Field of Psychoneuroimmunology, with a Special Note on AIDS

GEORGE F. SOLOMON

In 1964 the psychologist Rudolf H. Moos and I jointly published a paper called "Emotions, Immunity and Disease," which at the time we necessarily subtitled "A Speculative Theoretical Integration" (Solomon & Moos, 1964). Because this paper has a certain pioneer status, it is gratifying to me that when I wrote an identically titled "anniversary" review with the immunologist Alfred A. Amkraut, with whom I had collaborated for many years, the paper required no such subtitle (Solomon & Amkraut, 1983). Rapidly accumulating data from experimental and clinical research have significantly reduced resistance among clinicians and basic scientists (biological and behavioral) to the concept that the immune system, operating via the central nervous and neuroendocrine systems, may act as a "transducer" between experience and disease, in effect converting the signals that originate in psychological responses into the signals that affect health.

Various names have been applied to this process. My original term was psychoimmunology. A more comprehensive, more fitting term, coined by Robert Ader, a leading figure in this field, is psychoneuroimmunology, and this is the term I will use. Novera Spector, a champion of psychoneuroimmunological concerns at the National Institute of Neurological and Communicative Disorders and Stroke, prefers the term neuroimmunomodulation, since he feels that the psyche is but one aspect of neural function (personal

This chapter originally appeared in *Advances*, 1985, 2(1), 6-19. It is reprinted here with permission from the Institute for the Advancement of Health.

communication, 1983). Others, such as Steven E. Locke, co-editor of the annotated bibliography, *Mind and Immunity*, prefer the term behavioral immunology.

Psychoneuroimmunology is concerned with the interaction of the central nervous system (mediating both psychic and biological processes) and the immunologic system (responsible not only for disease resistance but also for newly recognized bioregulatory functions). Psychoneuroimmunology can be subdivided into several aspects. Psychoimmunology deals with the effects of personality, stress, and emotions on immune-associated diseases, both immunologically resisted diseases (infectious and neoplastic) and immunologically mediated diseases (related to immunologic aberration—allergies, autoimmune diseases). Immunopsychiatry deals with immunologic abnormalities found in conjunction with mental illnesses. Immunoneurology deals with the effects of immune factors on the central nervous system. Neuroimmunoregulation deals with the control and modulation of immune function by the central nervous system and the neuroendocrines, neurotransmitters, and neuropeptides that it produces or influences. Related but not intrinsic is neuroimmunopharmacology, the field concerned with the effects of drugs and hormones on the central nervous system and the immune system jointly.

An assumption or premise of psychoneuroimmunology, at least in relation to any clinical implication, is that *all* disease (including mental illnesses and also medical conditions not ordinarily considered "psychosomatic") is multifactoral in origin, the result of interrelationships among the genetic, endocrine, nervous and immune systems, and behavioral–emotional factors (Salk, 1962). Since ancient times, observant clinicians have commented upon the relevance of emotions to the onset and course of a disease. Sir William Osler, "the father of modern medicine," is reputed to have said that to predict the outcome of pulmonary tuberculosis it is as important to know what is going on in a man's head as what is going on in his chest.

In general, psychoneuroimmunology looks to the links between the central nervous system, where the psyche processes its perceptions and reactions, and the immune system. My aim here is to explore the significance and nature of these links, but I first want to point out some intriguing analogies between the immune and central nervous systems. Both have the capacity of memory. Both serve functions of adaptation and defense. In each system, inappropriate defenses can lead to pathological syndromes—to allergies in the immune system and to neurosis in the psychological system. (To the hay-fever sufferer or the phobic, respectively, neither ragweed pollen nor the garter snake is truly dangerous.) When turned against the self, the immune system can lead to autoimmunity and the central nervous system to depression (and perhaps suicide). In each system, inadequate defenses result in vulnerability. In each, prior exposure can induce sensitization or tolerance (Kangas & Solomon, 1975; Linscott, 1976). A pioneer in psychosomatic medicine, Peter H. Knapp, recently has also suggested that the eliminatory element of emotional responses, a characteristic emphasized in psychoanalytic theory by Sandor Rado, might have a psychophysiological concomitant in immune responses (personal communication, 1983).

The following are 14 hypotheses on the linkages between the central nervous system and the immune system. For each hypothesis, I provide illustrative supporting data from recent research. I do not consider the list of hypotheses complete, and I do not offer my citation of evidence as representing full proof of any one of them. To document fully the clinical and experimental evidence supporting each would be beyond the scope of this limited paper. The hypotheses cover the clinical implications (including the therapeutic significance) of central nervous system and immune interactions, and the mechanisms providing such links. (Another way of looking at this analysis is to treat the interaction of the central nervous and immune systems as a hypothesis with 14 corollaries. At this point, however, I consider the interaction between the systems a demonstrated fact.)

In a brief aside, I shall also discuss the challenges to psychoneuroimmunology raised by AIDS and infection with the human immunodeficiency virus. I pose researchable questions that follow from a psychoneuroimmunologic frame of reference, a perspective that seems particularly suitable because AIDS is both an infectious disease and a disease of immunologic aberration.

FOURTEEN HYPOTHESES ON THE LINKS BETWEEN THE IMMUNE AND THE CENTRAL NERVOUS SYSTEMS

1. *Enduring coping style and personality factors (so-called trait characteristics) should influence the susceptibility of an individual's immune system to alteration by exogenous events, including reactions to events.* Let us begin the discussion of this hypothesis by examining the autoimmune diseases, with which I have had the most clinical research experience. The genetic element in immunoregulation, the presence of clinical autoimmune diseases among members of a family, and the presence of autoantibodies among otherwise healthy family members all point to the influence of genetic factors in autoimmune diseases; some researchers suggest viral factors as well (Talal, Fye, & Moutsopoulos, 1976; Lawrence, 1962; Pollak, 1964). However, a considerable number of studies indicate that personality factors also seem to predispose an individual to develop autoimmune diseases. Moos and I found that female patients with the autoimmune disease rheumatoid arthritis show more masochism, self-sacrifice, denial of hostility, compliance–subservience, depression, and sensitivity to anger than their healthy sisters, and are

described as always having been nervous, tense, worried, highly strung, moody individuals. Physically healthy relatives with rheumatoid factor in their sera—which may dispose them to developing the autoimmune disease—are psychologically healthier than those lacking this autoantibody, the implication being that a combination of physical predisposition and a breakdown of psychological defenses leads to manifest disease (Solomon & Moos, 1965). Personality data similar to those obtained from rheumatoid arthritics have been reported for patients with other autoimmune diseases (Solomon, 1981a). The involvement of the central nervous system in autoimmunity is further suggested by the finding that left-handedness, determined by the brain, is associated with increased risk of autoimmune disease (Marx, 1982).

A number of recent studies of cancer patients have found personality traits that are roughly similar to those in patients with autoimmune diseases (Solomon & Amkraut, 1983; Bahnson, 1980, 1981) and older studies have found comparable traits in patients with infectious diseases, such as tuberculosis (Sparer, 1956). These personality characteristics tend to exemplify the concept of alexithymia—literally, the inability to find words for feelings—that Sifneos and Nemiah apply to individuals who are psychologically disposed to physical illness and who are out of touch with, unaware of, and unable to express emotions, particularly negative ones (Nemiah & Sifneos, 1970).

I have come to the tentative conclusion that there is not an "autoimmune-prone," "cancer-prone," or "infection-prone" personality but, rather, an "immunosuppression-prone" personality or coping pattern. This statement does not imply a totally nonspecific theory of the relationship of personality to disease, since an immunosuppressive personality pattern is quite different, say, from the personality pattern that is prone to coronary artery disease (the Type A personality) (Friedman & Roseman, 1974). Research into the personality correlates of variations in immunologic functions among "normals" might yield important clues regarding vulnerability to disease. It should also be noted that spontaneous behavior differences even among identical (inbred) animals may have immunologic consequences. Fighting female mice have smaller virus-induced tumors, which are immunologically resisted, than do nonfighters (Amkraut & Solomon, 1972).

2. *Emotional upset and distress (so-called state characteristics) should alter the incidence, severity, and/or course of diseases that are immunologically resisted (infectious and neoplastic diseases) or are associated with aberrant immunological function (allergies, autoimmune diseases, AIDS—also immunologically resisted).* Work documenting the existence prior to an illness of a high frequency of life change requiring adaptation is now familiar (Rahe & Arthur, 1978). More specifically, a variety of studies indicate that stress events and/or the breakdown of psychological defenses and adaptations are related to the onset of

allergic, autoimmune, infectious, and neoplastic diseases (Solomon & Amkraut, 1983; Solomon, 1981a; Bahnson, 1980, 1981). (In this context *distress* or even *strain* would be a more appropriate term than *stress*—one definition of which is an extraordinary demand on physiological and/or psychological defenses with concomitant neuroendocrine responses—since the individual's perception of the event is critical. A first parachute jump presumably is stressful to the uninitiated, whereas not being able to jump because of an injured ankle might be stressful to the inveterate sky diver.)

Moos and I found that the *course* of rheumatoid arthritis appears to be related to the integrity of an individual's psychological defenses; patients with weakened psychological defenses and consequent dysphoria are more likely to have rapidly progressing disease, to be more incapacitated, and to respond less well to medical treatment (Solomon, 1981a). Klopfer had similar findings in a predictive study of patients with metastatic carcinoma (Klopfer, 1957), as had other researchers in the case of several infectious diseases (Solomon & Amkraut, 1983).

More recently, interesting work has suggested that in some "hardy" individuals stress does not increase susceptibility to illness (Kobasa, 1979). Such individuals are characterized by a commitment to self, an attitude of vigorousness toward the environment, a sense of personal meaningfulness, and a feeling of being in control of their lives. In effect, the "hardiness" of these individuals appears to protect them against the immunologic effects of emotional upset and distress.

3. *Severe emotional disturbance and mental dysfunction should be accompanied by immunologic abnormalities.* This hypothesis is based on the supposition that if the central nervous system and the immune system are closely linked, then a major perturbation in one system should be reflected in the other.

A variety of immunologic abnormalities, some of which are confusing and contradictory, have been reported in conjunction with mental illness, particularly schizophrenia (Solomon, 1981b). It is my impression that the abnormalities found in conjunction with schizophrenia are epiphenomena not intrinsically related to this disturbance, but further research is certainly indicated. The immunologic abnormalities include the following: quantitative and (less convincingly) qualitative declines in the immunoglobulin agents that assist the immune response; weakened immune response to administered antigens; and increased incidence of a variety of autoantibodies that an individual produces against itself. (The argument of Heath—based on the presence of autoantibodies to specific cells in the septal area of the brain—that schizophrenia itself is an autoimmune disease is not convincing [Heath, 1969], but the recent suggestion of agonist-behaving autobodies to dopamine receptor sites is intriguing [Fudenberg, 1984]). A consistent finding has been the presence in some schizophrenic patients of morphologically—and, in some studies, functionally—abnormal lymphocytes (Fessel, 1963). These cells have some features of activated T cells (Hirata-Hibi, Higashi, Tachibana, & Watanabe, 1982).

Clinical depression (often a consequence of bereavement, whose immunologic consequences I examine in hypothesis 8) appears to be associated with immunosuppression (Kronfol, Silva, Greden, Dembiski, & Carroll, 1982). As Woody Allen said in one of his movies: "I don't get depressed; I grow a tumor instead."

4. *Diseases of immunologic aberration should, at times, be accompanied by psychological and/or neurological symptoms.* The most obvious example of this contention is the psychosis associated with the autoimmune disease systemic lupus erythematosus, which can be very similar symptomatically to schizophrenia. This psychological disorder can even be a presenting symptom of the disease, improving when the underlying physiological disorder is treated (Fessell & Solomon, 1960). In addition, AIDS can be accompanied by an acute organic brain syndrome (Nichols, 1983).

5. *Experimental behavioral manipulation—in terms, for example, of stress, conditioning, and early experiences—should have immunologic consequences.* Particularly at this point I shall be only illustrative, in view of the now-extensive literature supporting this hypothesis.

A number of reports, mostly retrospective and some epidemiologic, have linked stress to increased susceptibility to infectious diseases or to the aggravation of such diseases (Palmblad, 1981). However, retrospective studies of the influence of psychological factors in any disease are subject to the "chicken and egg" criticism that the psychic symptoms may have been caused by the disease rather than being causal factors in the development of the disease. Not until 1969 was I able to show that stress in rats, particularly stress resulting from overcrowding, can affect humoral immunity, in both the primary and the secondary response (Solomon, 1969). Shortly thereafter, my colleagues and I were able to demonstrate that stress affects cellular immunity (Amkraut, Solomon, Kasper, & Perdue, 1973). Monjan and Collector found that stress initially led to immunosuppression but, when continued, led to enhanced immune responsiveness (Monjan & Collector, 1977). Other researchers found that graded increases in acute stress led to graded degrees of immunosuppression (Keller, Weiss, Schleiffer, Miller, & Stern, 1981). Experimental and naturally occurring acute stresses were shown to be immunosuppressive in human beings (Palmblad, Petrini, Wasserman, & Akenstedt, 1979; Dorian, Keystone, Garfinkel, & Brown, 1981). New work suggests that control over stress is critical in modulating immune functioning, since animals subjected to inescapable—that is, uncontrollable—shock showed diminished lymphocyte proliferation in response to mitogens, whereas animals subjected to escapable shock did not (Laudenslager, Ryan, Drugan, Hyson, & Maier, 1983). Further, inescapable shock also had a greater effect than escapable shock on the activity of natural killer cells (Maier & Laudenslager, 1983). Such differential effects may be mediated by effects on endogenous opiates.

Recent work extends to research on primates regarding another aspect of stress effects on immunity. Preliminary research suggests that the agitation–depression reaction of infant monkeys to maternal or peer separation—a reaction that is considered a possible model of human grief—is associated with decreased lymphocyte proliferation in response to mitogens (Laudenslager, Reite, & Harbeck, 1982; Reite, Harbeck, & Hoffman, 1981). Most significant is the evidence, first shown by Bartrop et al., that human bereavement is accompanied by immunosuppression (Bartrop, Lagarus, Luckhurst, Kiloh, & Penny, 1977; Schleiffer, Keller, Camarino, Thornton, & Stein, 1983). Working through the loss is accompanied by recovery of the immune function. (It has been known for some time that bereavement is accompanied by increases in morbidity and mortality, especially in males [Parkes & Brown, 1972].)

In regard to conditioning, a Russian paper on the conditioning of immunity appeared as early as 1926 (Metalnikov & Chorin, 1926). But it was not until Ader and Cohen, in elegant work reported in 1975, suppressed humoral immunity through conditioning (using the immunosuppressive drug cyclophosphamide as the unconditioned stimulus and saccharin as the conditioned stimulus) that this phenomenon was clearly demonstrated, implicating convincingly the central nervous system in immunoregulation (Ader, 1975). Their work has been confirmed in other laboratories, some of which utilized other immunosuppressants (Kusnecov, Sivyer, King, Husband, & Cripps, 1983). It has also been found that cellular immunity can be conditioned (Borbjerg & Ader, 1983). Conditioned immunosuppression can prolong the lives of mice with systemic lupus erythematosus (Ader, 1982), and the enhancement of immunity can also be conditioned (Gorcynski, Macrae, & Kennedy, 1982). Early experience also affects immunity. In a study of adult rats, those handled during the first three weeks of life showed enhanced adult humoral immunity (Solomon, Levine, & Kraft, 1968).

6. *Experimental manipulation of appropriate parts of the central nervous system should have immunologic consequences.* The hypothalamus—which is rich in neural connections to the limbic system of the brain, has receptors for humoral influences from the blood and cerebrospinal fluid, and influences the pituitary through a variety of polypeptide-releasing factors (TRH, LHRH, CRF, and somatostatin)—serves as the interface between the brain and a range of critical peripheral regulatory functions. It has been implicated in immune function by direct research and has many neurohormones and neurotransmitters that may affect immune function.

Early work in humoral immunity demonstrated that the electrical stimulation of the lateral hypothalamus of rats led to alterations in their levels of immunoglobulins (Fessel & Forsythe, 1963). Significant Soviet work revealed that a destructive lesion in a specific portion of the dorsal hypothalamus of rabbits led to complete suppression of primary antibody response, prolonged retention of antigen in the blood, inability to induce streptococcal antigen myocarditis, and prolonged graft retention (Korneva & Khai, 1963); on the other hand, electrical stimulation of the same region enhanced antibody response (Korneva, 1967). Destruction of the posterior hypothalamus has been shown to aggravate experimentally induced allergic polyneuritis, an effect that is related to the absence of antibodies to protect the myelin sheath that surrounds some nerves (Konovalov, Korneva, & Khai, 1971).

Hypothalamic lesions affect cell-mediated immunity as well. One source of evidence is experiments on the cell-mediated reaction of delayed hypersensitivity. Anterior lesions in the guinea pig suppress the normal delayed cutaneous hypersensitivity to picryl chloride and tuberculin (Macris, Schiavi, Camarino, & Stein, 1972). Amkraut and I also found that electrolytic lesions of the ventromedial and posterior nuclei of the hypothalamus of hybrid rats impaired the graft-versus-host reaction in the recipient (unpublished data, 1970). Guinea pigs with anterior hypothalamic lesions had significantly smaller cutaneous tuberculin reactions than pigs without an operation or pigs who had undergone a sham operation, and there was decreased stimulation in vitro of lymphocytes from animals with hypothalamic lesions (Keller, Shapiro, Schleiffer, & Stein, 1982).

Other areas of the brain also affect immune reactions. Interesting recent French work implicates the cerebral cortex in immunoregulation in a laterally differential way. In mice an intact left cerebral cortex is necessary for the production of T-cell-inducing factors (Renoux, Biziere, Renoux, & Guillamin, 1983). The cortex does not affect B-cell activity, which is influenced by hypothalamic lesions, leaving the pathway for the production of B cells unclear. Forebrain ablation in the chick embryo alters the thymus (Jankovic, 1982/1984), the site of T lymphocytes and a source of control of many immune reactions.

The connection between the central nervous system and the immune system is clear also from the fact that portions of the immune system itself are significantly infiltrated with nerve endings (Spector, 1983). The thymus has nerve-end fibers from the vagus, which originates in the brainstem, and from other sources. The bone marrow, a source of B cells, also has a good neural supply (Calvo, 1968), and brain lesions affect marrow function (Baciu, 1962). The autonomic nervous system, which regulates such generally involuntary functions as blood pressure, heart rate, and hormone secretions, also appears significantly involved in immune response. During the immune response, noradrenaline decreases in the spleen but not in nonlymphoid organs (Besedovsky, Del Rey, Sorkin, Da Prada, & Keller, 1979).

7. Activation of the immune system (for example, through immunization) should be accompanied by altered phenomena in the central nervous system.

Further evidence that the hypothalmus is directly involved in regulation of immune response is provided by the work of Besedovsky and Sorkin in Switzerland and of Korneva in the U.S.S.R. (Besedovsky et al., 1979; Korneva, 1967). In animals that respond to an immunizing antigen, the firing rates of neurons (as determined by implanted electrodes) increase in the ventro-medial nuclei of the hypothalamus (Besedovsky et al., 1979).

8. *Hormones and other substances regulated or elaborated by the central nervous system should influence immune mechanisms.* The effect of hormones on immune response has been the subject of many reviews (Reichlin & MacLean, 1981). Most clearly implicated, of course, have been adrenal corticosteroids with their inhibitive effect. My initial foray into animal experiments dealing with stress-induced immunosuppression resulted from finding a breakdown of psychological defenses in patients with rheumatoid arthritis. I knew that such a breakdown is associated with an increase in the immunosuppressive adrenal cortical steroid hormones (Hamburg, 1962), and was aware of an association between autoimmunity and relative immunologic incompetence— which has now been related to decreased activity of suppressor T cells (Fudenberg, 1968). In vitro, low concentrations of corticosteroids stimulate lymphocyte proliferation, which strengthens the immune response, and high concentrations inhibit lymphocyte proliferation (Ambrose, 1964).

That stress and other experiential influences on immunity are not mediated merely by adrenal hormones has been made clear by recent work showing stress-induced suppression of immunity in rats from which the adrenal glands have been removed (Keller, Weiss, Schleiffer, Miller, & Stein, 1983). (Earlier, Amkraut and I had found that in a graft-versus-host model of cellular immunity stress is more immunosuppressive than is the corticoste-roid-releasing ACTH [Amkraut & Solomon, 1973].) A variety of other stress-affected neuroendocrines influence immune response, including growth, thyroid, and sex hormones; insulin; the catecholamines; histamine; and the prostaglandins. For example, infusions of the catecholamine norepineph-rine, the production of which rises under stress, increase the activity of natural killer cells, which play an important role in the immune system's surveillance against tumor cells (Locke et al., 1984). Similarly, prostaglandins (the release of which is inhibited by corticosteroids [Lewis & Pipen, 1975]) are immunosuppressive in normal animals but tend to restore immunocom-petence in immunosuppressed ones; the mechanisms for these different effects remain unknown (Jaffe et al., 1983).

Soviet work demonstrates that the neurotransmitter serotonin delays the primary immune response to an antigen and lowers the intensity of primary and secondary response (Devoino, Eremina, & Ilyutchenok, 1970). Removing the hypothalamus or the pituitary and lesions in the pituitary stalk abolish these inhibitory effects. In the hypothalamus, serotoninergic struc-tures appear to participate in the production of antibodies. (Such mechanisms may be involved in immunosuppression induced by psychological depression.) Administering the antidepressant iproniazid (which inhibits monoamine oxidase, thus elevating biogenic amines such as serotonin) as well as serotonin itself delays the involvement of helper T cells in stimulating IgG antibody production by B cells during the secondary immune response (Devoino & Idova, 1973). Similar serotonin-related drug effects are found in delayed hypersensitivity (reflecting cell-mediated immunity; (see Devoino & Ilyutchenok, 1968). There are claims that serotonin can ameliorate autoimmune disease (both multiple sclerosis and its probable analogue, experimental allergic encephalomyelitis) by affecting the distribution and quantity of suppressor T cells (Abramchik, 1982/1984). Neuropeptide levels appear altered in autoimmune disease—patients with rheumatoid arthritis have lower levels of beta-endorphin (Kangilaski, 1981).

It is probable that many of the effects of psychological events on the immune system are the result of the influences of neuroendocrines, neurotransmitters, and neuropeptides on nucleotide molecules within cells—particularly on the cyclic nucleotides (cAMP and cGMP), fittingly called the second messengers, and on adenosine triphosphate (ATP), the mechanisms of which may be parallel in the central nervous system and the immune system (Horowitz, Beer, Clody, Vogel, & Chasin, 1972). Neurotransmitters and neuroendocrine hormones that affect cGMP include acetylcholine, insulin, and serotonin; those that affect cAMP include beta-adrenergics, histamine, and prostaglandins; and those that affect ATPase include alpha-adrenergics, corticosteroids, insulin, growth hormone, and thyroxin (Hadden, 1983). Effects of cGMP and cAMP on the immune system are generally reciprocal: The former enhances and the latter suppresses lymphocyte proliferation, activities of killer cells, lymphokine production, motility, and rosetting (by T cells); and the former suppresses and the latter enhances differentiation of immune cells (Hadden, 1983).

It appears likely that the neuropeptides (particularly the opioid peptides), which modulate the reactions of the central nervous system, will be found to have an important and complex role in immunity. To date, their immune effects are not completely clear. Beta-endorphins increase the mitogen-stimulated proliferation of T cells, and enkephalins enhance active T-cell rossettes (Gilman, Schwartz, Milner, Bloom, & Feldman, 1981; Milner, Murgo, & Plotnikoff). The opiate blocker naloxone can prevent stress-induced immunosuppression (Shavit, Lewis, Terman, Gale, & Liebeskind, 1983).

9. *Immunologically competent cells should have receptor sites for neuroendocrines, neurotransmitters, and neuropeptides, and for substances regulated by them.* Cell receptors are the locks into which the keys of different chemical ligands fit to produce a change in cellular activity. A number of investigators have found (and continue to find) receptors on lymphocytes or thymocytes for hormones controlled by the central nervous system (research reviewed by

Solomon and Amkraut [1983]), including corticosteroids, insulin, testosterone, estrogens, beta-adrenergic agents, histamine, growth hormone, acetylcholine, and methionine-enkephalin (Zozulia, Patsakova, & Kost, 1982). Presumably, the presence of a receptor site implies a function for its substrate. Some substrates have been identified as playing a role in stimulating the differentiation of lymphocytes and in controlling their activity (Cantor & Gershon, 1979; Helderman & Strom, 1978).

10. *Feedback mechanisms in immune regulation should act, at least in part, via mediation of the central nervous system.* Serum levels of adrenal cortical steroid hormones are elevated in response to an antigen or graft rejection, presumably via the influence of ACTH, which is controlled by the hypothalamus (Besedovsky & Sorkin, 1977; Besedovsky, Sorkin, & Keller, 1978). This finding suggests a feedback loop between the immune system and the hypothalamic-endocrine system. Antigen stimulates immune response, which leads to a rise in cortisol, which, in turn, tends to suppress the immune response. Such an endocrine response has been postulated as an explanation for the phenomenon of antigenic competition, in which the response to one antigen inhibits the response to another (Besedovsky et al., 1979).

Another feedback mechanism is suggested by the finding that T cells not produced in response to an antigen are more sensitive to the inhibitory effects of steroids than T cells that are; this points to a modulating feedback loop that prevents such sensitized T cells from being overstimulated by the immunohormones (lymphokines) that are released after antigenic stimulation and that increase the activities of a variety of cells involved in immune responses (Hall & Goldstein, 1983a). Recent research strongly suggesting such a feedback mechanism found a decreased noradrenaline turnover in the hypothalami of rats at a peak of immune response (Besedovsky et al., 1983). This effect was duplicated by injecting into rats lymphokines released by immunologic cells in vitro. It thus appears that lymphokines, a product of the immune reaction, may induce autonomic and endocrine mechanisms that, controlled by the central nervous system, contribute to immunoregulation. (This possibility adds weight to the question: Can central nervous system influences lead to such immunologic dysfunction as autoimmunity, for which psychological correlates were pointed out in hypothesis I?)

11. *Factors elaborated by the immune system should affect the central nervous system and substances regulated by it.* Infused radioactive thymosin alpha$_1$, known to influence maturation of T cells, can be found in circumventricular areas of the brain involving neuroendocrine regulation (Hall & Goldstein, 1983b). Lymphocytes themselves are a source of gamma-endorphin and ACTH (Smith & Blalock, 1981). Antibrain antibodies are claimed in Yugoslav work to affect both conditioned learning and the immune response, and Russians claim that thymic hormones (important in T-cell function as

well as T-cell maturation) influence learning (Jankovic, 1982/1984). Animals from which the thymus has been removed showed delayed sexual maturation, presumably through neuroendocrine mediation (Besedovsky & Sorkin, 1974).

12. *Biochemical and functional similarities might be expected between the substances modulating the function and reactivity of the central nervous system (neuropeptides) and the substances with comparable effects on the immune system (lymphokines).* An ever-increasing number of low-molecular-weight proteins (polypeptides), about two dozen so far, are being identified as modulating the sensitivity of the central nervous system. These compounds have slower and more prolonged actions than neurotransmitters (chemicals transmitting nerve impulses across synaptic junctions and engendering electrical activity along the cell membrane of the adjacent neuron). Likewise, more than a dozen soluble products of immunologically competent cells—the lymphokines (which generally are polypeptides)—have so far been identified as amplifying, activating, and controlling immune response. (An analogy has been made between a synapse and the junction between a macrophage and a lymphocyte [E. M. Smith, personal communication, 1984].) Similarities between the two systems are also suggested by the fact that a variety of substances affect both. I have already noted in hypothesis 11 that the thymic hormones (among them, thymosin alpha$_1$) seem to affect the central nervous system as well as the immune system. In addition, enkephalin and endorphin affect both systems, ACTH stimulates corticosteroids that affect both systems. Both enkephalin and ACTH are part of the same precursor molecule. There are also antigenic and structural similarities among ACTH, beta-endorphin, and human leukocyte interferon (Smith & Blalock, 1981). Apparently, there are even some similarities in the structure of specific proteins of the thymus and the cerebral cortex (Valueva & Malyzchev, 1982).

13. *Thymic hormones regulating immune function should be influenced by the central nervous system.* If, as I am arguing, the central nervous system and the immune system are intimately interrelated, does it not seem likely that thymic hormones, so involved with T-cell activity, are true neuroendocrines—that is, under the direction of the central nervous system? What might be the controlling factor or factors of thymic hormones? Is there a "thymosin tropin" analogous to ACTH, and where might it be produced? There is growing evidence of bidirectional interactions between the thymus and the neuroendocrine system. Thymosin beta$_4$ elicits the release of luteinizing hormone-releasing factor, and injecting thymosin beta$_4$ intraventricularly increases the serum levels of luteinizing hormone (Rebar, Miyake, Low, & Goldstein, 1981). Thymectomy affects the pituitary, the "master" gland, itself controlled by releasing factors from the hypothalamus (Jankovic, 1982/1984). Neuroendocrines influence the production of thymic hormones (Fabris, 1982). Lethargic mice, a mutant strain, suffer from a neurologic

abnormality that develops before weaning, lasts 30 to 60 days, and then gradually disappears. This neurological disease is associated with thymic atrophy; the thymus returns to normal as soon as the neural disturbance disappears (Dung, 1977). Both thymectomized and nude mice, another mutant strain that shows thymic atrophy, display a profoundly disturbed neuroendocrine balance (Fabris, Mocchegianni, Muzzioli, & Imberti, 1983). There is an isolated report of the extraction from the anterior pituitary of a low-molecular-weight peptide with thymocyte-stimulating properties (Saxena & Talwar, 1977).

14. *Behavioral interventions (such as psychotherapy, relaxation techniques, imagery, biofeedback, and hypnosis) should be able to enhance or optimize immune function.* We have come full circle, back to clinical medicine: If "noxious affects" (such emotions as anxiety, grief, depression, and loneliness) are immunosuppressive, then it stands to reason that whatever psychotherapeutic or psychopharmacologic intervention makes for a distress-free state of mind might be expected to improve immune function. An important question is whether behavioral intervention can *enhance* immunity. Psychoneuroimmunologic research on the effects of such interventions on specific aspects of the immune response cries out to be done. Are the innumerable reports of successful behavioral interventions (from psychoanalysis to faith healing to visualizing "good" white blood cells eating up "bad" cancer cells) in a variety of physical diseases, particularly cancer and the autoimmune diseases, the result, at least in some cases, of psychoneuroendocrine effects on immune function? One unique recent study found that young, highly hypnotizable subjects were able to *increase* the in vitro proliferative response of their lymphocytes to pokeweed mitogen (which stimulates both B and T cells) when given the suggestion under trance that their white blood cells were like "powerful sharks" destroying "weak germs" (Hall, 1983). (Many studies have noted that hypnosis can moderate such inflammatory responses as histamine-induced wheals.)

Henry and Meehan conceptualize behavior as a continuum from effort to relaxation and mood as a continuum from euphoria to distress; and at different points of a continuum identify responses along the pituitary-adrenal cortical axis and the sympathetic-adrenal medullary axis (Henry & Meehan, 1981). Are happiness, security, sense of control, relaxation, and other positive emotions accompanied by immune enhancement? Again, the work remains to be done, work certainly likely to be of relevance to clinical medicine.

THE ACQUIRED IMMUNE DEFICIENCY SYNDROME AS A MODEL FOR PSYCHONEUROIMMUNOLOGY RESEARCH

As I noted earlier, AIDS, an apparently "new" acquired immune deficiency syndrome, is both an infectious disease and a disease of immunologic aberration, and so seems particularly suitable to be examined from a psycho-neuroimmunologic framework.

Since 1981, when 231 cases were reported, AIDS—accompanied by high risk for such opportunistic infections as pneumocystis carinii and Kaposi's sarcoma—has appeared among specific groups and spread among them in epidemic-like fashion. It now seems clear, with the discovery in the United States and France of the HTLV-III/LAV retrovirus, now called HIV, that an infectious agent is a necessary but probably not sufficient causal factor. According to the Centers for Disease Control, as of May 1989, the United States had a total of 94,280 cases. The distribution of the increasing number of single-mode transmission cases has remained relatively constant: 59% of those affected are gay or bisexual males, 18% drug abusers, 1% hemophiliacs, 2% recipients of blood transfusions, 4% recipients through heterosexual contact, and 3% others; 20.6% of the cases were reported in New York City and 6.6% in San Francisco (Centers for Disease Control, 1989).

AIDS is accompanied by a variety of immunologic abnormalities, includ-ing a decreased number of helper T cells with a reduced helper:suppressor T-cell ratio; decreased lymphocyte response to mitogens; lowered production of interleukin-2 and gamma interferon but elevated levels of thymosin alpha$_1$; lymphopenia; skin anergy to common allergens; hyperglobulinemia, reflect-ing hypepractive spontaneous B-cell responses; probable hyperactivity of suppressor T cells; some impairment of natural killer-cell activity; and some-times thrombocytopenia (Talal, 1983). There appears to be a correlation between total numbers of sexual contacts and history of infections with hepatitis B and cytomegalovirus.

It is also clear that far more individuals than those classified as having AIDS, according to the criteria established by the Center for Disease Control, have immunosuppression and a syndrome that can include: laboratory signs of lowered helper:suppressor T-cell ratio, lowered T-cell numbers, lowered responsivity of lymphocytes to stimulation in vitro, thrombocytopenia, and hyperglobulinemia; and clinical symptoms of infection (especially thrush [candidiasis], bullous impetigo, cytomegalovirus, severe genital herpes, or herpes zoster), fatigue, fever or night sweats, cough, and diarrhea (Abrams, Lewis, Beckstead, Easavant, & Drew, 1984). This syndrome of "lesser AIDS," referred to as AIDS-related complex (ARC), can persist, improve, or, progress to AIDS. It is now apparent that antibody indicating presence of the virus, is far more widespread, especially in some geographic areas, than AIDS or ARC and that asymptomatic persons without immune deficiencies may harbor the virus and transmit disease.

Norman Talal states, "AIDS teaches us that immunoregulatory diseases are truly multifactorial" (Talal, 1983). What questions might be addressed in taking a multifactorial, biopsychosocial, psychoneuroimmunologic frame of reference for research on HIV infection and AIDS.

1. Do stressful life experiences, coping style, affective states, personality, and/or social–cultural influences (psychosocial factors) relate to susceptibility to HIV infection?
2. Do psychosocial factors influence the course of HIV infection? Are such factors related to length of asymptomatic state or duration of life? Do such factors relate to rate and degree of decline in CD4 cell levels and/or to numbers and function of other components of the immune system?
3. How do sociocultural factors, particularly those relevant to particular groups whose behaviors place them at increased risk for HIV infection, influence immunologic and clinical manifestations of HIV disease? What is the impact on HIV-infected individuals of social interventions (e.g., educational campaigns) and social policy (e.g., laws relating to confidentiality or nondiscrimination)?
4. At any given level of HIV-induced immune deficiency, do psychosocial factors play a role in determination of clinical health status and degree of subjective well-being or illness?
5. Can stressors or other psychosocial factors activate HIV from a latent to an active, rapidly replicating form?
6. Are there relationships among psychosocial factors and neuropsychological/neuropsychiatric manifestations of HIV infection?
7. Do cytokines of the immune system play a role in neuropsychiatric aspects of HIV infection, and, conversely, do neuropeptides influence immunity in HIV infection?
8. What are the nature and consequences of HIV interactions with neuropeptide receptor sites?
9. Can behavioral, psychotherapeutic, or psychopharmacologic interventions affect immune functions and/or relieve symptoms in persons with HIV spectrum disorders?

In 1982 the University of California, San Francisco Biopsychosocial AIDS Project, coordinated by Jeffrey S. Mandel, conducted a pilot study of AIDS patients. Among the several themes to emerge were a few of particular relevance:

1. Coping styles, although variable, frequently included denial (for example, through perseverance and emotional stoicism) and suppression of dysphoric affect (for example, avoiding "negative" feelings, such as anger).
2. A number of stressful life events occurred in the year preceding diagnosis.

3. The patients manifested guilt about sexual identity and previous sexual activities.
4. There were unresolved or as yet untested feelings about "coming out" to family members or employers.
5. Longer survival appeared related to adaptive traits and coping patterns.

These observations are consistent with hypotheses 1 and 2. More systematic studies, including correlation of psychosocial factors with specific immunologic and clinical conditions are now underway at a number of cites.

CONCLUSION

I end this overview of the burgeoning and complex field of psychoneuroimmunology with the caveat that the time for such overviews is passing. The need now is to focus on specific aspects of the field, from the underlying molecular biological mechanisms that mediate between the central nervous system and the immune system to the behavioral correlates—clinical and experimental—of particular features of the immune response. The study of interdisciplinary fields is always difficult. The investigation of psychoneuroimmunology is made more difficult by the fact that both behavioral medicine and immunology are growing exponentially in knowledge and complexity. In a sense, psychoneuroimmunology is at a point that neuroendocrinology had reached decades ago. We should remember that the psychological effects on endocrine function were understood before the pituitary-releasing factors of the hypothalamus had been discovered! Clinically, we can expect important developments in the prevention and treatment of disease to emerge from the further exploration of psychoneuroimmunology. The possible role of psychological interventions in immune enhancement must be studied systematically.

It is appealing to postulate a cooperative evolutionary development of the immune system and the central nervous system. If the immune system and the central nervous system are closely linked, then not only may understanding of psychophysiology enhance understanding of immune mechanisms but, as both Jonas Salk (personal communication, 1981) and Gerald Edelman (Edelman, 1982) suggest, cellular and molecular immunology may enhance understanding of mechanisms within the nervous system.

REFERENCES

Abramchik, G. N. (1983). *Clinical aspects of serotonin treatment for autoimmune diseases.* Paper presented at Soviet Academy of Sciences conference, "Regulation of Immune Homeostasis," in Leningrad. (Published in 1984)

Abrams, D. I., Lewis, B. J., Beckstead, J. H., Casavant, C. A., & Drew, W. L. (1984). Persistent diffuse lymphadenopathy in homosexual men: Endpoint or prodome? *Annals of Internal Medicine, 100,* 801–808.

Ader, R. (1975). Behaviorally conditioned immunosuppression. *Psychosomatic Medicine, 37,* 333–340.

Ader, R. (1982). Behaviorally conditioned immunosuppression and murine systemic lupus erythematosus. *Science, 215,* 1534–1536.

Ambrose, C. T. (1964). The requirement for hydrocortisone in antibody forming tissue cultivated serum-free medium. *Journal of Experimental Medicine, 119,* 1027–1049.

Amkraut, A. A., & Solomon, G. F. (1972). Stress and murine sarcoma virus (Maloney)—induced tumors. *Cancer Research, 32,* 1428–1433.

Amkraut, A. A., & Solomon, G. F. (1973). Effects of stress and hormonal intervention on the graft versus host response. In B. D. Jankovic & K. Isokovic (Eds.), *Microenvironmental aspects of immunity* (pp. 667–674). New York: Plenum Press.

Amkraut, A. A., Solomon, G. F., Kasper, P., & Perdue, A. (1973). Effects of stress on the graft versus host response. *Advances in Experimental Medicine and Biology, 29,* 267–274.

Baciu, I. (1962). La régulation nerveuse et humorale de l'erythropoiese. *Journal of Physiology* (Paris), *54,* 441.

Bahnson, C. B. (1980). Stress and cancer: State of the art. Part 1. *Psychosomatics, 21,* 975–981.

Bahnson, C. B. (1981). Stress and cancer: State of the art. Part 2. *Psychosomatics, 22,* 207–220.

Bartrop, R. W., Lagarus, L., Luckhurst, E., Kiloh, L. G., & Penny, R. (1977). Depressed lymphocyte function after bereavement. *Lancet, 1,* 834–836.

Besedovsky, H. O., Del Rey, A., Sorkin, E., Da Prada, M., Burri, R., & Honneger, C. (1983). The immune response evokes changes in brain noradregenergic neurons. *Science, 221,* 564–565.

Besedovsky, H. O., Del Rey, A., Sorkin, E., Da Prada, M., & Keller, H. H. (1979). Immunoregulation mediated by-the sympathetic nervous system. *Cell Immunology, 48,* 346.

Besedovsky, H. O., & Sorkin, E. (1974). Thymic involvement in female sexual maturation. *Nature, 249,* 356–358.

Besedovsky, H. O., & Sorkin, E. (1977). Network of immune-neuroendocrine interactions. *Clinical and Experimental Immunology, 27,* 1–12.

Besedovsky, H. O., Sorkin, E., & Keller, H. H. (1978). Changes in the concentration of corticosterone in the blood during skin graft rejection in the rat. *Journal of Endocrinology, 76,* 175–176.

Borbjerg, D., & Ader, R. (1983). Acquisition and extinction of conditioned suppression of a graft versus host response in the rat. *Psychosomatic Medicine, 45,* 369. (*Abstract*).

Calvo, W. (1968). The innervation of the bone marrow in laboratory animals. *American Journal of Anatomy, 123,* 315.

Cantor, H., & Gershon, R. K. (1979). Immunological circuits. Cellular compositions. *Federal Proceedings, 39,* 2058–2064.

Centers for Disease Control (1989, May). *HIV/AIDS surveillance report* (pp. 1–16). Atlanta, GA: Author.

Devoino, L. V., Eremina, O. F., Ilyutchenok, R., & Yu. (1970). The role of the hypothalamo-pituitary system in the mechanism of action of reserpine and 5-hydroxytryptophan on antibody production. *Neuropharmacology, 9,* 67–72.

Devoino, L. V., & Idova, G. V. (1973). Influence of some drugs on the immune response. IV. Effect of serotonin, 5-hydroxytryptophan, iproniazid and p-chlorphenylalanine on the synthesis of IgM and IgG antibodies. *European Journal of Pharmacology, 22,* 325–331.

Devoino, L. V. Ilyutchenok, R., & Yu. (1968). Influence of some drugs on the immune response. II. Effects of serotonin, 5-hydroxytryptophan, reserpine and iproniazid on delayed hypersensitivity. *European Journal of Pharmacology, 4,* 449–456.

Dorian, B. J., Keystone, E., Garfinkel, P. E., & Brown, G. M. (1981). Immune mechanisms in acute psychological stress. *Psychosomatic Medicine, 43,* 84. (*Abstract*)

Dung, H. C. (1977). Deficiency in the thymus-dependent immunity in "lethargic" mutant mice. *Transplantation, 23,* 39.

Edelman, G. M. (1982). Through a computer darkly: Group selection and higher brain function. *Bulletin of the American Academy of Arts and Sciences, 23,* 36–49.

Fabris, N. (1982). *Endocrine control of thymic factor production in young adults and old mice.* Paper presented at Soviet Academy of Sciences conference, "Regulation of Immune Homeostasis," at Leningrad.

Fabris, N., Mocchegianni, E., Muzzioli, M., & Imberti, R. (1983). Thymusneuroendocrine network. In N. Fabris, E. Garaci, J. Hadden, & N. A. Mitchison (Eds.), *Immunoregulation* (pp. 341–362). New York: Plenum Press.

Fessel, W. J., & Forsythe, R. F. (1963). Hypothalamic role in control of gamma globulin levels. *Arthritic and Rheumatism, 6,* 770. (*Abstracts*)

Fessel, W. J., & Hirata-Hibi, M. (1963). Abnormal leukocytes in schizophrenia. *Archives of General Psychiatry, 9,* 601–613.

Fessel, W. J., & Solomon, G. F. (1960). Psychosis and systemic lupus erythematosus: A review of the literature and case reports. *California Medicine, 92,* 266–270.

Friedman, M., & Roseman, R. H. (1974). *Type A behavior and your heart.* New York: Alfred A. Knopf.

Fudenberg, H. H. (1968). Are autoimmune diseases immunologic deficiency states? *Hospital Practice, 3,* 43–53.

Fudenberg, H. H. (1984). Is schizophrenia an immunologic receptor disorder? *Medical Hypotheses,* 85–93.

Gilman, S. C., Schwartz, J. M., Milner, R. J., Bloom, F. E., & Feldman, J. D. (1981). Enhancement of lymphocyte proliferation responses by beta-endorphin. *Society for Neuroscience Abstracts, 7,* 880.

200 / Part IV. Psychoneuroimmunology

Gorcynski, R. M., Macrae, S., & Kennedy, M. (1982). Conditioned immune response associated with allogenic skin grafts in mice. *Journal of Immunology, 29,* 704–709.

Hadden, J. W. (1983). Cyclic nucleotides and related mechanisms in immune regulation: A mini review. In N. Fabris, E. Garaci, J. Hadden, & H. A. Mitchison (Eds.), *Immunoregulation* (p. 201–230). New York: Plenum Press.

Hall, H. H. (1983). Hypnosis and the immune system: A review with implications for cancer and the psychology of healing. *American Journal of Clinical Hypnosis, 25,* 92–103.

Hall, N. R., & Goldstein, A. L. (1983a). Role of thymosin and the neuroendocrine system in the regulation of immunity. In N. Fabris, E. Garaci, J. Hadden, & N. A. Mitchison (Eds.), *Immunoregulation* (pp. 141–163). New York: Plenum Press.

Hall, N. R., & Goldstein, A. L. (1983b). The thymus–brain connection: Interactions between thymosin and the neuroendocrine system. *Lymphokine Research, 2,* 1–6.

Hamburg, D. A. (1962). Plasma and urinary corticosteroid levels in naturally occurring psychologic stresses. *Research Publication of the Association for Research in Nervous and Mental Diseases, 40,* 406–413.

Heath, R. G. (1969). Schizophrenia: Evidence of a pathologic immune mechanism. *Proceedings of the American Psychopathology Association, 58,* 234–236.

Helderman, J. H., & Strom, T. B. (1978). Specific binding site on T and B lymphocytes as a marker of cell activation. *Nature, 274,* 62–63.

Henry, J. P., & Meehan, J. P. (1981). Psychosocial stimuli, physiological specificity and cardiovascular disease. In H. Weiner, M. A. Hofer, & A. J. Stunkard (Eds.), *Brain, behavior, and bodily disease* (pp. 305–333). New York: Raven Press.

Hirata-Hibi, M., Higashi, S., Tachibana, T., & Watanabe, N. (1982). Stimulated lymphocytes in schizophrenia. *Archives of General Psychiatry, 39,* 82–87.

Horowitz, Z. P., Beer, B., Clody, D. E., Vogel, J. R., & Chasin, M. (1972). Cyclic AMP and anxiety. *Psychosomatics, 13,* 85–92.

Jaffe, B. M., Santoro, M. G., Le Port, P., Favelli, C., Hofer, D., & Garaci, E. (1983). Prostaglandins and immunoregulation. In N. Fabris, E. Garaci, J. Hadden, & N. A. Mitchison (Eds.), *Immunoregulation* (pp. 271–281). New York: Plenum Press.

Jankovic, B. D. (1982). *Immunodulation of neutral structures and functions.* Paper presented at Soviet Academy of Sciences Conference, "Regulation of Immune Homeostasis," at Leningrad. (Published in USSR, 1984)

Jankovic, B. D., & Isokovic, K. (1973). Neuro-endocrine correlates of immune response: 1. Effects of brains on antibody production, arthus reactivity, and delayed hypersensitivity in the rat. *Int. Allergy, 45,* 360–372.

Kangas, J. H., & Solomon, G. F. (1975). *The psychology of strength.* Englewood Cliffs, NJ: Prentice Hall.

Kangilaski, J. (1981). Beta-endorphin levels lower in arthritis patients. *Journal of the American Medical Association, 246,* 203.

Keller, S. E., Shapiro, R., Schleiffer, S. J., & Stein, M. Hypothalamic influences on anaphylaxis. *Psychosomatic Medicine, 44,* 302. (*Abstract*)

Keller, S. E., Weiss, J. M., Schleiffer, S. J., Miller, N. E., & Stein, M. (1981). Suppression of immunity of stress: Effect of a graded series of stressors on lymphocyte stimulation in the rat. *Science, 213,* 1397–1400.

Keller, S. E., Weiss, J. M., Schleiffer, S. J., Miller, N. E., & Stein, M. (1983). Stress-induced suppression of immunity in adrenalectomized rats. *Science, 221,* 1301-1304.

Klopfer, B. (1957). Psychological variables in human cancer. *Journal of Projective Techniques, 21,* 331-340.

Kobasa, S. C. (1979). Stressful life events, personality and health: An inquiry into hardiness. *Journal of Personality and Social Psychology, 37,* 1-11.

Konovalov, G. V., Korneva, E. A., & Khai, L. M. (1971). Effect of destruction of the posterior hypothalamic area on the experimental allergic polyneuritis. *Brain Research, 29,* 283-286.

Korneva, E. A. (1967). The effects of stimulating different mesencephalic structures on protective immune response pattern. *Fiziologicheskii Zhurnal SSSR Imeni I. M. Sechenova (Leningrad), 53,* 42-45.

Korneva, E. A., & Khai, L. M. (1963). Effects of destruction of hypothalamic areas on immunogenisis. *Fiziologicheskii Zhurnal SSSR Imeni I. M. Sechenova (Leningrad), 49,* 42-46.

Kronfol, Z., Silva, J., Greden, J., Dembiski, S., & Carroll, B. J. (1982). Cell-mediated immunity in melancholia. *Psychosomatic Medicine, 44,* 304. (*Abstract*)

Kusnecov, A. W., Sivyer, M. G., King, A. J., Husband, A. W., & Cripps, R. L. (1983). Behaviorally conditioned suppression of the immune response by antilymphocyte serum. *Journal of Immunology, 180,* 2117-2120.

Laudenslager, M. L., Reite, M., & Harbeck, R. J. (1982). Suppressed immune response in infant monkeys associated with maternal separation. *Behavioral and Neural Biology, 36,* 40-48.

Laudenslager, M. L., Ryan, S. M., Drugan, R. C., Hyson, R. L., & Maier, S. F. (1983). Coping and immunosuppression: Inescapable but not escapable shock suppresses lymphocyte proliferation. *Science, 221,* 568-570.

Lawrence, J. S. (1962). Genetic studies on rheumatoid arthritis. *American Journal of Public Health, 52,* 1689-1696.

Lewis, G. P., & Pipen, P. (1975). Inhibition of release of prostaglandins as an explanation of some of the actions of antiinflammatory corticosteroids. *Nature, 254,* 308.

Linscott, W. D. (1976). Specific immunologic unresponsiveness. In H. H. Fudenberg, D. P. Stites, J. L. Caldwell, & J. V. Wells (Eds.), *Basic and clinical immunology* (pp. 146-150). Los Altos: Lange Medical Publications.

Locke, S., Kraus, K., Kutz, I., Edbril, S., Phillips, K., & Benson, H. (1984, November). *Altered natural killer cell activity during norepinephrine infusion in humans.* Paper presented at First International Workshop on Neuroimmunomodulation.

Macris, N. T., Schiavi, R. C., Camarino, M. S., & Stein, M. (1972). Effect of hypothalamic lesions on immune processes in the guinea pig. *American Journal of Physiology, 210,* 1205-1209.

Maier, S. F., Laudenslager, M. L., & Ryan, S. M. (1983). *Stressor controllability, immune function and endogenous opiates.* Unpublished manuscript.

Marx, J. L. (1982). Autoimmunity in left-handers. *Science, 217,* 141-144.

Metalnikov, S., & Chorin, V. (1926). The role of conditioned reflexes in immunity. *Annals of the Pasteur Institute, 11,* 1-8.

Miller, G. C., Murgo, A. J., & Plotnikoff, N. P. (1983). Enkephalins enhancement of active T-cells rosettes from lymphoma patients. *Clinical Immunology and Immunopathology, 26*, 446-451.

Monjan, A. A., & Collector, M. I. (1977). Stress-induced modulation of the immune response. *Science, 196*, 307-308.

Nemiah, J. C., & Sifneos, P. E. (1970). Affect and fantasy in patients with psychosomatic disorders. In O. W. Hill (Ed.), *Modern trends in psychosomatic medicine* (pp. 26-31). New York: Appleton-Century-Crofts.

Nichols, S. E. (1983). Psychiatric aspects of AIDS. *Psychosomatics, 24*, 1083-1089.

Palmblad, J. Stress and immunologic competence: Studies in man. In R. Ader (Ed.), *Psychoneuroimmunology* (pp. 229-257). New York: Academic Press.

Palmblad, J., Petrini, B., Wasserman, J., & Akenstadt, T. (1979). Lymphocyte and granalocyte reactions during sleep deprivation. *Psychosomatic Medicine, 41*, 273-278.

Parkes, C. M., & Brown, C. J. (1972). Health after bereavement: A controlled study of young Boston widows and widowers. *Psychosomatic Medicine, 34*, 449-461.

Pollack, V. E. (1964). Antinuclear antibodies in families of patients with systemic lupus erythematosus. *New England Journal of Medicine, 271*, 165-171.

Rahe, R. H., & Arthur, R. J. (1978). Life change and illness studies: Past history and future directions. *Journal of Human Stress, 4*, 3-15.

Rebar, R. W., Miyake, A., Low, T. L. K., & Goldstein, A. L. (1981). Thymosin stimulates secretion of luteinizing hormone-releasing factor. *Science, 213*, 669-671.

Reichlin, S., & MacLean, D. B. (1981). Neuroendocrinology and the immune process. In R. Ader (Ed.), *Psychoneuroimmunology* (pp. 475-520). New York: Academic Press.

Reite, M., Harbeck, R., & Hoffman, A. (1981). Altered cellular immune response following peer separation. *Life Sciences, 29*, 1133-1136.

Renoux, G., Biziere, K., Renoux, M., & Guillamin, J. M. (1983). The production of T-cell-inducing factors in mice is controlled by the brain neocortex. *Scandinavian Journal of Immunology, 17*, 45-50.

Salk, J. (1962). Biological basis of disease and behavior. *Perspectives in Biology and Medicine, 5*, 198-206.

Saxena, R. K., & Talwar, G. P. (1977). An anterior pituitary factor stimulated thymidine incorporation in isolated thymocytes. *Nature, 268*, 57.

Schleiffer, S. J., Keller, S. E., Camarino, M., Thornton, J. C., & Stein, M. (1983). Suppression of lymphocyte stimulation following bereavement. *Journal of the American Medical Association, 250*, 374-377.

Shavit, Y., Lewis, J. W., Terman, G. W., Gale, R. P., & Liebeskind, J. C. (1983). Endogenous opioids may mediate the effects of stress on tumor growth and immune function. *Proceedings of the Western Pharmacology Society, 26*, 53-56.

Smith, E. M., & Blalock, J. E. (1981). Human lymphocyte production of corticotropin and endorphin-like substances: Association with leukocyte interferon. *Proceedings of the National Academy of Science USA, 78*, 7530-7534.

Solomon, G. F. (1969). Stress and antibody response in rats. *International Archives of Allergy and Applied Immunology, 35*, 97-104.

Solomon, G. F. (1981a). Emotional and personality factors in the onset and course of autoimmune disease, particularly rheumatoid arthritis. In R. Ader (Ed.), *Psychoneuroimmunology* (pp. 159–182). New York: Academic Press.

Solomon, G. F. (1981b). Immunologic abnormalities in mental illness. In R. Ader (Ed.), *Psychoneuroimmunology* (pp. 259–278). New York: Academic Press.

Solomon, G. F., & Amkraut, A. A. (1983). Emotions, immunity and disease. In L. Temoshok, C. Van Dyke, L. S. Zegans (Eds.), *Emotions in health and illness: Theoretical and research foundations* (pp. 167–186). New York: Grune & Stratton.

Solomon, G. F., Levine, S., & Kraft, J. K. (1968). Early experience and immunology. *Nature, 220,* 821–822.

Solomon, G. F., & Moos, R. H. (1964). Emotions, immunity and disease. A speculative theoretical integration. *Archives of General Psychiatry, 11,* 657–764.

Solomon, G. F., & Moss, R. H. (1965). The relationship of personality to the presence of rheumatoid factor in asymptomatic relatives of patients with rheumatoid arthritis. *Psychosomatic Medicine, 27,* 350–360.

Sparer, P. J. (Ed.). (1956). *Personality, stress, and tuberculosis.* New York: International Universities Press.

Spector, N. H. (1983). Anatomic and physiological connections between the central nervous and immune systems (neuroimmunomodulation). In N. Fabris, E. Garaci, J. Hadden, N. A. Mitchison (Eds.), *Immunoregulation.* New York: Plenum Press.

Talal, M. (1983). A clinician and a scientist looks at acquired immune deficiency syndrome, AIDS: A validation of immunology's theoretical foundation. *Immunology Today, 4* (Suppl.), 180–183.

Talal, H., Fye, K., & Moutsopolous, H. (1976). In H. H. Fudenberg, D. P. Stites, J. L. Caldwell, & J. V. Wells (Eds.), *Basic and clinical immunology* (pp. 151–159). Los Altos: Lange Medical Publishers.

Valueva, T. K., & Malyzchev, V. A. (1982). *The role of various humoral thymic factors in antigen-independent T-lymphocyte differentiation.* Paper presented at Soviet Academy of Sciences, "Regulation of Immune Homeostasis," at Leningrad.

Zozulia, A. A., Patsakova, E. K., & Kost, N. V. (1982). Reaction between methionine enkaphalin and human lymphocytes. *Akad. Med. Nauh. SSSR, 1,* 28–32.

·V·

THE BRAIN'S REGULATION
OF THE BODY

·17·

Impact of Age on Weight Goals

R. ANDRES, D. ELAHI, J. D. TOBIN,
D. C. MULLER, and L. BRANT

Although the health hazards due to excessive obesity and excessive leanness are multiple and diverse, weight recommendations for over 40 years have been based solely on the risk of dying. The weight recommendation tables in nearly universal usage have been derived from the experience of the life insurance industry. Those tables have not recommended any weight adjustments for age. An analysis of the actuarial data on which the most recent tables are based shows that minimal mortality occurs at progressively increasing body weight as age advances (20 to 29, through 60 to 69 years). There is, furthermore, no systematic sex difference in those weights. We have prepared height–weight tables that are age-specific and delete sex and body frame type as variables. These weight standards are lower for young adults and higher for older adults than those previously recommended. A review of 23 other reported populations confirms the need to adjust weight standards for age.

The most widely used weight goals in the United States for over 40 years have undoubtedly been those provided by the Metropolitan Life Insurance Company. Three sets of tables have been published: the Ideal Weight Tables in 1942 and 1943; the Desirable Weight Tables in 1959; and the 1983 Height-Weight Tables. These tables have all had the same basic structure, but the weight ranges have been modified over the years. There are separate tables for men and women; weight ranges are given for a wide range of heights; and separate but overlapping weight ranges are provided for each of three body frames, small, medium, and large. The 1942-43 and 1959 tables were sug-

This chapter originally appeared in *Annals of Internal Medicine*, 1985, *103*(6, Pt. 2), 1030–1033.

gested for adults 25 years of age and older, the 1983 tables for those aged 25 to 59 years.

The grouping of ages into a single table of weights prompted us to analyze independently the actuarial data published in the Build Study 1979 (Society of Actuaries and Association of Life Insurance Medical Directors of America, 1980), which summarizes the database used in the construction of the Metropolitan 1983 tables. In all three sets of the Metropolitan tables, weights were given with clothes and heights with shoes. Corrections for nude height and weight were suggested for the 1983 tables. Tables were also published in which 1 inch (2.54 cm) was subtracted from the height as a shoe correction for men and women; 5 pounds (2.27 kg) were subtracted from the weight for men and 3 pounds (1.36 kg) were subtracted for women as clothing corrections. It is however the "clothed" tables that have received wide dissemination.

The rationale for the construction of the 1942–43 tables was not provided. The weight ranges were probably based on the weights of the insured 20- to 29-year-old subjects (Society of Actuaries and Association of Life Insurance Medical Directors of America, 1980). The weight ranges in the 1959 and 1983 tables were based on the actuarial mortality data of specific height–weight groups, presumably from pooled data from ages 25 to 69 for the 1959 tables and from ages 25 to 59 for the 1983 tables.

The division of the overall recommended weight range into separate ranges for three body frames was not based on actual measurements of body frame in the insured population. Neither the rationale for, nor the details of the computation of the ranges for the three frames, or indeed for the overall ranges in weight for individual heights, has been presented. Until the 1983 tables were published, the selection of the appropriate body frame was left to the judgment of the person or the physician. The publication of the 1983 tables provided two cutpoints for elbow breadth for men and for women at different height ranges that placed subjects into one of the three frame categories. However, because elbow breadth was not measured in the insured population, the weight adjustments for frame must have been set by unexplained empirical rules.

Since 1959 there has been a steadily increasing number of body weight–mortality reports from other populations. Although some studies are technically flawed, there are now about 50 different populations that merit attention. The studies include populations in the United States, Europe, Japan, Israel, Australia, New Zealand, and the South Pacific. The populations are not only geographically disparate but also differ widely in the occupation, race, and age of the populations selected. In addition, the studies differ with respect to duration of study; consideration of associated variables; rules for initial exclusion of subjects from the study; and techniques of assessing obesity.

ANALYSIS OF ACTUARIAL DATA FOR AGE EFFECTS

The Build Study 1979 (Society of Actuaries and Association of Life Insurance Medical Directors of America, 1980) collated data from 25 life insurance companies in the United States and Canada, including 4.2 million policies issued from 1950 to 1971 and traced to 1972. There were 106,000 deaths during this period. Data were presented for ages 20 to 29 through 60 to 69, and for 15 to 16 and 17 to 19 years, but the data in the latter two groups are sparse and will not be considered. Subjects were placed into 1 of 5 height groups and into 1 of 18 10-pound weight groups. The mortality ratios (actual/expected deaths) and number of deaths were reported for each of the height–weight groups in which at least ten deaths occurred.

Corrections were done for shoe height (1 in. [2.54 cm] for men and women) and for weight of indoor clothing (5 lb. [2.27 kg] for men and 3 lb. [1.37 kg] for women). For each height–weight group the body mass index (BMI) was calculated (kg/m^2). Plots of the body mass index versus mortality ratio showed that, as others have found for this and for other populations (Dyer, Stamler, Berkson, & Lindberg, 1975; Keys, 1980; Bray, 1982), the data are much better fit by a quadratic (U-shaped) curve than by a simple linear regression. The computation of the regression equation was weighted statistically for the number of deaths in each height–weight category. For each of the five age groups, for men and for women, the following equation was computed: mortality ratio $= a + b$ (BMI) $+ c$ (BMI)^2.

Parabolic curves for each of the ten age–sex groups were constructed and the body mass index nadirs of the U-shaped curves were computed. The body mass index values at the two points of intersection of the curve with the 100% level of the mortality ratio were also computed. Thus not only were the single "best" body mass indices (those associated with lowest or minimal mortality) calculated, but the range of body mass indices associated with less than expected mortality were determined for each age–sex group. For both men and women, there was a powerful effect of age on the body mass index associated with minimal mortality (Table 17.1).

It is remarkable that the calculated body mass index values for men and women did not show any consistent sex difference. Regression lines relating the "best" body mass index to age are nearly identical (Andres, 1985). Thus if recommendations are to be based on weights associated with lowest mortality, separate tables for men and women are not necessary.

Based upon the above regression analyses, a new age-specific weight-for-height table (Table 17.2) has been constructed (Andres, 1985). It is no more complex than the 1983 Metropolitan tables. Even though age has been added as a variable, sex and body frame have disappeared—sex because of its lack of significant effect and frame because no data are available. Thus

TABLE 17.1. Effect of Age on Body Mass Index Associated with Lowest Mortality[a]

Age group	Body mass index (kg/m^2)	
	Men	Women
20–29	21.4	19.5
30–39	21.6	23.4
40–49	22.9	23.2
50–59	25.8	25.2
60–69	26.6	27.3

[a]Data from Build Study 1979 (see Society of Actuaries and Association of Life Insurance Medical Directors of America, 1980).

instead of six weight ranges for each inch of height, the age-specific table has five weight ranges, one for each of the five decades of age.

ANALYSIS OF OTHER POPULATIONS FOR AGE EFFECTS

Among the other populations that have been studied, 23 populations have been presented in a suitable format and in enough detail that the body weight-for-height value associated with the lowest mortality can be ascertained (Dyer et al., 1975; Keys, 1980; Avons, Ducimetiere, & Rakotovao, 1983; Belloc, 1973; Borhani, Hechter, & Breslow, 1963; Garrison, Feinleib, Castelli, & McNamara, 1983; Jarrett, Shipley, & Rose, 1982; Larsson, Bjorntorp, & Tibblin, 1981; Lew & Gortinkel, 1979; McGee & Gordon, 1976; Noppa, Bengtssonn Wedel, & Wilhelmsen, 1980; Pettitt, Lisse, Knowler, & Bennett, 1982; Rhoads & Kagan, 1983; Tyroler, Knowles, Wing, et al., 1984; Vandenbroucke, Mauritz, de Bruin, Verheesen, van der Heide-Wessel, & van der Heide, 1984; Waaler, 1984; Westlund & Nicolaysen, 1972). To compare the data reported in these studies, the various indices of overweight used must be converted to a common scale. The body mass index was selected as the most appropriate reference base. A large number of the more recent studies have used the body mass index as their measure. Furthermore, a range of 20 to 25 kg/m^2 on the index is now frequently recommended as the standard of normality for body weight. Table 17.3 shows the populations included in the 23 studies that provided satisfactory data.

Nineteen of the populations studied are white men, followed by seven studies of white women. There are two studies of Japanese men, one in Japan and one in Hawaii, but no studies of Japanese women. Nor are they any studies of any other Asiatic population group. Only one study of Native

TABLE 17.2. Comparison of the Weight-for-Height Tables from Actuarial Data (Build Study): Non-Age-Corrected Metropolitan Life Insurance Company and Age-Specific Gerontology Research Center Recommendations[a]

Height (ft-in)	Metropolitan 1983 weights (lb) for ages 25-59[b]		Gerontology Research Center weight range (lb) for men and women by age[c]				
	Men	Women	25	35	45	55	65
4-10	...	100-131	84-111	92-119	99-127	107-135	115-142
4-11	...	101-134	87-115	95-123	103-131	111-139	119-147
5-0	...	103-137	90-119	98-127	106-135	114-143	123-152
5-1	123-145	105-140	93-123	101-131	110-140	118-148	127-157
5-2	125-148	108-144	96-127	105-136	113-144	122-153	131-163
5-3	127-151	111-148	99-131	108-140	117-149	126-158	135-168
5-4	129-155	114-152	102-135	112-145	121-154	130-163	140-173
5-5	131-159	117-156	106-140	115-149	125-159	134-168	144-179
5-6	133-163	120-160	109-144	119-154	129-164	138-174	148-184
5-7	135-167	123-164	112-148	122-159	133-169	143-179	153-190
5-8	137-171	126-167	116-153	126-163	137-174	147-184	158-196
5-9	139-175	129-170	119-157	130-168	141-179	151-190	162-201
5-10	141-179	132-173	122-162	134-173	145-184	156-195	167-207
5-11	144-183	135-176	126-167	137-178	149-190	160-201	172-213
6-0	147-187	...	129-171	141-183	153-195	165-207	177-219
6-1	150-192	...	133-176	145-188	157-200	169-213	182-225
6-2	153-197	...	137-181	149-194	162-206	174-219	187-232
6-3	157-202	...	141-186	153-199	166-212	179-225	192-238
6-4	...	...	144-191	157-205	171-218	184-231	197-244

[a]Values in this table are for height without shoes and weight without clothes. To convert inches to centimeters, multiply by 2.54; to convert pounds to kilograms, multiply by 0.455.

[b]The weight range is the lower weight for small frame and the upper weight for large frame.

[c]Data from Andres (1985).

TABLE 17.3. Geographic, Racial, and Sexual Characteristics in Studies Reporting Weight-Mortality Data

Location of study	Race	Number of populations Men	Number of populations Women
United States	Caucasian	11	4
	Japanese	1	0
	Black	1	0
	Native American	1	1
Japan	Japanese	1	0
Europe	Caucasian	8	3
Total		23	8

Americans has been reported; only one study of black men has been reported and none of black women. These deficiencies must strike a note of caution concerning the applicability of weight tables generated from these data to populations other than white men and women.

It is important to know whether the data from the 23 population studies agree with the weight recommendations of the Metropolitan 1959 and 1983 tables or with the age-specific table of weights we have generated. We compared the body mass indices associated with the lowest mortality from these studies with the body mass indices of the Metropolitan tables. Because the mid-point of the medium frame of the Metropolitan tables is the most commonly used reference standard, this value was taken for each height for men and for women. Corrections in those tables for shoes and clothes were made as recommended (Metropolitan Height and Weight Tables: 1983): For the 1959 tables, for men and women, 1 inch (2.54 cm) and 2 inches (5.08 cm), respectively, were deducted from the heights and 7 pounds (3.18 kg) and 4 pounds (1.81 kg) from the weights to correct for shoes and clothes. Comparable values for the 1983 tables, as noted above, were 1 inch (2.54 cm) for both men and women and 5 pounds (2.27 kg) and 3 pounds (1.36 kg), respectively. Because the metric system is now almost universally used in expressing the body mass index, the computation was: BMI $(kg/m^2) = (wt[lb.]/ht[in.]^2) \times 703.1$. The variance in the body mass index for individual heights for men and women in the 1959 tables is relatively small. The mean body mass index (weighted for the height distribution of the United States population) for men is 21.6 kg/m^2 and for women 21.2 kg/m^2. The body mass index variance among individual heights for men and women in the 1983 tables is greater, but a high percentage of persons fall within a relatively narrow range. On average, again weighted, the mean body mass index for men is 22.4 kg/m² and for women is 22.5 kg/m².

Among the 23 male populations, there are 65 individual age groups reported; among the 8 female populations, there are 33 individual age groups reported. Of these, the body mass index associated with minimal mortality falls below the 1959 cut-points of 21.6 and 21.2 kg/m² in only 4 male and 4 female groups, and 6 of these 8 groups are below age 40. Thus 61 male and 29 female groups fall above those cut-points.

If the body mass index cut-points are raised to those of the 1983 tables (22.4 and 22.5 kg/m²) then 7 male and 8 female groups lie below those limits, whereas 58 male and 25 female groups exceed those limits. Thus a strong consensus of various populations in addition to the insured population suggests that above age 40 the Metropolitan weight recommendations are too low.

It is important to stress that this analysis has considered the impact of body weight on total mortality only. There is no question that severe obesity is a serious threat to life. Furthermore, obesity is associated, probably causally, with other significant risk factors for coronary artery disease, such as hypertension, hyperlipidemia, and glucose intolerance. These disorders and obesity itself have a strong familial component. Thus weight tables derived from populations without risk factors for coronary artery disease should be used by persons without these risk factors. Persons with other risk factors or a significant family history for those disorders should not use standard tables.

RECOMMENDATIONS

The 1983 Metropolitan tables have erred, apparently in an effort to simplify the weight recommendations, by not entering age as a variable. The recommended weights are too liberal for young adults, accurately reflect the life insurance experience for those about age 40 to 45 years, and are too restrictive for persons in their 50s and 60s. For persons over age 40 and especially over age 50, a large number of other epidemiologic studies show that a body mass index in the range of 22.5 kg/m² (the midpoint for the medium frame in the 1983 Metropolitan tables) is associated with a higher mortality rate than body mass indices 10% to 20% higher than that value. The body mass index associated with minimal mortality does not differ in any systematic manner between men and women; thus separate weight tables for men and women may not be necessary. Weight-for-height tables should be advised for otherwise healthy persons. Persons with specific illnesses should have their weight goals set in accordance with established medical information.

More studies are required, especially in persons over age 70; the data are too sparse to make any recommendations with confidence to elderly persons.

Although there are no obvious systematic differences in the results of American and European studies among whites, there is only fragmentary information on Oriental, black, and Native American populations. Prospective studies among those groups are required. Genetic differences in the pattern of fat distribution suggest that weights associated with minimal mortality will show significant racial differences. The changing patterns of mortality with time among diverse diseases associated with overweight suggest that periodic monitoring of the body weight–mortality association will be required and that modifications of weight standards will be necessary in the future.

REFERENCES

Andres, R. (1985). Mortality and obesity: The rationale for age-specific height–weight tables. In R. Andres, E. L. Bierman, & W. R. Hazzard (Eds), *Principles of geriatric medicine* (pp. 311–318). New York: McGraw-Hill.

Avons, P., Ducimetiere, P., & Rakotovao, R. (1983). Weight and mortality. *Lancet, 1,* 1104.

Belloc, N. B. (1973). Relationship of health practices and mortality. *Preventative Medicine, 2,* 67–81.

Borhani, N. O., Hechter, H. H., & Breslow, L. (1963). Report of a ten-year follow-up study of the San Francisco longshoremen. *Journal of Chronic Disorders, 16,* 1251–1266.

Bray, G. A. (1982). *Obesity.* Kalamazoo, MI: Upjohn Company.

Dyer, A. R., Stamler, J., Berkson, D. M., & Lindberg, H. A. (1975). Relationship of relative weight and body mass index to 14-year mortality in the Chicago Peoples Gas Company Study. *Journal of Chronic Disorders, 28,* 109–123.

Garrison, R. J., Feinleib, M., Castelli, W. P., & McNamara, P. M. (1983). Cigarette smoking as a confounder of the relationship between relative weight and long-term mortality: The Framingham Heart Study. *Journal of the American Medical Association, 249,* 2199–2203.

Ideal weights for men. (1943, June). *Statistical Bulletin, 24,* 6–8.

Ideal weights for women. (1942, October). *Statistical Bulletin, 23,* 6–8.

Jarrett, R. J., Shipley, M. J., & Rose, G. (1982). Weight and mortality in the Whitehall Study. *British Medical Journal, 285,* 535–537.

Keys, A. (1980). Seven countries: A multivariate analysis of death and coronary heart disease. Cambridge, MA: Harvard University Press.

Larsson, B., Bjorntorp, P., & Tibblin, G. (1981). The health consequences of moderate obesity. *International Journal of Obesity, 5,* 97–116.

Lew, E. A., & Garfinkel, L. (1979). Variations in mortality by weight among 750,000 men and women. *Journal of Chronic Disorders, 32,* 563–576.

McGee, D., & Gordon, T. Section 31: The results of the Framingham Study applied to four other U.S.-based epidemiologic studies of cardiovascular disease. In W. B. Kannel & T. Gordon (Eds.), *The Framingham Study: An epidemiological investiga-*

tion of cardiovascular disease (DHEW Publication No. NIH 76-1083). Washington, DC: U.S. Government Printing Office.

Metropolitan Height and Weight Tables: 1983. (1983, January–June). *Statistical Bulletin, 64,* 2.

New weight standards for men and women. (1959, November–December). *Statistical Bulletin, 40,* 1–3.

Noppa, H., Bengtsson, C., Wedel, H., & Wilhelmsen, L. (1980). Obesity in relation to morbidity and mortality from cardiovascular disease. *American Journal of Epidemiology, 111,* 682–692.

Pettitt, D. J., Lisse, J. R., Knowler, W. C., & Bennett, P. H. (1982). Mortality as a function of obesity and diabetes mellitus. *American Journal of Epidemiology, 115,* 359–366.

Rhoads, G. G., & Kagan, A. (1983). The relation of coronary disease, stroke, and mortality to weight in youth and in middle age. *Lancet, 1,* 492–495.

Society of Actuaries and Association of Life Insurance Medical Directors of America. (1980). *Build Study 1979.* Chicago: Author.

Tyroler, H. A., Knowles, M. G., Wing, S. B., et al. (1984). Ischemic heart disease risk factors and twenty-year mortality in middle-age Evans County black males. *American Heart Journal, 108,* 738–746.

Vandenbroucke, J. P., Mauritz, B. J., de Bruin, A., Verheesen, J. H. H., van der Heide-Wessel, C., & van der Heide, R. M. (1984). Weight, smoking, and mortality. *Journal of American Medical Association, 252,* 2859–2860.

Waaler, H. T. (1984). Height, weight and mortality: The Norwegian experience. *Acta Medica Scandinavica, 679* (Suppl.), 1–56.

Westlund, K., & Nicolaysen, R. (1972). Ten-year mortality and morbidity related to serum cholesterol: A follow-up of 3,751 men aged 40–49. *Scandinavian Journal of Clinical and Laboratory Investigation, 30* (Suppl. 127), 1–24.

·VI·

COPING WITH STRESS

·18·

Stress-Resistant Personality

SUZANNE C. OUELLETTE KOBASA

Since 1975 I have been involved in studies of the question of who stays healthy under stress. Specifically, I have been concerned with identifying the personality characteristics that distinguish those people who have encountered a number of significant stressful life events and stayed healthy.

To understand this research, it is important first to describe some stress research in general. This will provide some background and also some sense of how this line of research came to be. For the last 20 years or so a great number of medical and social science researchers have been interested in the connection between the appearance of stressful life events and the onset of illness. A great deal of time, energy, and money has been spent on the notion of a causal link between stressful life events and illness. This includes psychiatric illness as well as physical illness. In the late 1950s and early 1960s a major advance took place in the form of a new definition of stress and some measurement tools for this definition.

Thomas Holmes and Richard Rahe (1967) defined stress in terms of stressful life events. Stress became a matter of the environment or the situation. A stressful life event was defined as any event that caused change or demanded readjustment in the life of the average person. Using that definition, a whole variety of both positive and negative events, minor and major events become stressful. A job demotion is stressful, but so is a promotion. A promotion with a salary increase can cause one to buy a new house or to make many possible changes in one's life. A minor event like getting a traffic ticket is a stressful life event, but not as powerful as a major change such as the death of a spouse.

Holmes and Rahe developed a scale to measure these life events. Subjects were asked to check off those events that had occurred to them in the recent past. Sample items were events such as a job transfer, death of a spouse, and a vacation. For each event, Holmes and Rahe provided a weight indicating how stressful the event was. They then tested the list of life events with several populations and asked people to rate each event on a scale of 0 to 100, with marriage getting a score of 50. Large groups of judges were able to agree fairly well on their evaluation of the stressfulness of these events. With such a scale, it then became easy to go to large populations and measure their stress levels. It was no longer necessary to perform intensive interviews; researchers could merely have people self-administer the checklist.

There have been literally thousands of studies reported in the research journals using Holmes and Rahe's Schedule of Recent Events, Social Readjustment Rating Scale, or scales similar to these. Two of Holmes and Rahe's classic studies, which have spawned many similar ones, were done in the 1960s. In the first study, the list of stressful events was given to a hospitalized population, and the patients with heart attacks, depression, hysterectomy, etc., checked off events that had happened to them. The same list was then given to people who were not ill. The hospitalized people checked off significantly more life events than those who were not ill.

A second study, somewhat more sophisticated, was prospective in design. Rahe took a group of young sailors beginning a 6-month cruise. He asked them to fill out the stressful life events questionnaire and then divided the sailors into two groups: the high-stress sailors who had undergone a large number of stressful life events in the past year; and the low-stress sailors who had not had many stressful life events in the past year. Rahe then followed the two groups through the next 6 months of the cruise. His findings were that sailors in the high-stress group reported to sick bay more often, and complained more often of symptoms. That is, his findings suggest a connection between stressful life events and illness onset.

Many studies like these have appeared in research journals. Holmes and Rahe's instruments have been used for similar studies by many researchers. The media have made much of these results. There have been television and radio broadcasts about stress, Sunday supplement reports, and newspaper articles with the approximate message that stress kills. They all suggest that people should avoid stress if they want to stay healthy. Some articles tell us what professions are most stressful, so people can get some sense of how much at risk they are.

An article in *Family Circle Magazine* got me started on this line of research. In this article, the reader was provided with a stressful life events test and told how to take it and how to interpret it. The answers were to be checked off and then the scores of each item added together. A score of 300 or above was supposed to mean that a person had an 80% probability of getting seriously ill in the near future. A score between 200 and 300 meant that a person had about a 60% probability of getting seriously ill in the near future.

My score was higher than 300, and I was still breathing and feeling all right, and it seemed to me that that was not the only way to interpret those results. The writer of the article also gave some advice at the end of the article. The reader was told that if his or her score was above 300, to watch out. One more stressful life event could be quite dangerous, and therefore a high-scoring reader should avoid further major life changes.

In reviewing the research literature and the popular literature such as this article, three points were troublesome. First, the statistics were problematic. They did not justify the inference of causality. The correlations between stress and illness were around .24 in many of the studies, and fell below .12 in some. What this means is that many people do not show this high-stress-high-illness pattern. There are indeed people who have a great deal of stress and no illness, and people who have a great deal of illness and no stress. The equation is not as simple as that when stress happens, illness always happens. The statistics did not seem to justify what we were being told.

My second problem had to do with the kind of advice that was coming out of this research. We were told to avoid stressful life events. That may be possible sometimes, but there are also times when we cannot avoid stressful life events. One might say no to a job promotion, but one cannot avoid a serious illness in the family. Also, it seemed that the advice was somewhat limiting. Implicit in the message to avoid stressful life events was the idea that you should also walk away from positive life events, because positive life events require adjustment too. So we were being told to say no to this job promotion because it would lead to a great deal of stress. This kind of advice struck me as both unrealistic and really limiting people's opportunities.

My third problem had to do with what I call the fundamental view of people at work in much of stress research. It seemed to me that this research had looked only at stressful events and illness; that it assumed a view of people as passive victims in their environment. People were portrayed as poor victims of the environment, which contains these events that affect us.

What of views of human nature that address creativity? What of views of human nature that portray the person as causing the stress in his or her life? It seemed that the life-events researchers were being much too narrow in their understanding of human behavior and this alternative view of human behavior that I was looking for. This is not just philosophical speculation. Psychological data abound about the need for novelty, the importance of risk-taking, and the value of change and new and interesting experiences. This was lacking in the life-change research.

Given these three problems with the life-change research, I decided to start a stress project of my own, and in that project I wanted to find a group of individuals who had had a number of significant stressful life events in their recent past, but who stayed healthy in the face of them. I wanted to locate the kind of people who were being forgotten in a good deal of the research I had reviewed.

The first research was a study with telephone company executives. I chose executives in part because executives had been portrayed, in the popular media especially, as the classic stress victims. They seemed likely to be under high stress. It also seemed likely that, since the economy had not fallen apart, there was a good chance that many of these executives were handling the stress well.

It might have been that the people who were staying healthy were simply different physiologically. They might be constitutionally predisposed to deal well with stress. They might have better genes than those people who were getting sick in the face of stressful life events. It might also be that their social situations were different. The people who stay healthy under stress might have more resources. They might have more money or a better education. They might have stronger support networks. They might be different psychologically. My investigation focused on this possible psychological difference initially. As a personality and social psychologist, I was looking for the personality distinctiveness of these people. It seemed that the people who stay healthy under stressful life events should have distinctive kinds of personalities, distinctive orientations towards life. They might have a set of general attitudes that would allow them to approach stressful life events as not necessarily so bad, and make them easier to cope with.

I brought to those executives three hypotheses concerning personality. The three personality hypotheses had to do with commitment, control, and challenge. This has been referred to as the three C's, a mnemonic that I am not certain I like, but a mnemonic nonetheless. The first hypothesis was that those executives who reported a great number of stressful life events but no illness were executives who would be more committed to what they were doing, while executives who were getting sick under stress would have what I would call a lack of commitment, or alienation from what they were doing. The second hypothesis had to do with control. The notion was that those executives who stayed healthy under stressful life events would show a greater sense of personal control over what was happening in their lives, while those who were getting sick would be more likely to report powerlessness or an external locus of control. The third hypothesis had to do with challenge. Those executives who stayed healthy would report a greater sense of challenge, a greater interest in new and different things in their lives. Those who got sick would be much more attracted to the status quo and threatened by the notion of change.

In 1975 I went to Illinois Bell Telephone and administered to middle and upper level executives a stressful life events and illness questionnaire like the Holmes and Rahe list, but adding to those items ones that were distinctive to the telephone company situation. These additions came from interviews with the executives about the distinctive stresses that existed in their lives. After we compiled the final list, we gave it to about 800 executives and also asked them to fill out an illness checklist, which provided about 150 commonly recognized diseases and symptoms. When the results came back, I was able to divide the subjects by their responses into four groups. There were indeed those executives who had been written about so much in the popular media. These executives reported high numbers of stressful life events and were also getting sick. I called them the high-stress–high-illness executives.

There were also, however, an equal number of executives who reported as much stress but no illness change, and those were the people I was looking for. I called them high-stress–low-illness executives. There were also executives who had gotten sick without any stressful life events, or a low number of stressful life events, and executives who had very little stress and very little illness. These two groups will be considered later.

Of greatest interest are the two high-stress groups: One gets sick, but the other does not. The important question is what is the difference between them. There were about 350 men in question. I had intended for the study to concern stress resistance in men and in women, but when the 800 questionnaires came back from the telephone company, there were only 20 women represented. The proportion is different now, but it turned out that there were only 20 women in the middle and upper ranks in 1975 when the data were collected.

We then administered a very lengthy questionnaire that contained a great number of questions designed to assess the personality variables of commitment, control, and challenge. The questionnaire also asked a number of demographic questions regarding age, job level, and other items to provide information about the social context people operate in. The responses to the personality part of the questionnaire were then subjected to discriminant function analysis, which selects the items that differentiate people getting sick from people staying healthy.

We found that things like age, income, religion, and job level did not distinguish the two groups from one another. A crucial finding was that age did not discriminate: It was not the case that the people who were staying healthy were younger. There were as many old executives in the high-stress–low-illness group as there were in the high-stress–high-illness group. Other demographic characteristics did not make a difference, but the personality characteristics did significantly differ between the two groups.

Those executives who reported a lot of stress and were staying healthy were indeed more committed, more in control, and more challenged than the executives who were getting sick. Commitment to self was the most important discriminator in this executive group. Those executives who stayed healthy reported in interviews, as well as on the questionnaire, knowing who they were. They were able to talk about their values and priorities. They were in touch with their feelings. They knew what was important to them. They were able to say, "I can see how these values and priorities get played out in both my family life and my work." That was different from the alienation from self that I found in those executives who were getting sick. The executives who were getting sick were not sure what their values or priorities were any more. They told stories about having come to work for the telephone company 10 years ago and now found themselves in a totally different kind of environment because of their having been tricked by the telephone company in its new, emerging form. They did not know why they were the way they were any more.

The second most important variable had to do with sense of control. Those executives who stayed healthy were indeed able to influence what was going on in their lives. In interviews after the questionnaire administration, I asked the executives about matters such as Affirmative Action and equal opportunity. At that point the telephone company was being put under pressure by the government to make some changes. Those executives who were in the high-stress–low-illness group made such statements as, "The policy comes down from above that I'd better change the makeup of my office, but how that's going to work is up to me." They felt some ability to control the messages they were getting. Those executives in the high-stress–high-illness group saw no way that they could influence changes. To them, pressures were just being exerted on them, and they felt they were only pawns carrying out the wishes of powerful others in New York or Washington.

Another variable that made a difference was a sense of vigorousness that appeared in the high-stress–low-illness group. People who were staying healthy expressed more eagerness about what they were doing. They were interested in what was going on in the telephone company and felt engaged by that. On the other hand, the people who were getting sick wanted to pull back from change and wanted things to be the way they were before.

Other people have considered the roles of commitment, control, and challenge to be important to health. René Dubos has considered commitment as related to autoimmune disease. Martin Seligman's work on learned helplessness concerns several species other than human, but it may be that some of the same dimensions are at work. The kind of challenge that I see as crucial may be similar to the work on the effects of enriched environments for rats on their brain growth that Marian Diamond has described (see Chapter 2).

One example of a person who illustrated these variables in our studies is especially noteworthy. After the executives were studied in the initial retrospective project, they were told that if they wanted to hear about their results, they could. One called and said, "Look, I don't believe in this kind of psychological stuff you do, but I'm thinking of making a major change; I'm thinking of leaving the phone company and going to this little electronics company that's a much more risky operation, and I figure if what you're going to do is free, I'll come and get the advice. Maybe it'll be helpful."

This man's protocol showed high stress and high illness. He was only in his 30s, but he had hypertension, peptic ulcer, and migraine headaches, and other symptoms as well as these diseases. What stood out from his personality questionnaire was alienation, not only from himself but also from other people. He also showed some low control, but the main factor was the alienation, the lack of commitment that was striking. He arrives 45 minutes late, trench coat flying behind him, papers under his arm. Then he makes a beeline for my secretary's desk and begins calling people. He's got to call many people to let them know where he's going to be in the next 45 minutes, while I'm in my office waiting, hearing all these phone calls. He comes in and I've prepared what's going to be a fairly difficult conversation with him about his alienation from other people, but it's difficult to do that because the phone keeps ringing and every time it does he jumps up because he's convinced it's for him and he can't talk in my office so he has to run out to the secretary's office. This happens three times, and we're not getting anywhere. He says to me, "Look, I really need to take all these calls, they're very crucial. But you may have something here. So why don't you talk into my tape recorder?" So he pulls out a tape recorder, puts it on my desk and says, "I'll listen to it at night when I have a chance." That was the clearest case of someone who I would call low in hardiness.

These three characteristics—commitment, control, and challenge—fit together in such a way as to form the constellation I call hardiness. From doing that first study, it seemed to me that there was indeed something else that could be said about stressful life events. It seemed to me that one could say there are people not avoiding stressful life events who are not dropping dead. There is a possibility of living a very active, changing life, and what's crucial may be the development of these three kinds of characteristics.

That message got out, the research was written up, and the executives were told about these three kinds of characteristics. But there was a problem with the research design. I was assuming that the executives, when given something like a job transfer, would bring to that transfer a sense of commitment to the work and to themselves, a sense of control, and a sense of challenge. Perhaps the reverse is true, that the hardiness is only there as a result of having stayed healthy under stress. The high-stress–low-illness executive fills out the questionnaire, checks off all the stresses, doesn't check off any symptoms or diseases, and then says to himself, "Boy, I went through all these things and I didn't get sick. I must be committed, in control, and challenged!"

The high-stress–high-illness person, who checks off all the stresses and many illnesses, looks at what he's written and says to himself, "Oh boy, I don't want to be part of this situation any more. I must be out of control to allow these things to happen to me, and why can't things stay the way they are?" The only way to determine the direction of causality was to perform a prospective study. Salvatore Maddi of the University of Chicago and I began a prospective study with the same executives in 1975. We found that hardiness does indeed continue to have an influence on illness reports. Even controlling for prior illness, in looking not just to illness but to an illness change, from 1975 to 1977 and 1977 to 1980 we found that hardiness still had an impact (Kobasa, 1979; Kobasa, Maddi, & Kahn, 1982).

This prospective study made us much more optimistic that the hardiness was there initially, influencing the way people look at stress and the way they cope with it. Since the prospective study, the majority of work has concentrated on other possible buffers, such as a constitutional difference, a social difference, and pairing personality hardiness with other such possible buffers or mediators of stress. One study examines constitutional predisposition (Kobasa, Maddi, & Courington, 1981). For all of the executives, in addition to having the questionnaires they sent us, we also have their medical records, since they are provided with free medical examinations every year. We looked at the medical records for family histories of illnesses thought to have some genetic component. These were merely gross indicators, but we counted the number of illnesses the person reported having experienced in terms of hardiness. Those executives who reported high family illness histories were sicker than those who did not. But family history does not explain all the illness variance. Hardiness still explains a considerable amount of the variance, and combining the two, looking at both, is significantly better than looking at either one alone.

The same sort of finding emerged regarding exercise. We asked how much exercise the executives did, what kind they did, how strenuous they thought it was, and how many hours they did it, and constructed an exercise composite score. Exercise significantly predicted current illness in the face of stressful life events. This effect was independent of hardiness, and combining the two significantly increased prediction of illness.

The third buffer we examined was social support. The findings here are more complex. The literature on stressful life events now is much more concerned with mediators and buffers of the stress–illness relationship than it was in the 1960s. Social support is the most commonly studied mediator. However, exactly what social support consists of is not always clear. One definition of social support is that it consists of instrumental help, dealing with the stress of the other person. Another definition is that of emotional support, the wife not helping fix the situation of the difficult job transfer, but simply patting the husband on the head and saying, "Whatever you do, I'll love you." Another definition is that social support is just getting from someone else the information needed to deal with stressful life events. It could be all these factors and others as well. Definitions are often not specified in the research.

I also had some concern about the absolute good of social support. It is possible that social support might interfere with commitment, control, and challenge. With a great deal of social support, does one need to exercise personal control? So I examined the social support question with some skepticism about the absolute benefit. We asked the executives about three kinds of social support: social assets, boss support, and family support. Social assets were defined as how much money they had, their early upbringing, parents' education, how many times they had moved as children, how they did in school, etc. These are sociological questions and represent assets that are typically valued in this society. Boss support was defined as the degree of support the executives were perceiving that they were getting from their bosses. We also asked about family support. This was defined as how the executives perceived their families in terms of cohesiveness and expressiveness.

We found that social assets did not make any difference in stress resistance for this group of executives. This may be because they were fairly homogeneous. It may be that if one makes $40,000 a year, stress resistance is not increased significantly by making $80,000 a year; $40,000 may be enough. Boss support did make a difference. Those executives were healthier who were able to say, "My boss is behind me, I see my boss as someone that I can go to when I need some information. I also see him as the kind of person who is going to stand behind me when I make a decision." Executives under high stress situations were much more likely to stay healthy if they had both personality hardiness and a perception of the boss as supportive.

Family support worked in a completely different way. We found that the executives who had the most illness were those who reported high stress, low personality hardiness, and very high family support. We are still studying just how this works. It may be that the kind of support he gets at home, the ability to perceive the home as cohesive and expressive, is not the kind of support he needs to deal with the stresses at work. It may be that he needs the kind of support that will help him with problem-focused coping, rather than emotion-focused coping. What is crucial here is the combination of low hardiness and high family support. Family support is not necessarily bad, it is only bad if one is low in hardiness. How can a person feel alienated from his family, out of control, and at the same time feel that his family is wonderful? These two things do not seem to go together, and high family support may actually get in the way of developing personality hardiness. Instead of going to work and facing the challenges, he may stay home and say he has a headache or his ulcer is acting up, and he is taken care of, is escaping instead of working on his sense of involvement or control. His family support could be a way of avoiding both the confrontation with stress and his ability to develop hardiness.

The preceding findings have to do primarily with business executives. I have also begun to look at other groups. I have studied lawyers, army officers, and to remedy the lack of women in these samples, I began a study of people with cervical cancer. The cervical cancer study is an examination of the degree to which personality hardiness and stressful life events might be precursors to the development of cervical cancer. We started with healthy women and are following them. The results are not yet in. We have looked at the baseline data in terms of working women versus nonworking women, and we find that if we are just looking at things like anxiety, depression, and strain complaints that these hardiness results hold up with women. Dividing the women into those who are doing well under stress and those who are getting sick, commitment, control, and challenge again differentiate the two. The same finding holds for lawyers and army officers.

There are also some interesting differences among the professional groups. These differences are strong enough that we need to consider occupational membership as another kind of buffer. Comparing the executives and the lawyers, the initial correlation between stressful life events and illness was stronger in executives than it was in lawyers, meaning that executives are much more likely to report strain symptoms and illnesses after their encounters with stressful life events than are lawyers. This may have to do with occupational ideology or mythology about stress. The executives talked about how bad stress is, that they know it causes illness. They pointed to the top floor of their building and said that an emergency cardiac unit was being installed there, because they know that many of them will have myocardial infarctions and at least the company will treat them quickly when it happens.

The lawyers, on the other hand, told stories about how they put off doing work until the last minute, because they like the kind of charge they get. For them, stress is part of the business, it is part of why they are lawyers. Simple conceptualization of stress is being reinforced by the kind of occupation people are involved in. The lawyers also reported more pure hardiness than the executives. This seems also to have to do with their occupational context. Law school may be a kind of socializing for stress resistance. Law school is also an opportunity for learning how to cope with stress. The executives have not had that kind of socializing experience.

Recently we looked at religion by accident. We looked at a group of Utah lawyers, and Mormonism became an unexpected variable. The Mormon lawyers did better under stress than the non-Mormon lawyers. Listening to them, they seemed to be living out the Protestant ethic, which has similarities with hardiness. Both share the sense that working hard, struggling, is important, and allow one to be challenged and feel in control.

We keep adding to the notion of stress resistance. Personality, occupational factors, exercise, and health habits may all play some part. One question many people have asked is whether hardiness is something one is born with or whether it can be developed. It may be that it can be developed. We have begun a series of hardiness groups. We take a group of executives who report a good number of stresses, especially in the workplace, and who also report some kind of risk factor, such as hypertension or elevated serum cholesterol levels, and put them in one of three groups. In one group we try to induce commitment, control, and challenge. In another group we simply do a relaxation exercise. In the third group we give them something to read. We are looking at whether we can, in a group situation, increase a person's sense of hardiness.

Other stress-management approaches also seem relevant to hardiness. Getting people to examine stress, look at their reactions to it as, for example, Ethel Roskies of the University of Montreal does in her stress-management groups, seems relevant to commitment to self. Even the more physiologically oriented stress-management techniques such as relaxation and biofeedback through getting people to pay a little more attention, to be a little more self-aware, and pay more attention to feelings as well as thoughts, should have some role in increasing commitment. These same techniques should also help people increase their sense of control. These factors of commitment, control, and challenge may well underlie many techniques of psychological change. It may augment our understanding of change to consider them, and such consideration may lead both to better theoretical insight and to improved techniques of change.

REFERENCES

Holmes, T. H., & Rahe, R. H. (1967). The social readjustment rating scale. *Journal of Psychosomatic Research, 11,* 213-218.

Kobasa, S. C. (1979). Stressful life events, personality, and health: An inquiry into hardiness. *Journal of Personality and Social Psychology, 37,* 1-11.

Kobasa, S. C. (1982). The hardy personality: Toward a social psychology of stress and health. In G. S. Sanders & J. Suls (Eds.), *Social psychology of health and illness* (pp. 3-32). Hillsdale, NJ: Erlbaum.

Kobasa, S. C., Maddi, S. R., & Courington, S. (1981). Personality and constitution as mediators in the stress–illness relationship. *Journal of Health and Social Behavior, 22,* 368-378.

Kobasa, S. C., Maddi, S. R., & Kahn, S. (1982). Hardiness and health: A prospective study. *Journal of Personality and Social Psychology, 42,* 168-177.

Kobasa, S. C., Maddi, S. R., & Puccetti, M. C. (1982). Personality and exercise as buffers in the stress-illness relationship. *Journal of Behavioral Medicine, 5,* 391–404.

Kobasa, S. C., & Puccetti, M. C. (1983). Personality and social resources in stress resistance. *Journal of Personality and Social Psychology, 45,* 839–850.

Maddi, S. R., Kobasa, S. C., & Hoover, M. (1979). An alienation test. *Journal of Humanistic Psychology, 19,* 73–76.

Wiebe, D. J., & McCallum, D. M. (1986). Health practices and hardiness as mediators in the stress-illness relationship. *Health Psychology, 5*(5), 425–438.

·19·

The Salutogenic Model of Health

AARON ANTONOVSKY

Given that the human condition is stressful, the question is how any of us manage to stay healthy. This is the question of salutogenesis. The core of the question can be put as the need to explain the location of a person near the ease end of the health ease/dis-ease continuum. If we consider—and reject—the hypothesis that the answer could be stressor avoidance, an initial alternative answer can be presented: the availability of generalized resistance resources (GRRs). The initial question can be broadened to consider maintenance or improvement of one's position on the breakdown continuum, irrespective of location at any given time. Analysis of the nature of generalized resistance resources, of why they are hypothesized to facilitate tension management and avoid stress, leads to the formulation of the central construct of my book, *Health, Stress, and Coping*, and the concept of the sense of coherence. "The sense of coherence is a global orientation that expresses the extent to which one has a pervasive, enduring though dynamic feeling of confidence that (1) the stimuli deriving from one's internal and external environments in the course of living are structured, predictable, and explicable; (2) the resources are available to one to meet the demands posed by these stimuli; and (3) these demands are challenges, worthy of investment and engagement. These three components are called, respectively, comprehensibility, manageability and meaningfulness" (Antonovsky, 1987, p. 19).

This chapter originally appeared in *Health, Stress, and Coping: New Perspectives on Mental and Physical Well-Being* by Aaron Antonovsky, 1979, pp. 182–197. It is reprinted here with permission from Jossey-Bass, Inc. Other than minor editorial changes in the first paragraph only one significant change has been made from the original version. The formal definition of the sense of coherence construct has been taken from Antonovsky's *Unraveling the Mystery of Health* (1987). In this book, Antonovsky develops in greater detail issues raised in the earlier volume and includes the instrument designed to measure the SOC. We have, however, with the author's approval, preferred to include the present selection, which gives an overall view of the salutogenic model. Readers would be well advised to turn to this book.

The final block in what I call the salutogenic model is the evidence for linking the sense of coherence and health status.

Inevitably, detailed consideration of each building block obscures the integral character of the model as a whole. Paradoxically, further, it oversimplifies a complex of interrelationships. Finally, it tends to obscure the links between the variables in the model. The function of this discussion, then, is to overcome these difficulties. The full picture, as I see it, is presented in Figure 19.1. A model frozen in a diagram unfortunately has a static character. It takes a leap of the imagination to transform both the elements in the model and the arrows and lines indicating their interrelationships into a dynamic whole in space and particularly in time. But the diagram is the best I can do, and I would ask the reader to refer to it as each element and link is discussed.

SENSE OF COHERENCE

Studying a diagram or discussing it in words requires an element of arbitrariness in selecting a point of departure. It is nonetheless not accidental that I start the discussion from the sense of coherence. That is, after all, the core of my answer to the problem of salutogenesis. The sense of coherence is measurable; each of us is located at some point on the sense-of-coherence continuum, which can be seen as an ordinal scale. Sense of coherence is an orientation that is not situation- or role-specific. Although there may be situations or issues with regard to which a person with a strong sense of coherence can be utterly perplexed, these are essentially peripheral to one's life or mark minor fluctuations around a fairly stable location on the continuum. Given the nature of human existence, it is difficult to conceive of anyone being extremely high on the continuum. This would require an unimaginably stable world, an inconceivably unchanging internal and external environment. Only someone who is totally out of touch with reality could claim to have an absolute sense of coherence. In fact, I suggest that a good clue to a fake sense of coherence would be an extremely high score. Most of us, then, would score from extremely low to moderately high.

To say that the sense of coherence is stable, enduring, and pervasive does not, however, compel us to say that it is immutable. In what sense, then, is it dynamic? We would do well to divide the answer to this question into two parts. The first focuses on the development of the orientation in childhood, adolescence, and early adulthood. The second considers modifications throughout subsequent life. The two parts overlap: there can be sharp changes of direction in childhood; there is development throughout life until death. But it is analytically useful to deal separately with the emergence of a sense of coherence and then with its modification.

LIFE EXPERIENCES

As indicated in the diagram, life experiences (Arrow A) are crucial in shaping a sense of coherence. From the time of birth, or even earlier, we constantly go through situations of challenge and response, stress, tension, and resolution. The more these experiences are characterized by consistency, participation in shaping outcome, and an underload-overload balance of stimuli, the more we begin to see the world as being coherent and predictable. When, however, one's experiences all tend to be predictable, one is inevitably due for unpleasant surprises that cannot be handled, and one's sense of coherence is weakened accordingly. Paradoxically, then, a measure of unpredictable experiences—which call forth hitherto unknown resources—is essential for a strong sense of coherence. One then learns to expect some measure of the unexpected. When there is little or no predictability, there is not much one can do except seek to hide until the storm (of life) is over, hoping not to be noticed. Or else one strikes out blindly and at random until exhaustion sets in. No defense mechanisms can be adequate.

We must note an implicit assumption here. If a strong sense of coherence is to develop, one's experiences must be not only by and large predictable but also by and large rewarding, yet with some measure of frustration and punishment. The outcome depends on the underload–overload balance. But what if one's life experiences are largely consistent and predictable but frustrating and punishing? Again, the answer is a matter of degree. Frustration and punishment can be so devastating that survival is put into question. If they are not so extreme, then defense mechanisms become possible and a reasonably strong sense of coherence begins to form.

One emerges from childhood, then, with some formed albeit tentative sense of coherence. In adolescence, the crucial stage for ego identity, tentativeness begins to be transformed into definitiveness. If one's experiences continue to be by and large cut of the same cloth as earlier experiences, one's sense of coherence is reinforced. Yet considerable change is possible. The important point is that there is increasing room for choice. The child maintains a small number of salient relationships. He gets feedback from relatively few people. The stimuli are not too variable. The adolescent has greater options in choosing or encountering experiences that enhance or weaken his or her sense of coherence.

Entering young adulthood, one has acquired, as it were, a tentative level of the sense of coherence, a picture of the way the world is. One now makes major commitments: marriage and a new nuclear family; the work at which one will spend most of one's waking hours; a style of life; a set of social relationships. These provide one with a relatively stable set of life experiences, day after day and year after year. By the time a decade or so has passed, if not sooner, the tentativeness has been transformed into a considerable degree of permanence.

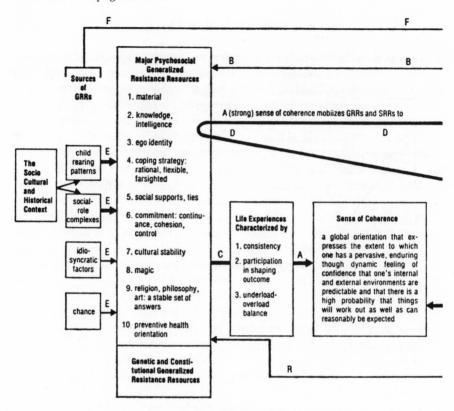

Key to Figure 1

Arrow A: **Life experiences shape the sense of coherence.**

Arrow B: Stressors affect the generalized resistance resources at one's disposal.

Line C: **By definition, a GRR provides one with sets of meaningful, coherent life experiences.**

Arrow D: **A strong sense of coherence mobilizes the GRRs and SRRs at one's disposal.**

Arrows E: **Childrearing patterns, social role complexes,** idiosyncratic factors, and chance **build up GRRs.**

Arrow F: The sources of GRRs also create stressors.

Arrow G: Traumatic physical and biochemical stressors affect health status directly; health status affects extent of exposure to psychosocial stressors.

Arrow H: Physical and biochemical stressors interact with endogenic pathogens and "weak links" and with stress to affect health status.

Arrow I: Public and private health measures avoid or neutralize stressors.

Line J: A strong sense of coherence, mobilizing GRRs and SRRs, avoids stressors.

FIGURE 19.1. The salutogenic model.

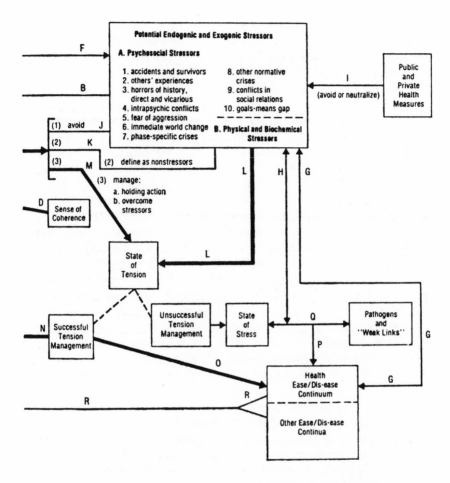

Line K: A strong sense of coherence, mobilizing GRRs and SRRs, defines stimuli as nonstressors.

Arrow L: **Ubiquitous stressors create a state of tension.**

Arrow M: **The mobilized GRRs (and SRRs) interact with the state of tension and manage a holding action and the overcoming of stressors.**

Arrow N: **Successful tension management strengthens the sense of coherence.**

Arrow O: **Successful tension management maintains one's place on the health ease/dis-ease continuum.**

Arrow P: Interaction between the state of stress and pathogens and "weak links" negatively affects health status.

Arrow Q: Stress is a general precursor that interacts with the existing potential endogenic and exogenic pathogens and "weak links."

Arrow R: Good health status facilitates the acquisition of other GRRs.

Note: The statements in bold type represent the core of the salutogenic model.

One selects and interprets experiences to conform to the established level of the sense of coherence. It is unlikely, then, that one's sense of coherence, once formed and set, will change in any radical way. Fluctuations will be minor.

But unlikelihood is not certainty, which brings us to the second part of our answer to the question about the dynamic nature of the sense of coherence: modification of the sense of coherence. We can point to two major ways in which an adult's sense of coherence can undergo fairly significant transformations. First, there is the cataclysmic stressor, in either a broad or a personal sphere, which transforms a great variety of life experiences, often in a brief period of time, through a considerable change in one's GRRs (Arrow B). One has had no hand, no choice, in this experience and often no preparation for it. Perhaps the classic example is sudden widower-hood. War, forced migration, the death of one's child, losing one's job because the plant closed down, a natural disaster—central to all these events is not primarily that they are largely unanticipated, in a personal sense, but that they bring in their wake a variety of unpredictable experiences. Inevitably, then, they result in a significant weakening of one's sense of coherence.

Is such weakening necessarily permanent? To ask this question is to point to the second major way one's sense of coherence can undergo a significant modification. By contrast to the first, it is never sudden, almost always has an element of choice (conscious or unconscious), and can result in movement in either direction on the sense-of-coherence continuum. Let us take widowerhood as an example. Whatever one's previous level of sense of coherence, this is inevitably a major disruption of one's life, particularly when there has been no anticipatory socialization. Slowly and painfully, one can choose experiences that, offering meaningful stimuli, rebuild one's sense of coherence. Or, if one is lucky, such experiences are thrust on one. No less can the opposite pattern characterize one's life (see Parkes, 1972; Parkes, Benjamin, & Fitzgerald, 1969). In parallel fashion, and not necessarily as a result of a catacylsmic stressor, a woman can go out to paid work after decades of being a housewife; an illiterate person can learn to read and write; one can undergo psychotherapy; one can embark on a substantially different kind of work; one can marry or divorce. Change, then, can take place. But change of this type is always within the context of one's previous level of the sense of coherence, is always slow, and is always part of a web of life experiences that transmit stimuli that are more or less coherent. Movement toward the strong end of the continuum always requires hard work.

GENERALIZED RESISTANCE RESOURCES

If one's life experiences, then, shape one's sense of coherence, what shapes one's life experiences? What determines whether they consist of coherent or incoherent stimuli and are characterized by consistency, participation in shaping outcome, and neither underload nor overload? Part of the answer— the effect of stressors—was given above (Arrow B). But the greatest part of my answer is one's generalized resistance resources (Line C). By definition, a GRR provides one with sets of meaningful, coherent life experiences. Thus Line C is a symbol more for tautology than for causality. If material resources or a flexible coping strategy or social supports by definition provide coherent life experiences, if that is their hallmark, one cannot quite say that the relationship is causal, for there is no way of testing the truth of the statement. The value, however, of separating GRRs from life experiences in the diagram, and the meaning of Line C, is that we are thereby provided with a theoretical criterion, a culling rule, for identifying GRRs. The empirical prediction, which can be tested, is the relationship between GRRs and the sense of coherence, which can be defined and measured independently.

At the present stage in the development of the salutogenic model and without considerable empirical research, we have no basis for predicting the structure of the relationship between GRRs and the sense of coherence. Is a given GRR—for example, a clear, stable ego identity or social supports—a necessary or even a necessary and sufficient condition for a strong sense of coherence? Or, if such generalizations are impossible, are some GRRs more useful than others in coping with certain stressors (Arrow D)? One of the advantages of the salutogenic model is that it allows us—indeed, even stimulates us—to ask such questions, whatever the answers turn out to be.

SOURCES OF GRRs

We can now move further "back" in the diagram. Arrows E point to the sources of the GRRs. These have been discussed at length; I would only briefly point up a number of issues that may have been slighted earlier. First, whatever the somewhat cavalier approach I may seem to have taken with regard to the role of stressors in influencing health status, I did so only to offset the strong current concern with stressors. As will be evident shortly, this position must be qualified. I take it here in order to point out that there are also direct links between the sources of GRRs and stressors (Arrow F). Someone growing up and living in a society with an annual per capita income of $250 confronts different stressors and has different GRRs at his or her disposal than does someone growing up and living in a society with a per capita income of $2,500. Living in a world with limited means of transportation and communication and weapons of destruction is quite different from living in a "civilized" world of satellites, 747s, and nuclear weapons. Whether one's society has pacific or hostile relations with its neighbors matters a great deal both for the GRRs and the stressors in one's life. It is perhaps even more important, in these terms, to distinguish between people who are members of different social classes, sexes, or ethnic groups within one society.

Second, I see no grounds for assigning priority to one or the other of the two major sources of GRRs (childrearing patterns and social-role complexes) in shaping the GRRs at one's disposal. At first sight, it might seem clear that there is a greater affinity between childrearing patterns and ego identity and between present social class position and material resources. But ego identity and adult major role activity and role set are deeply intertwined, as are parental social class and present material resources. The relationships, then, are complex. Then again, they may well be not as complex as seems to be the case. There is at least some reason and empirical evidence to think that there is a wholeness in the direction in which one is constrained to go by the complex of one's childrearing patterns and social-role complexes, in a given sociocultural and historical setting. The strain toward consistency among these acts pushes one in the direction of a greater or lesser degree of GRRs. This consistency enables us to speak of the prototypical life chances of an individual in a given subculture—for example, of a poor, white housewife in Appalachia.

The relationship between cultural and individual factors brings us to a third point. Whatever the very major power of sociocultural and historical factors in shaping the GRRs at one's disposal, we are witness to substantial individual differences. Intelligence, however it may be measured, is distributed on a normal curve. Beauty, charm, strength, and a myriad of other personal characteristics, however these are measured, vary from person to person. Of course these are measured and evaluated differently in different cultural settings. Of course they are influenced and perceived differently depending on the social context. But these idiosyncratic characteristics and tendencies are not therefore irrelevant in shaping the GRRs at one's disposal. One can make reasonable probabilistic predictions knowing a person's sociocultural world as to where he or she will rank on GRRs. But the prediction will never be close to perfect for a given individual.

Finally, we must note the role of chance as a source of GRRs. The luck that confronts us is often far from a matter of luck. Further, one person may take advantage of a lucky opportunity while another may not. One may even be so strong a determinist as to claim that everything that happens had to happen. There are, nonetheless, chance events that may often be of considerable significance in shaping one's GRRs. Rarely does one buy a sweepstakes ticket, chat with a stranger while waiting for a train, register for a class because it is held at a convenient hour, leaf through the personal ads in a magazine, or get invited to a party and thereby embark on a chain of events that substantially alters one's life. Rare. Far less important than childrearing patterns and social-role complexes. But it does happen.

STRESSORS

Let us now assume that we have accounted adequately for the emergence of a given level of the sense of coherence that characterizes a person at a given time and return to the center of the diagram. Before we can explicate the relationship between the sense of coherence and health, we must focus on the place of stressors in the salutogenic model. I touched on this issue above in considering the impact stressors can have on GRRs (Arrow B). Now we look elsewhere.

The relationship between stressors and movement toward the dis-ease end of the health ease/dis-ease continuum requires some clarification. Biochemical and physical stressors—droughts, bombings, invasion, pests—much as psychosocial stressors, can have an impact on GRRs. But unlike psychosocial stressors, whose impact is always mediated through GRRs and the sense of coherence, biochemical and physical stressors can be of such direct traumatic magnitude as to bypass interaction with the sense of coherence. A noxious gas, a poisonous substance, a bullet, or a car can act directly on the health status of an individual (Arrow G; double arrow shows two-way causation). Alternatively, a cumulative harsh overload of such stressors (smoking or exposure to asbestos or to high noise levels) can act indirectly on health by exploiting the endogenic potential pathogens and "weak links" in interaction with a state of stress (Arrow H; double arrow shows interaction).

There is, indeed, good reason for the pathogenic model to have dominated thinking about disease for most of human history. The three-pronged power of stressors (Arrows B, G, and H), which included perhaps above all nutritional deprivation and the most primitive level of sanitation, was sufficient to overcome even substantial resistance resources.* When, however, the standard of living in a society (or in some segments of a society) reaches a rough level of adequacy, differences in health level no longer are overwhelmingly determined by biochemical and physical stressors. At this point psychosocial stressors and, above all, the sense of coherence become crucial variables. And at this point salutogenesis becomes at least as intriguing and important a question as pathogenesis.

MANAGEMENT OF TENSION

Having analyzed the sense of coherence as a dependent variable, we now turn to consider it as an independent variable. The achievement of a roughly

---

*Yet even during the worst plagues, some remained healthy and some recovered. Had our focus been salutogenic, we might have learned much more about GRRs than we know today. For a brilliant if tongue-in-cheek paper analyzing the remarkable plague immunity of an ethnic minority in ancient Egypt thanks to a powerful GRR technically called Bohbymycetin, see Caroline and Schwartz (1975) on chicken soup.

adequate standard of living does not do away with physical and biochemical stressors. They remain ubiquitous. For the first time in history on a large scale, however, it has now become possible to cope with them. Success has been remarkable. The triumphs of public health and of the microbiological sciences have been great (Arrow I). But there is a built-in limitation, which Dubos (1960) has profoundly analyzed. The bugs, as I have put it, are smarter. Not always, not every bug, and they have retreated. In this era of chronic diseases (and not much less applicable to infectious diseases in such an era) the single-bullet approach can no longer be seen as viable in and of itself or even as the dominant weapon. In this context the sense of coherence becomes important.

As shown in the model, the role of the sense of coherence is three-directional. First, by mobilizing the GRRs at one's disposal (Arrow D), as well as specific resistance resources (SRRs), a strong sense of coherence can avoid one's being subjected to some stressors (Line J). Second, it allows us to define some stimuli, which others might perceive as stressors, as innocuous or even as welcome (Line K). But whether we like it or not, none of us can in such ways keep stressors out of our lives. Day in, day out, throughout our lives, we find that stressors put us repeatedly in a state of tension (Arrow L). Periods of calm and stability, of homeostasis, are rare in human existence. At this point the third direction in which a strong sense of coherence operates is decisive. It would hardly be important were stressors reducible to an occasional experience (which is almost never the case), much as it is not very important when stressors are overwhelming. We respond to a state of tension, if we have a strong sense of coherence, by mobilizing those GRRs that we have at our disposal and that we judge to be appropriate in seeking to resolve the tension by overcoming the stressor (Arrow M; double arrow shows interaction). (See Pearlin & Schooler, 1978, pp. 6–7, for a discussion of the three functions of coping responses: to modify situations, to control the meaning of situations, and to control the stress.)

We can now clarify the dual function of GRRs. Earlier we noted their function in creating life experiences that produce a strong sense of coherence. In this sense, they are constantly active. But they also function as a potential. Someone with a strong sense of coherence, whatever its sources, confronted with tension, can call on the GRRs to manage the tension successfully. One brings to bear one's wealth, one's knowledge, one's strong ego identity, one's social supports, and so forth. Note that this approach does not obviate the need for GRRs of the internal environment to perform a holding action. Physical and biochemical resources are required to prevent too rapid a transformation of tension into stress (Selye's stage of exhaustion). But the crucial role of GRRs is in overcoming the stressor and thereby resolving the tension. One must add that the person with a strong sense of coherence can also directly mobilize SRRs appropriate to the particular stressor. Finally, it bears repeating in the present context that overcoming a stressor and resolving tension is a life experience that in turn reinforces the sense of coherence (Arrow N). By overcoming a stressor we learn that existence is neither shattering nor meaningless.

From a dynamic, historical point of view, the dual function of GRRs can now be seen as one. Since conflict and stressors are ubiquitous throughout life and hence tension is at least as characteristic of human beings as is homeostasis, one is from earliest infancy calling on whatever GRRs are at one's disposal. When they suffice to provide a life experience that makes sense to us—that is consistent with our expectations, allows us some participation in determining outcome, and has neither too few nor too many stimuli for us to handle—and thus allow us to resolve tension, another building block is added to our sense of coherence. This theoretical approach, it should be noted, underlies my analysis of the relations between people and communities and the health care institution.

STRESS

Given the initial statement of the problem as that of salutogenesis, there remains but one issue to consider at this point, the feedback impact of health status. That is, in the never-to-exist society in which people are never harmed by traumatic or cumulative physical and biochemical insults, protected as they are by public and private health measures; in which all persons have a very strong sense of coherence and hence are capable of mobilizing GRRs and SRRs—in such never-never land, one knows much tension but never stress. And so all would be on the extreme ease end of the health ease/ dis-ease continuum, at least until one emulates Oliver Wendell Holmes' wonderful one-horse shay in a dramatic ending. Over and over again, we would manage tension successfully, thereby reinvigorating our sense of coherence (Arrow N) and at least maintaining our easeful health status (Arrow O). But given the brilliance of the bugs and the inevitable inadequacies of the sense of coherence and of exogenous GRRs, even the most fortunate are bound, on occasion, to fail to manage tension well.

There is no need here—particularly since I do not intend to deal with theories of diseases—to discuss the relationship between a state of stress and movement toward the dis-ease end of the health continuum (Arrow P). This is the focus of attention of almost the entire stress literature. I can make no contribution. Of far greater significance, the thrust of my entire book is to propose a shift in concern to the study of successful tension management. Two points are germane here.

First, it seems clear to me that stress is a general precursor. Only when stress interacts with the existing potential endogenic and exogenic pathogens do pathological consequences occur (Arrow Q). As Selye (1975) puts it (notwithstanding his unclear use of the word *tension*): "Although stress itself is defined as the 'non-specific response of the body to any demand,' the weakest link in a chain will be the one that selectively breaks under tension. Similarly, the weakest part of any animate or even inanimate machine will be the one that fails when a nonspecific, general demand is made upon the performance of the whole" (p. 41). A most important corollary of this approach is the rejection of the concept of psychosomatic disease. Other than the massive traumata that leave none unscathed (Arrow G), all diseases are usefully understood as psychosomatic. In other words, almost all breakdown involves stress. Stress, however, does not determine the particular expression of the breakdown.

My second point is crucial to the salutogenic approach. The pathogenic orientation asks: What causes a person to become ill with a particular disease? The salutogenic orientation, by contrast, asks: Whatever the person's particular location at any given time on the health ease/dis-ease continuum, what are the factors that facilitate his or her remaining at that level or moving toward the more salutary end of the continuum? Thus no assumption is made that one is well and becomes sick. On the contrary, the commitment is to seeing people at some point on the health continuum at any given time and continually confronted with stressors and hence with the problem of preventing tension from becoming stress. In this way, the sense of coherence is always hypothesized to be a relevant factor.

HEALTH

Which brings us to the final issue. Heretofore, we have viewed one's location on the health ease/dis-ease continuum as a dependent variable. We have seen it as the final outcome of a long chain of phenomena. Such analytic albeit complex neatness is distorting. One's health status can be usefully viewed as an independent variable in three ways. First, it can affect the extent to which one is exposed to stressors (hence Arrow G points in both directions). At a high health level, conflicts in social relations may be attenuated or phase-specific crises borne with equanimity. Second, good health is in itself a significant generalized resistance resource by the definition of a GRR as a factor that fosters meaningful and sensible life experiences. Third, in the same way that the other GRRs are interrelated, being on the healthy end of the health continuum can facilitate the acquisition of other GRRs (Arrow R).

Throughout, I have insisted that the health ease/dis-ease continuum is not to be regarded as coextensive with the entire realm of well-being. Other ease/dis-ease continua exist. To have entered into a systematic discussion of what these continua are, how our locations on them are determined, and how they relate to our concern with health would have been an impossible and unnecessary task within the scope of a book. Suffice it to say, then, that a nod has been made in their direction; they are highly relevant to and intertwined with health, but they are distinct. If our interest is in understanding health, then location on the family-relations or social-relations or material-resources ease/dis-ease continua can usefully be viewed as a GRR.

Reality, for better or for worse, is complex. The attempt to understand reality of necessity oversimplifies in that it must select and abstract. I have sought to minimize such oversimplification. Hence the perhaps bewildering array of arrows and lines and boxes in Figure 19.1. Doubtless the attempt has fallen short in one sense or another. Thus, for example, I have certainly dealt inadequately with genetic and constitutional GRRs and with public and private health measures. Genetic and constitutional GRRs are too complex and are beyond my capacities to explore here; public and private health measures are considered elsewhere. I would be troubled, however, only if the central paradigm was not clear. This paradigm finds its graphic expression in the diagram. Stripped of all qualifications and complexities, the thick lines in the diagram and the boldface words in its key are what I have to say.

REFERENCES

Antonovsky, A. (1987). *Unraveling the mystery of health*. San Francisco: Jossey-Bass.

Caroline, N. L., & Schwartz, H. (1975). Chicken soup rebound and relapse of pneumonia. *Chest, 67,* 215–216.

Dubos, R. J. (1960). *The mirage of health*. London: Allen & Unwin.

Parkes, C. M. (1972). *Bereavement: Studies of grief in adult life*. New York: International Universities Press.

Parkes, C. M., Benjamin, B., & Fitzgerald, R. G. (1969). Broken heart: A statistical study of increased motality among widowers. *British Medical Journal, 1,* 740–743.

Pearlin, L. I., & Schooler, C. (1978). The structure of coping. *Journal of Health and Social Behavior, 19,* 2–21.

Selye, H. (1975). Confusion and controversy in the stress field. *Journal of Human Stress, 1,* 37–44.

·20·

Coronary-Prone Behavior

CHARLES SWENCIONIS

JEANNE MOSCA

Coronary-prone behavior is a pattern of hostility, competitiveness, and time-urgency that many people show in stressful situations and that predisposes them to CHD, coronary heart disease (Matthews & Haynes, 1986). Coronary-prone behavior seems to predispose one to a particular illness, rather than generally making one more susceptible to disease (Cooper, Detre, & Weiss, 1981).

People have long thought that a relationship exists among personality, stress, and heart disease. William Harvey, the discoverer of the blood's circulation, said in 1628, "Every affection of the mind that is attended with either pain or pleasure, hope or fear, is the cause of an agitation whose influence extends to the heart" (Eastwood & Trevelyan, 1971). The German physician Von Dusch wrote in 1868 that people who had heart disease spoke loudly and were excessively involved with work. John Hunter, an English surgeon who discovered the connection between the placenta and the uterus, himself afflicted with angina, said, "My life is in the hands of any rascal who chooses to annoy me." Hunter died suddenly during a heated board meeting at St. George's hospital in London in 1793 (Jenkins, 1978). Sir William Osler in the 1897 Lumlean Lectures (Friedman, 1969) said that the coronary patient was "not the delicate, neurotic person . . . but the robust, the vigorous in mind and body, the keen and ambitious man, the indicator of whose engine is always at full speed ahead" (p. 269).

The Meningers, Arlow, Dunbar, and others (Jenkins, 1971, 1976) have noticed a tendency for CHD patients to be aggressive, ambitious, compulsive, striving, hard-driving, and goal-directed. However, these observations were made of people who already had CHD, making it impossible to tell if this

244

behavior was not somehow a product of heart disease. In addition, such behavior was not described in such a way as to allow prediction of people who were likely to develop CHD, nor was the statistical relationship between behavior and CHD strong enough to compel the attention of the medical community.

In the 1950s two San Francisco cardiologists, Ray Rosenman and Meyer Friedman (Friedman & Rosenman, 1974), became convinced of the importance of behavior in causing CHD. They had conducted a study of the relationship of diet, exercise, and other standard risk factors on the development of CHD, and found that the factors they expected to predict CHD were not very powerful. The people studied were husbands of women in the Junior League. Several wives of the men in the study told Rosenman and Friedman that it was not surprising they did not get good results because they had not studied the important factor in the lives of the men who had developed CHD: stress. The wives suggested the men who had become ill had been working too hard, or been under great pressure at work or at home for some time before getting their heart attacks.

In addition, at about this time, Rosenman and Friedman's receptionist told them she could predict who their CHD patients were, as opposed to other patients, just by observing them in the waiting room. These people were loud, spoke quickly, and were very concerned with time. "When they arrive at the office," she said, "they're very worried about whether we're running late. They want to use the phone. They're always looking at the clock."

When these cardiologists had their waiting room chairs reupholstered, the upholsterer remarked to them that their chairs had the most unusual pattern of wear he had ever seen. While most chairs wore out at the back of the seat, these chairs were worn out at the front edge: Their patients were in such a hurry that they were literally sitting on the edge of their seats.

Rosenman and Friedman began to call this pattern of being aggressive, hostile, competitive, and time-urgent "coronary-prone behavior." They began to study it formally with retrospective studies. They found that people who had died of CHD and showed advanced atherosclerosis were described by their surviving relatives and friends as more hostile, competitive, and time-urgent than were people who had died of other diseases.

In several of their studies, they found that the amount of cholesterol in the blood is affected by stress. They studied the serum cholesterol of tax accountants and found that levels peaked at April 15, even when diet was controlled. Rosenman and Friedman also observed a peak in serum cholesterol levels in medical students at examination time (Friedman, Byers, Diamant, & Rosenman, 1975; Friedman, George, Byers, & Rosenman, 1960; Friedman, Hellerstein, Jones, et al., 1968). Other investigators have found, in more than 50 separate students in humans, monkeys, and rats, that stress increases the amount of cholesterol and fatty acids in the blood. In monkeys, stress increases the rate of development of atherosclerosis, characterized by fatty deposits that build up inside the arteries and are the cause of CHD and stroke (Manuck, Kaplan, & Clarkson, 1983; Selye, 1976).

Rosenman and Friedman continued small-scale retrospective studies through the 1960s, until they had marshalled enough evidence to justify a long-term prospective study of the relationship between coronary-prone behavior and CHD. A retrospective study looks back on people once they have contracted a disease. A prospective study follows a large number of initially healthy people over time and attempts to predict who will become ill. Prospective studies are more rigorous, but require enormous amounts of time, effort, and money. Anticipating resistance to their ideas, Rosenman and Friedman renamed this personality pattern the Type A behavior pattern (TABP), a more neutral term, which they hoped would gain acceptance more easily.

Rosenman and Friedman began an 8 1/2-year prospective study of 3,154 initially well men, the Western Collaborative Group Study (Rosenman, Brand, Jenkins, et al., 1975). They typed each man as either coronary-prone (Type A), or not coronary-prone (Type B). The Type B person speaks more slowly and softly than the Type A person and is not in such a hurry. He or she does not react automatically with hostility, competitiveness, or time-urgency when challenged.

The results showed that Type A men are 2.37 times more likely than Type B men to develop CHD. This difference is not totally attributable to Type A men smoking more, having higher blood pressure, higher serum cholesterol or triglycerides, being overweight, having diabetes, or having more CHD in their families. When all these standard risk factors were statistically removed, the added risk due to TABP was still 1.97 greater than that for Type B men. Type A is a risk factor as powerful as high blood pressure, cigarette smoking, or excess serum cholesterol, the other most powerful risk factors.

The Western Collaborative Group Study was a population-based study, that is, it was performed on a group of people expected to have a typical incidence of heart disease for their population. The standard risk factors for the people in this study were not elevated, and they were about evenly divided between Type A's and Type B's.

Other researchers have found this relationship between TABP and CHD as well. A long-term prospective study of the development of CHD has been carried out for many years among the residents of Framingham, Massachu-setts. This study was begun before the Western Collaborative Group Study and focuses more on the standard risk factors. It is also a population-based study. However, extensive psychological and social data were also gathered on the participants from the time they entered the study. Suzanne Haynes selected questions that reflected the Type A pattern from those people who had been asked about their psychological and social lives in the Framingham study, and found that Type A employed women and housewives in the Framingham study were more likely to develop CHD than Type B women. Type A men were also found to be at higher risk for CHD than Type B men, but only among white-collar workers (Haynes, Feinleib, & Kannel, 1980).

Two other prospective population-based studies, the Belgian–French Cooperative Heart study (French–Belgian Collaborative Group, 1982), and the Belgian Heart Disease Prevention Trial (DeBacker, Kornitzer, Kittel, et al., 1983), found a positive relation between Type A personality and the development of CHD. One prospective population-based study, the Honolulu Heart Program, found no association between CHD and Type A behavior (Cohen & Reed, 1985). This may have been because this population, men of Japanese descent living in Hawaii, had both a low incidence of CHD and a low prevalence of Type A personalities.

ASSESSING TYPE A BEHAVIOR

Rosenman and Friedman were more successful in demonstrating a relationship between personality and CHD than past investigators had been, in part because they developed a better test for the coronary-prone personality than others had. Being cardiologists, they were not hampered by the confusing and confused training in personality that psychologists and psychiatrists receive. They did not think they had to uncover a deeply hidden construct; nor did they rush to develop a paper-and-pencil test. They naively believed that since they had observed their patients behave in hostile, competitive, and time-urgent ways in situations of stress, they could put people in a stressful situation and tell by watching their behavior whether they were coronary-prone. This naiveté allowed them to develop a highly advanced and sophisticated method of behavioral personality assessment.

Rosenman and Friedman got working men to take time away from work for a specific appointment, and come to their medical center. There, an interviewer kept them waiting beyond the appointed time without explanation. When they were finally seen, the interviewer offered no apology for being late and was somewhat abrasive. The interviewer asked questions that made them think about situations that provoke hostility, competitiveness, and time-urgency in practically everyone, such as waiting in bank lines, supermarket lines, post office lines; driving behind a slow car you cannot pass; and people or situations that are repeatedly irritating. The interviewer was brusque, interrupted, and seemed unconcerned with the person's answers.

The interview is recorded on audiotape, or preferably, on videotape. Only 25% of the assessment is scored on the basis of the content of the person's responses. Seventy-five per cent of the assessment is based on the person's behavior: how much he or she shows evidence of hostility, competitiveness, or time-urgency during the interview.

For example, Type A persons talk in an explosive, bombastic manner. They speak louder and more rapidly than Type B persons. Type A's modulate their voices to emphasize the importance of their points, often raising volume to talk over the interviewer. Their answers are frequently one-word or brief responses, given as quickly as possible. They do not like to be interrupted, and they speak with vigor. Type A's try to control the interview and hurry the interviewer with head nods or "uh-huhs."

Type A's look tense, have a facial grimace or extreme jaw tension, fidget, and move their lips even when not talking. Type A's are in so much of a hurry their speech is clipped or telegraphic, in incomplete sentences with the terminal words often elided. The Type A person sighs frequently, especially when discussing work, probably to indicate sorrow over failing to attain poorly defined, vague goals. Overall, the Type A person gives a sense of energy, purpose, and control. The Type B person shows a lesser degree of all these characteristics, and gives an overall sense of being subdued and lethargic.

The interview method for assessing TABP is known as Type A Structured Interview. Although one can observe these characteristics in anyone in a stressful situation, administration and assessment of the structured interview is highly technical and requires as much training by a person experienced in this test as any other psychological test. That is, proper administration of the Structured Interview requires as much training as does the Wechsler Adult Intelligence Scale, for example.

What is sophisticated about the structured interview method of assessing Type A behavior is that it puts persons into a situation similar to the stressful situations that provoke hostility, competitiveness, and time-urgency and then observes whether they show these behaviors.

Would a scaled paper-and-pencil test be more objective? An extremely elegant paper-and-pencil test has been devised for measuring Type A behavior, the Jenkins Activity Survey. The Jenkins test has been constructed using the most sophisticated psychometric procedures available, yet it is less successful in identifying people who will develop CHD than the Type A Structured Interview. About one third of the Type A's identified by the structured interview are classified by the Jenkins test as Type B's (Matthews, Krantz, Dembroski, et al., 1982; MacDougall, Dembroski, & Musante, 1979). On the other hand, the Jenkins test shows a dose–response relationship between Type A behavior and CHD (Jenkins, Rosenman, & Zyzanski, 1974), while the structured interview does not (Rosenman et al., 1975). That is, the greater the Type A behavior as measured by the Jenkins test, the greater the incidence of CHD.

Why should a "subjective" observation of people's voices and gestures be more accurate than an "objective" paper-and-pencil test? When people answer questions about themselves, as they do on written tests, everything is passed through a filter of self-perception. That is, the way people see themselves is distorted and their biases influence what they report about themselves.

Thus, persons who are quite hostile may believe everyone is as hostile as they are and report themselves as only ordinary in hostility. In this way, a test that observes what people do in a structured stressful situation can be more objective than believing what people write about themselves.

Friedman and associates have tried to make their structured interview even more objective by breaking the Type A pattern into 38 components, each of which is scored from 0 to 3 on intensity or frequency, and then taking a sum. However, this interview is conducted in an empathic rather than a challenging fashion, and it is unlikely that each component of Type A behavior should have equal weight. This approach is called the Videotaped Structured Interview. It has yet to be validated.

Despite the fact that the Framingham Type A Scale and the Jenkins Activity Survey are self-report scales, they have successfully predicted CHD in prospective studies. A third scale has done so as well, the Bortner Rating Scale (Bortner, 1969), which has been used mainly in European studies. A number of other self-report scales have been used to measure Type A behavior, but none have been validated in prospective studies.

Agreement among the different methods has been poor. If agreement between the Type A Structured Interview and the Jenkins Activity Survey has been found to be about 66%, and we assume the population consists of 50% Type A's and 50% Type B's, then the agreement is only 16% above chance. Agreement among the Framingham Type A Scale, the Type A Structured Interview, and the Jenkins Activity Survey has been reported at essentially chance levels. This phenomenon, in which different methods of measuring a construct yield different results, is called method variance. It means that we are not measuring the same thing with the different methods and strongly suggests that we do not yet know which components of Type A behavior are responsible for its association with CHD.

REDUCING TYPE A BEHAVIOR

The most important question about Type A behavior is whether stress management will prevent the development of CHD or, once someone has CHD, whether further heart attacks or angina attacks can be prevented. Meyer Friedman, Carl Thoresen, and associates have completed a 3 1/2-year study in which they tried to reduce Type A behavior in people who had already had one myocardial infarction (MI), or heart attack. The nonfatal reinfarction rate among people who received both Type A treatment and cardiologic counseling was 4.1% compared with 10.6% among people who received only cardiologic counseling, a highly significant difference. No significant differences occurred between the groups in terms of percentages of people with fatal reinfarction (Friedman et al., 1984). Several approaches have been taken to treating Type A behavior, but this project of Friedman and associates is the only one to use CHD as an outcome measure. Discussion of these approaches is beyond the scope of this chapter.

MECHANISMS OF TYPE A BEHAVIOR

How does Type A behavior cause CHD? Psychological and physiological differences exist between Type A people and Type B's. Psychologically, Type A's perceive all challenges as four-alarm fires and rush to put them out. Type B's are more measured in their response to challenge. In one experiment, Rosenman and Friedman gave Type A and Type B men an insoluble Chinese wooden puzzle. They were given a time limit, and were shown an excellent vintage bottle of Château Lafite-Rothschild, which they would win if they solved the puzzle. While they were working on the puzzle, loud rock music was played.

The Type A men worked feverishly the whole time they were allowed for the puzzle. The Type B men, however, worked for a while, realized the puzzle was insoluble, and gave up, spending the rest of the time relaxing. The Type A men also secreted more norepinephrine into their blood than the Type B men (Friedman et al., 1975). Norepinephrine speeds heart rate, raises blood pressure, and speeds the deposition of plaque on the inner walls of the arteries.

In another study, David Glass and collaborators (1980b) put Type A and Type B men on a treadmill of the type used to measure the exercise tolerance of CHD patients. These men were exercised to their cardiovascular capacity. The Type A men denied they were exhausted at capacity, while the Type B men admitted they were tired.

In addition to the psychological differences between Type A's and Type B's, there are biological differences as well. In another study by Glass and colleagues (1980a), Type A's and Type B's played a video game, a version of Super Pong, a simulated tennis game. They played against a confederate experimenter of Glass's who was very experienced in Super Pong and could not be beaten. In the competition, Type A's secreted more epinephrine and norepinephrine into their blood than the Type B's. Epinephrine and norepinephrine, in addition to encouraging the deposition of plaque on arterial walls, also make it more likely that the heart will beat out of rhythm, which could be life-threatening in a person with chronic arrhythmia.

In another study, Theodore Dembroski and colleagues (Dembroski, MacDougall, & Herd, 1979) found that when Type A's were given mental arithmetic to perform or were given an oral quiz on American history, their heart rates and blood pressures rose more than those of Type B's. The Type A's at rest showed more variation in their heart rates and blood pressures, although these were not higher at rest than those of the Type B's.

Whether there is an innate biological difference between Type A's and Type B's is unclear. The finding that recurrence of myocardial infarction can be reduced by reducing Type A behavior suggests that the major difference is a psychological one: Type A's see all challenges as extremes and are always gearing up excessively for every possible threat, while Type B's choose their battles more carefully.

In either case, the physiological result is the same. With every call to arms, the blood pressure rises and falls, putting stress on the inner walls of the arteries, possibly causing small tears in the walls. As these tears heal, blood clots form. The increased epinephrine and norepinephrine in the blood cause these clots to form quickly. As they form, cholesterol and other fats and solid matter in the blood adhere to the clot and become part of it. After the tear in the arterial wall is healed, part of this accumulation remains stuck to the artery wall and forms atherosclerotic plaque. If enough plaque forms on the walls of the coronary arteries, which supply blood to the heart muscle, blood flow to the muscle is restricted or cut off entirely. This causes that part of the heart muscle to be unable to work as hard as it once did, to produce pain on exertion (angina), or even to die and become replaced by noncontractile scar tissue (myocardial infarction).

NEGATIVE FINDINGS

Negative findings in the Type A literature come primarily from two areas: studies of people at high risk for CHD, and coronary angiography studies, which are performed on people at high risk for CHD or who already have some other cardiac disease.

Several sets of negative findings have come from prospective studies of people at high risk for CHD. The Multiple Risk Factor Intervention Trial (Shekelle, Hulley, Neaton, et al., 1985) and the Aspirin Myocardial Infarction Study (Shekelle, Gale, & Norusis, 1986) involved thousands of high-risk people with assessment by the Type A Structured Interview in the first and by the Jenkins Activity Survey in the second. The Multicenter Post-Infarction Program (Case, Heller, Case, et al., 1985) and studies by Dimsdale et al. (1978, 1979) involved fewer patients, but all had negative findings. Dimsdale and colleagues even found a greater incidence of recurrences among Type B's. The only positive finding among the prospective studies of high risk is from the follow-up of people from the Western Collaborative Group Study who had a CHD event during the course of that study (Jenkins et al., 1976).

Fifteen studies of the relationship between Type A personality and coronary atherosclerosis, as measured by coronary angiography, have been published with positive and negative findings almost equally distributed. Perhaps the most interesting among these is the study by Williams et al. (1988), which seems to untangle the conflicting findings. This was by far the largest angiographic study of Type A behavior, with 2,289 patients. Multivariate analyses showed that Type A behavior as assessed by the structured interview is significantly associated with CAD severity after age, sex, hyperlipidemia, smoking, hypertension, and their various significant interactions were controlled for. The relationship is, however, dependent on age. Patients aged 45 or younger had more severe CAD if they were Type A's. Among patients aged 46–54, Type A's and Type B's had about equal CAD severity. Among patients 55 years of age and older, there was a trend toward more severe CAD among Type B's than among Type A's. Type A behavior as measured by the Jenkins Activity Survey was not related to CAD severity. The reversal of the relationship between Type A behavior and CAD among older patients may be due to survival effects. The failure of other studies to find this relationship is probably due to inadequate sample sizes, use of assessment tools other than the structured interview, and failure to consider the Type A by age interaction. Williams and colleagues conclude that Type A behavior is involved in the pathogenesis of CAD, but only in younger age groups. The effect of Type A behavior is small relative to the effects of smoking and hyperlipidemia, and Williams and colleagues suggest future research should focus more on the hostility and anger components of the Type A personality, particularly in younger people.

FUTURE DIRECTIONS

Type A behavior is a broad personality–environment–behavior–physiology complex. Not all its parts can be pathogenic, and methods of assessing it disagree. The most critical research to advance the field must be in the area of determining the most pathogenic components. Matthews et al. (1986) have most recently advanced the argument begun by Rosenman and Friedman that sympathetic nervous system responsivity is important. Williams et al. (1980), Matthews et al. (1977), and Shekelle et al. (1983) in separate studies have identified hostility as the most powerful factor in Type A behavior for predicting CHD. Scherwitz, Berton, and Leventhal (1978), and Mosca and Swencionis (manuscript in preparation), in separate studies, have identified preoccupation with the self as more powerful than global Type A behavior in predicting occlusion in angiography. Haynes et al. (1980) found that holding anger in predicted CHD in white-collar men, and not discussing anger predicted CHD in women.

All these areas hold potential for discovering the pathogenic components of Type A behavior. Once the concept of coronary-proneness is refined to its most pathogenic parts, and once we are able to accurately assess it in women, blacks, and Hispanics, we will be able to devise more effective treatments and determine if the contribution of coronary-prone behavior to CHD can be reduced.

REFERENCES

Bortner, R. W. (1969). A short rating scale as a potential measure of Pattern A behavior. *Journal of Chronic Disease, 22,* 87-91.

Case, R. B., Heller, S. S., Case, N. B., et al. (1985). Type A behavior and survival after acute myocardial infarction. *New England Journal of Medicine, 312,* 737-741.

Cohen, J. B., & Reed, D. (1985). Type A behavior and coronary heart disease among Japanese men in Hawaii. *Journal of Behavioral Medicine, 8,* 343-352.

Cooper, T., Detre, T., & Weiss, S. M. (1981). Coronary prone behavior and coronary heart disease: A critical review. *Circulation, 63,* 1199-1215.

DeBacker, G., Kornitzer, M., Kittel, F., et al. (1983). Behavior, stress, and psychosocial traits as risk factors. *Preventive Medicine, 12,* 32-36.

Dembroski, T. M., MacDougall, J. M., Herd, J. A., et al. (1979). Effects of level of challenge on pressor and heart responses in Type A and Type B subjects. *Journal of Applied Social Psychology, 9,* 209-228.

Dimsdale, J. E., Hackett, T. P., Hutter, A. M., et al. (1978). Type A personality and extent of coronary atherosclerosis. *American Journal of Cardiology, 42,* 583-586.

Dimsdale, J. E., Hackett, T. P., Hutter, A. M., et al. (1979). Type A behavior and angiographic findings. *Journal of Psychosomatic Research, 23,* 273-276.

Eastwood, M. R., & Trevelyan, H. (1971). Stress and coronary heart disease. *Journal of Psychosomatic Research, 15,* 289-292.

French-Belgian Collaborative Group. (1982). Ischemic heart disease and psychological patterns: Prevalence and incidence studies in Belgium and France. *Advances in Cardiology, 29,* 25-31.

Friedman, M. (1969). *Pathogenesis of coronary artery disease.* New York: McGraw-Hill.

Friedman, M., Byers, S. O., Diamant, J., & Rosenman, R. H. (1975). Plasma catecholamine response of coronary-prone subjects (Type A) to a specific challenge. *Metabolism, 24*(2), 205-210.

Friedman, E. H., Hellerstein, H. K., Jones, S. E., et al. (1968). Behavior patterns and serum cholesterol in two groups of normal males. *American Journal of Medical Science, 255,* 237-244.

Friedman, M., & Rosenman, R. H. (1974). *Type A behavior and your heart.* New York: Alfred A. Knopf.

Friedman, M., St. George, S., Byers, S. O., & Rosenman, R. H. (1960). Excretion of catecholamines, 17-ketosteroids, 17-hydroxy-corticoids and 5-hydrosyindole in men exhibiting a particular behavior pattern (A) associated with high incidence of clinical coronary artery disease. *Journal of Clinical Investigations, 39,* 758-764.

Friedman, M., Thoresen, C. E., Gill, J. J., Powell, L. H., Ulmer, D., Thompson, L., Price, V. A., Rubin, D. D., Breall, W. S., Dixon, T., Levy, R., & Bourg, E. (1984). Alteration of Type A behavior and reduction in cardiac recurrences in postmyocardial infarction patients. *American Heart Journal, 108*(b), 237-248.

Glass, D. C., Krakoff, L. R., Contrada, R., Hilton, W. F., Kehoe, K., Manucci, E. G., Collings, C., Snow, B., & Elting, E. (1980a). Effect of harassment and competition upon cardiovascular and catecholamine responses in Type A and B individuals. *Psychophysiology, 17,* 453-463.

Glass, D. C., Krakoff, L. R., Finkelman, J., Snow, B., Contrada, R., Kehoe, K., Mannucci, E. G., Isecke, W., Collins, C., Holton, W. F., & Elting, E. (1980b). Effect of task overload upon cardiovascular and plasma catecholamine responses in Type A and B individuals. *Basic and Applied Social Psychology, 1,* 199-218.

Haynes, S. G., Feinleib, M., & Kannel, W. B. (1980). The relationship of psychosocial factors to coronary heart disease in the Framingham Study. III. Eight-year incidence of coronary heart disease. *American Journal of Epidemiology, 111,* 37-58.

Jenkins, C. D. (1971). Psychologic and social precursors of coronary disease. *New England Journal of Medicine, 284,* 244-255, 307-317.

Jenkins, C. D. (1976). Recent evidence supporting psychologic and social risk factors for coronary disease. *New England Journal of Medicine, 294,* 987-994, 1033-1038.

Jenkins, C. D. (1978). Behavioral risk factors in coronary artery disease. *The Annual Review of Medicine, 29,* 543-562.

Jenkins, C. D., Rosenman, R. H., & Zyzanski, S. J. (1974). Prediction of clinical coronary heart disease by a test for the coronary-prone behavior pattern. *New England Journal of Medicine, 23,* 1271-1275.

MacDougall, J. M., Dembroski, T. M., & Musante, L. (1979). The structured interview and questionnaire methods of assessing coronary-prone behavior in male and female college students. *Journal of Behavioral Medicine, 2,* 71-83.

Manuck, S. B., Kaplan, J. R., & Clarkson, T. B. (1983). Behaviorally-induced heart rate reactivity and atherosclerosis in cynomolgus monkeys. *Psychosomatic Medicine, 45,* 95-108.

Matthews, K. A., Glass, D. C., Rosenman, R. H., et al. (1977). Competitive drive, pattern A, and coronary heart disease: A further analysis of some data from the Western Collaborative Group Study. *Journal of Chronic Disease, 30,* 489-498.

Matthews, K. A., & Haynes, S. G. (1986). Type A behavior pattern and coronary disease risk. *American Journal of Epidemiology, 123,* 923-960.

Matthews, K. A., Krantz, D. C., Dembroski, T. M., et al. (1982). Unique and common variance in structured interview and Jenkins Activity Survey measures of the Type A behavior pattern. *Journal of Personality and Social Psychology, 42,* 303-313.

Matthews, K. A., Weiss, S. M., Detre, T., Dembroski, T. M., Falkner, B., Manuck, S. J., & Williams, R. B. (Eds.). (1986). *Handbook of stress, reactivity, and cardiovascular disease.* New York: Wiley.

Mosca, J., & Swencionis, C. *Self-involvement, hostility, Type A behavior, and angiography.* Manuscript in preparation.

Rosenman, R. H., Brand, R. J., Jenkins, C. D., et al. (1975). Coronary heart disease in the Western Collaborative Group Study: Final follow-up experience of 8½ years. *Journal of the American Medical Association, 233,* 872–877.

Scherwitz, L., Berton, K., & Leventhal, H. (1978). Type A behavior, self-involvement, and cardiovascular response. *Psychosomatic Medicine, 40,* 593–609.

Selye, H. (1976). *Stress in health and disease.* Boston: Butterworths.

Shekelle, R. B., Gale, M., & Norusis, M. (1986). Type A score (Jenkins Activity Survey) and risk of recurrent coronary heart disease in the Aspirin Myocardial Infarction Study. *American Journal of Cardiology.*

Shekelle, R. B., Gale, M., Ostfeld, A., et al. (1983). Hostility, risk of coronary heart disease and mortality. *Psychosomatic Medicine, 45,* 109–114.

Shekelle, R. B., Hulley, S. B., Neaton, J. D., et al. (1985). The MRFIT behavior pattern study. II. Type A behavior and incidence of coronary heart disease. *American Journal of Epidemiology, 122,* 559–570.

Williams, R. B., Barefoot, J. C., Haney, T. L., Harrell, F. E., Blumenthal, J. A., Pryor, D. B., & Peterson, B. (1988). Type A behavior and angiographically documented coronary atherosclerosis in a sample of 2,289 patients. *Psychosomatic Medicine, 50,* 139–152.

Williams, R. B., Haney, T. L., Lee, K. L., et al. (1980). Type A behavior, hostility, and coronary atherosclerosis. *Psychosomatic Medicine, 42,* 539–549.

·VII·

CONCLUSION

·21·

Where Do We Go from Here?

ROBERT ORNSTEIN
CHARLES SWENCIONIS

This is by no means the end of the story. Research is continuing at a rapid pace in the fields described in this book and in other, related areas. The more we know about the healing capabilities of the human brain, the clearer it is that we are the same animals that evolved several million years ago on the African plains. However, there is a difference. If knowing about something gives one some power over it, it may be possible for humankind to evolve consciously.

For example, knowing that there is a stress-resistant personality enables us to emulate those qualities and improve our resistance. Knowing that the healthiest weight is closer to the average weight for a given age group, than to the Metropolitan Life Insurance Company ideal weight enables many people to relax about their weight. Knowing that social networks improve health gives us another reason to talk to one another.

This does not suggest that there is an ideal "healing brain" personality, a person who eats protein and drinks coffee in the morning, eats only carbohydrates at night, lives among plenty of negative air ions, and has the right neuropeptides and emotions.

This growing body of knowledge does suggest that even more research into the maintenance of health by the brain will continue to yield insights into how we can live more healthfully and free our consciousness to become whatever humankind may yet become.

Index

acetylcholine, 109ff, 191, 192
acquired immune deficiency syndrome
    (AIDS), 184, 185, 193, 195
adaptation, 7, 15, 137ff
adenosine, 124
advice-seeking, 92
air ions, 103ff
alcoholism, 94, 96
alertness, 6, 116, 120, 126
alexithymia, 185
allergies, 177, 183
alpha-methyldopa, 107
alternative medicine, 44, 54
Alzheimer disease, 111
amygdala, 150ff
angina, 65
angiography, 92
angiotensin, 152
antidepressant drugs, 109
anxiety, 67, 178, 194
arteriosclerosis, 34, 92, 246
arthritis, 65, 88, 175–178, 185, 186, 190
asthma, 65
autoantibody, 178
autoimmune diseases, 175–178, 181, 183,
    185
autonomy, 91

B-cells, 153, 165, 175, 189, 191, 195
belief, 68, 69
bereavement, 95, 164, 180–181, 187,
    188
beta-endorphin, 149, 165, 166, 191
biofeedback, 81, 194
biomedicine, 47ff, 58
blood-brain barrier, 107, 109, 116
blood pressure, 80ff

body mass index, 209, 212
brainstem, 12, 161
buffering, 39, 89ff, 225ff

caffeine, 114, 124ff
cancer, 70, 72, 77, 185, 194, 228
carbohydrates, 6, 107ff, 111ff, 121ff
cardiovascular disease, 75, 77ff
catecholamines, 109ff, 117ff, 190
catharsis, 17
cell-mediated system, 175
challenge, 8, 164, 222ff, 231, 234
ching, 56
cholesterol, 89, 245, 246
choline, 109ff
cholinergic transmitters, 161
cirrhosis, 77
codeine, 148
coherence, 8, 91, 97, 231ff
commitment, 8, 222ff
communication, 75ff
control, 8, 91, 180, 194, 222ff
coping, 94, 184, 196, 231
coronary heart disease, 88, 95, 213,
    244ff
coronary-prone behavior, 244ff
cortex, 13, 23ff, 103ff, 189
corticosterone, 163, 166, 190
cortisol, 192
creative adaptation, 137ff
crowding, 37ff, 144, 187
crying, 17
cultural allegiance, 95
cure, 137
cyclic adenosine monophosphate (AMP), 6,
    104, 167, 191
cytokines, 175

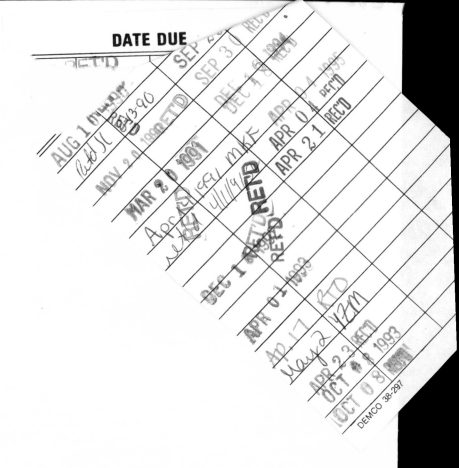